The Party's Over

*the text of this book is printed
on 100% recycled paper*

Also by David S. Broder

The Republican Establishment:
   The Present and Future of the G.O.P. (with Stephen Hess)

THE
PARTY'S OVER

The Failure of Politics in America

DAVID S. BRODER

HARPER COLOPHON BOOKS
HARPER & ROW, PUBLISHERS
New York · Evanston · San Francisco · London

For Ann, George, Josh, Matt and Mike

The table on page xxii is from an unpublished paper, *The Election Time Analysis of Attitudes of Trust in Government* by Warren E. Miller, November 2, 1971. Reprinted with permission of Warren E. Miller, Director of Center for Political Studies, Institute for Social Research, University of Michigan, Ann Arbor.

The table on page 117 is from a *Newsweek* Survey conducted by The Gallup Organization, Inc. Reprinted by permission.

The tables on pages 208 and 209 are from *Rich Man, Poor Man* by Herman P. Miller. Copyright © 1971 by Thomas Y. Crowell Company, Inc. Reprinted with permission of Thomas Y. Crowell Company, Inc., publishers.

The table on page 210 is by Roger A. Herriot and Herman P. Miller, "Changes in the Distribution of Taxes Among Income Groups: 1962 to 1968." Paper presented at the August 1971 meetings of the American Statistical Association.

Portions of this book have previously appeared in *The Atlantic* and *The Washington Monthly*.

First HARPER COLOPHON edition published 1972.

STANDARD BOOK NUMBER: 06-090288-4

A hardcover edition of this book is available from Harper & Row, Publishers.

Contents

Preface

This is a book about American politics and the American political condition, seen from the limited, personal perspective of a Washington-based political reporter. Like most books, it is the outgrowth of the author's experiences. For the last sixteen years I have been covering candidates, campaigns, politics and government in Washington and across the country for the *Congressional Quarterly*, the Washington *Evening Star*, the *New York Times* Washington bureau and—since 1966—for the Washington *Post*. My debt to those organizations for letting me take this long post-graduate course in American politics, at their expense, is too large to be calculated.

The bias of the book is that of one enamored of politics, American style. The clash and confusion of our free and open system of self-government fascinate me. There have been so many marvelously diverse and eccentric personalities; so much high comedy, intended and unintended; and there have been moments of magnificence. But, along with others who were personal witnesses to the terrible events that began with the assassination of John Kennedy and culminated in the 1968 campaign year, I have found my comfortable assumptions about the stability of American society and the responsiveness of American politics badly shaken.

The events of those years drove me to consider fundamental and uncomfortable questions, to re-examine the ideas about our country, its values and its method of government that had resided, undisturbed, in my head since college days at the University of Chicago. In the autumn of 1969, the *Post* generously allowed me to take a leave, so that I could accept a fellowship at the Institute of Politics of the John Fitzgerald Kennedy School of Government at Harvard University.

For nine months, I had leisure to reread some old books and study some new ones, to listen in on government courses and to talk with the men and women who taught them. Once a week, between thirty and forty Harvard and Radcliffe students would come by the Institute for an afternoon study group, where we talked and argued about the workings of our political and governmental institutions—the parties, the Congress and the presidency, state and local governments—and their responses to the issues facing America.

At many of our sessions during the year, we were joined by men and women from the political and governmental worlds. Listening to the challenges my student friends threw at them and the questions the visitors from the arena of practical politics raised themselves disabused me of any notion I might have had that we could easily return to politics as usual.

When I went back to work at the *Post* in the summer of 1970, the first assignment from Ben Bagdikian, then the national news editor, was to join Haynes Johnson in a survey of voter opinion on the 1970 election. Guided by Johnson, who is probably the most sensitive reporter of everyday American life in our time, I spent a month knocking on doors in precincts scattered across the nation. The pessimism we found about the American future and the cynicism toward American government and politics made it evident that the crisis of confidence was every bit as urgent on Main Street as in Harvard Yard.

It was in reaction to these experiences, and with the awareness that my own concerns about the failings of our political system were exceeded by those of many fellow Americans, that this book was written.

It is not a cheerful book, I am afraid. It argues that the challenge facing our society and institutions is far more critical than most of us find comfortable to believe. It seems quite possible that the crisis may deepen before we stir ourselves to make the effort and sacrifice that may be needed to redeem the original promise of this nation. But I hope the book is not so pessimistic that it leaves the reader with a greater sense of futility or impotence than many people already feel in the face of the external forces, including government, which are shaping their lives. I do not believe that we are powerless, either as individuals or as a people, to direct our future. On the contrary, it is my conviction—and the central argument of this book—that if we engage ourselves in politics, and particularly concern ourselves with the workings of those strangely neglected institutions, the political parties, that we may find the instrument of national self-renewal is in our hands.

The fundamental ideas in this book are not new. Whatever I may have grasped about the workings of American politics has been put in my head by others, by the scholars and critics of our governmental system, going back to De Tocqueville, and by my own mentors—the dozens of politicians, journalistic colleagues and academic friends who have taken time over the years to help me understand what was happening in an election or a legislative fight, and why. No student ever had a better faculty from which to learn.

In the circumstances leading up to the writing of this particular book, I owe a special debt to Katharine Graham, the publisher of the *Post*, and Benjamin C. Bradlee, its executive editor, for their constant encouragement to examine the hard questions about American politics, wherever that search might lead. Richard E. Neustadt, professor of government at Harvard, arranged the fellowship at the Institute of Politics and, like many of his colleagues, was generous with his time and thoughts in making that sabbatical year so rewarding. I am specially grateful to Janet Fraser, the director of the Institute's student program, for suggesting that a portion of that year be spent leading a study group at the Institute, and to the "regulars" in that group, who taught me so much more about politics, by their questions and comments, than I could ever tell them.

The special research and writing involved in this book could never have been accomplished, under the time pressures of my regular work, without yeoman assistance from the entire library staff of the Washington *Post*, under Mark Hannan, and our two doughty national news researchers, Joan Shorenstein Spiegel and Wendy Siegel. The research facilities of *Congressional Quarterly* and the *National Journal* were also of great assistance.

Rochelle Stanfield, the information director of the Advisory Commission on Intergovernmental Relations, provided both information and insights on local government problems and Federal-state relations, as she has done so often over the years. Early drafts of some sections were read and criticized by Gail Bensinger of *Congressional Quarterly*, William Small and Sylvia Westerman of CBS and James L. Sundquist of the Brookings Institution. Their suggestions were very helpful, but errors of information and interpretation are, of course, solely my responsibility.

Jan Krause Wentworth worked with me in the summer of 1971, researching a number of areas and making innumerable helpful editorial suggestions on succeeding drafts. Donna Crouch typed the final manuscript with speed and skill. Elizabeth McKee handled the arrangements for publication with her customary professional dexterity and, as she has before, Jeannette Hopkins brought to her role as editor a sense of personal commitment to the book that went well beyond the call of duty. To all of them, I say, "Thank you."

DAVID S. BRODER

November 1, 1971
Washington, D.C.

Introduction:
Anatomy of an Impasse

In the autumn of the pre-presidential year—the time at which these words are being written—the residents of the nation's capital have reason to recall the Founding Fathers' warnings against the "danger of factions." Partisanship runs riot and Washington begins to turn testy. However much he may insist that he is governing as President of all the people, the first-term incumbent begins to measure policy decisions by their effect on his re-election chances. He gauges the opposition field and finds occasion to point up the contrast between his statesmanship and his potential challengers' unseemly scrambling for office. Those gentlemen protect themselves as best they can against the President's intimations of unwarranted ambition, meanwhile elbowing each other for advantageous position in the spring primaries and the public opinion polls.

All these are just facts of life in Washington, as inescapable as the humidity of August or the spring inundation of tourists. If this year has been a bit testier than usual, it is undoubtedly because the government itself is divided, with a Republican in the White House and Democrats in control of Capitol Hill. The Senate is a-swarm with presidential and vice presidential hopefuls, all trying to make partisan points at the expense of the Administration. Richard M. Nixon has lobbied for passage of the Administration's program, cajoling conservative Republicans to stay in line and seeking whatever support he can find on the Democratic side of the aisle. But, despite cooperation from the Democratic leadership on some issues, the output of Congress is dwindling as election day draws closer and partisan considerations dominate.

The Republicans feel they deserve to be re-elected. They were called back into power three years ago by a public impatient to wind up another nasty Asian war which the Democrats seemed incapable of ending. By and large, the Republicans have done what they were meant to do, although there is still a sizable American army in the field and no formal peace treaty is in sight. The war news is off the front page, they note, and, mercifully, so is the constant agitation from and about the radical groups who want to turn the country upside down.

The problem is that the war's after-effects linger. The inflation which the Republicans inherited, though somewhat abated, remains a major preoccupation of Administration economists and average citizens. And the cutback in defense spending has slowed the economy and brought higher unemployment than anyone finds satisfactory. The Democrats argue that these are not problems of transition, as the President maintains, but the results of typical Republican mismanagement of the economy. This case was persuasive enough for them to win the midterm election, despite the President's and Vice President's all-out effort to elect a Republican Congress.

In the coming election, Republicans will run on the slogan of Peace and Prosperity—if they can reduce the unemployment figure and bring inflation under control; and if the protracted disarmament talks with the Russians do not end in disagreement; and if the tense Middle East situation does not explode into war; and if the India-Pakistan conflict can be kept within bounds.

The latest Supreme Court decision on school desegregation is causing the Republicans some problems and jeopardizing their prospects for further political gains in the South. Despite the President's evident coolness to the ruling, his critics do not let him forget the decision was written by the Republican he appointed as Chief Justice.

Richard Nixon is working as doggedly as ever, trying to keep one step ahead of his problems. Busy as he is with the duties of his office, he manages to take an active hand in political affairs. He has to, for there are threats on every side. In addition to the Senate Democrats, who rarely miss a chance to denounce him, there are restive conservatives in his own party, unhappy about the course of the Administration; a Republican Governor in his home state of California whose ambitions must be placated; and a millionaire Governor in New York who, instead of resting on the laurels of a long and distinguished career, seems always to be seeking new worlds to conquer.

Since the last presidential race, the Democrats have made a strong comeback in the state capitals. They now control Ohio and Pennsylvania, among other states important to the Administration's re-election. But there is a friendly Republican Governor in Illinois to help offset some of Mayor Daley's power. And there are high-level intrigues in Texas, whose top Democrat could not be more helpful to the President if he were a member of the GOP.

All things considered, Richard Nixon feels he can look forward with some confidence to 1956.

That is right—1956. This is history, not last year's events. Every item just referred to is sixteen years out of date, even if it seems to apply to the autumn of 1971. The President referred to is Dwight D. Eisenhower, not Richard Nixon. The war is Korea, not Vietnam. The Republican Chief Justice is Earl Warren, not Warren Burger. The school decision that is causing the controversy is the original 1954 ruling that "separate is not equal," not the more recent call for widespread busing to end segregation.

The California Governor whose ego needs constant attention is Goodwin J. Knight, not Ronald Reagan. The ambitious millionaire in Albany is Averell Harriman, not Nelson A. Rockefeller. The Administration's Texas friend is Allan Shivers, not John B. Connally. And the Senate Democratic hopefuls are named Kefauver and Gore and Kennedy and Johnson, not Muskie, McGovern, Jackson and Humphrey.

But if this short catalogue of the similarities of 1955 and 1971 produces a sensation of *déjà vu*, an impression that we are seeing a rerun of a not very good movie, then you understand what impels me to write this book. My view is that American politics is at an impasse, that we have been spinning our wheels for a long, long time; and that we are going to dig ourselves ever deeper into trouble, unless we find a way to develop some political traction and move again. I believe we can get that traction, we can make government responsible and responsive again, only when we begin to use the political parties as they are meant to be used. And that is the thesis of this book.

It is called *The Party's Over*, not in prophecy, but in alarm. I am not predicting the demise of the Republicans or the Democrats. Party loyalties have been seriously eroded, the Democratic and Republican organizations weakened by years of neglect. But our parties are not yet dead. What happens to them is up to us to decide. If we allow them to wither, we will pay a high price in the continued frustration of government. But, even if we seek their renewal, the cost of repairing the effects of decades of governmental inaction will be heavy. The process will be painful and expensive. Whatever the fate of our political parties, for America the party *is* over.

". . . *Government Will Go On as Usual*"

In 1955, when I came to Washington, the Eisenhower Administration and the Democratic Congress confronted each other like two overage, out-of-shape, arm-weary club fighters (the President was sixty-five that year; Speaker of the House Sam Rayburn, seventy-two). Neither could take command of the struggle for control of national policy, let alone score a knockout blow. So they leaned on each other and held each other up for eight months, until the final adjournment bell released them from their embarrassment.

By the deadpan reckoning of *Congressional Quarterly*, Eisenhower won approval of just over 46 percent of his 207 legislative requests to the 1955 session of Congress. He was awarded points on such mighty issues as his bid to "repeal the ban on purchases of foreign-made spun silk yarn," to "restore funds for the President's Commission on Veterans' Pensions," and to "authorize a memorial to the late Senator Robert A. Taft." He lacked the strength, however, to put over any faintly controversial measure, even statehood for Hawaii or a start on the Interstate Highway System. So static was the situation that we noted as "the most unusual aspect of the 1955 session" the fact that, for the first time since such records had been kept, no member of the House or Senate resigned or died between opening day and adjournment.

Despite the remarkable suspension of the mortality tables, health was a matter of major concern that autumn; for a time, the nation's leadership appeared quite literally stricken. Eisenhower was hospitalized in Denver, the victim of his first heart attack. Lyndon B. Johnson, the majority leader of the Senate, customarily described as the second-most-powerful man in Washington, was at home on the LBJ Ranch in Texas, recovering from his own severe coronary, suffered that summer. John F. Kennedy, then just a promising young Senator, was barely walking again, after back surgery earlier in the year that caused him to miss the first five months of the session and very nearly cost him his life. Only Richard M. Nixon was healthy, and, as always, looking on the brighter side of things. The day after the President's heart attack, the Vice President said, "The business of government will go on as usual." In that, he spoke truer than he knew.

From that day to this, our government has suffered from crippled leadership, from a slowdown of decision making, an impairment of its vital processes. The result has been an accumulation of unresolved problems and a buildup of public frustration so great that our quintessential American characteristics—our optimism and self-confidence—have now been shaken. Millions of Americans now feel they have lost control of the government and that government has lost its capacity to act, to respond, to move on the challenges that confront our nation. In an era of rapid and accelerating scientific, technological, social and cultural change, our governmental and political system has been operating in superslow motion. Time has not stood still, but the processes of politics have, as Richard Nixon knows better than most men.

On the day of Eisenhower's heart attack in 1955, he stood in momentary expectation of succession to the presidency. But he was to wait more than thirteen years to occupy the office. Not until each of the 1955 invalids, Eisenhower, Kennedy and Johnson, had had his turn did Richard Nixon finally step forward. And, when he did, he found, as he would have in 1955, that it was indeed "government as usual" that confronted him. Lacking an electoral mandate, facing a division in party control of Congress and the Executive, plagued by the inflexibility of the machinery of government, Richard Nixon has been as frustrated as his three predecessors in his efforts to move ahead on the national agenda.

In a real sense, Nixon is the symbol as well as the victim of our long period of political impasse. Our sense that we are trapped on a single spool of film, constantly being rerun on the projector of history, is heightened by the fact that every episode seems to end with Richard Nixon. No matter how many events or personalities intervene, it is always Nixon's face we see as the scene fades.

I am, like my Washington *Post* colleague Meg Greenfield, a member of the "Nixon Generation," of which she wrote:

At regular intervals now, ever since that first vote in 1952, our generation has either been supporting or opposing Richard Nixon. The psychological implications of this fact are staggering: half of us have lived our whole adult life as a series of dashed hopes and disappointments, while the other half have passed the same period in a condition of perpetual anxiety over the prospect that he would succeed. . . . What distinguishes us as a group from those who came before and those who have come after is that we are too young to remember a time when Richard Nixon was not on the political scene, and too old reasonably to expect that we shall live to see one.

But there is more to our frustration than just Nixon Generation neurosis. The politics of the last sixteen years has been a politics of fits and starts, of careers launched then cut off; of legislation passed but not implemented; of court decrees issued but not enforced; of programs authorized but not financed; of reforms begun but not completed; of wars started but not won; of great ventures sketched and then abandoned.

If history recalls any American achievement of this period, I suppose, it will be the flight to the moon. But that was remarkable just because it *was* unique. We actually set our goal, established a timetable for reaching it, and held to it. In almost every other instance, we have left our targets unattained. As a result, very few problems have moved off the national agenda, and a great many more have moved onto it. An exaggeration? To be sure, but not so much of one as you might think. Look down the list of topics at the Eisenhower press conference of January 25, 1956:

The first question, inevitably, was about Richard Nixon's political future. "Mr. President, if you should decide to seek re-election, would you favor Vice President Nixon as your running mate again?" Well, we all know the answer to that one, but the question of Nixon's future recurs endlessly.

Question 2: "Secretary Dulles is trying to exclude certain matters involving foreign affairs, including the Israeli-Arab situation, from being disputed in the coming campaign. Do you think it is possible, sir . . . and do you think it should be done?" Eisenhower came down foursquare for bipartisanship in "the great principles and policies that guide our foreign policy," but the question comes back to haunt us again and again.

Question 3: Why should Congress authorize foreign aid on a long-term basis? Sixteen years later, the Senate was still pretending that the need was temporary, and that the United States could withdraw at will from its obligations to the underdeveloped world. The program was limping along on a year-by-year, or even month-by-month basis, defying any hope of rational planning.

Question 4: Should desegregation standards be written into the

Federal school-aid bill? Does anyone feel that issue has been settled?

Several questions on Eisenhower's health and political plans intervened. Then:

"Mr. President, Senator Johnson of Texas says your farm program has been a failure. Do you have any comment?"

And: "Mr. President, in light of Khrushchev's disparagement of your aerial inspection plan . . . do you still have hopes for . . . a disarmament agreement with the Russians sometime soon?"

And: "Mr. President, would you say what you consider a correct definition of the desirable basis for a common American-British policy regarding the Middle East?"

And: "Mr. President, most of the farm legislation deals with helping the farmer. I would like to put in a plea for the consumer. Can you do nothing so that American people can eat the surpluses cheap?"

And that is where I came in.

The Decline and Fall of Party Government

The reason we have suffered governmental stalemate is that we have not used the one instrument available to us for disciplining government to meet our needs. That instrument is the political party.

Political parties in America have a peculiar status and history. They are not part of our written Constitution. The Founding Fathers, in fact, were determined to do all they could to see they did not arise. Washington devoted much of his Farewell Address to warning his countrymen against "the dangers of party in the state." And yet parties arose in the first generation of the nation, and have persisted ever since. Their very durability argues that they fill a need. That need is for some institution that will sort out, weigh, and, to the extent possible, reconcile the myriad conflicting needs and demands of individuals, groups, interests, communities and regions in this diverse continental Republic; organize them for the contest for public office; and then serve as a link between the constituencies and the men chosen to govern. When the parties fill their mission well, they tend to serve both a unifying and a clarifying function for the country. Competitive forces draw them to the center, and force them to seek agreement on issues too intense to be settled satisfactorily by simple majority referendum. On the other hand, as grand coalitions, they are capable of taking a need felt strongly by some minority of the population and making it part of a program endorsed by a majority.

When they do not function well, things go badly for America. The coming of the Civil War was marked by a failure of the reconciling function of the existing parties. Long periods of stagnation, too, can be caused by the failure of the parties to bring emerging public questions to the point of electoral decision. When the parties fail, individual citizens feel they have lost control of what is happening in politics and in government. They find themselves powerless to influence the course of events. Voting seems futile and politics a pointless charade. These are the emotions millions of Americans express today, after sixteen years of government impasse. By any measure you can take, public opinion is markedly more disenchanted with government and its leaders today than it was in 1955. The Gallup Poll reported in August of 1955 that 79 percent of the adults approved the way President Eisenhower was handling his job. At a comparable point in his term, in August, 1971, President Nixon enjoyed the confidence and approval of 49 percent of the American people. Nor was Nixon alone in public opprobrium. A bit earlier in the year, the Harris Survey reported that Congress got a favorable rating for its work from only 26 percent of the people, the lowest figure it had ever recorded in that category. The credibility of our highest officials is deeply suspect. In February, 1967, 65 percent of the American people told Dr. Gallup they did not believe the Johnson Administration was telling the public all it should know about the Vietnam war. Exactly four years later, with a new President in office, the same survey showed 69 percent did not believe they were getting the facts from Nixon.

"What we are witnessing," said Dr. Warren Miller, director of the Center for Political Studies at the University of Michigan in November, 1971, "is a massive erosion of the trust the American people have in their government." Cynicism about government has increased dramatically. The survey on which Miller was reporting showed that roughly half as many whites and blacks believed in the reality of "government of the people, by the people and for the people" in 1970 as had believed in it in 1958. By 1970 there was virtually a three-fold increase among whites and more than a five-fold increase among blacks who thought government was run by the big interests for their own benefit. The figures show an appalling rise in public distrust and alienation.

Believe Government Is Run By:	Whites			Blacks		
	1958	1966	1970	1958	1966	1970
People's Representatives For Benefit Of All	74%	51%	41%	78%	63%	34%
Big Interests For Themselves	18	34	48	12	23	63

The cynicism about government combines with a strong sense that the country is not solving its problems to produce a degree of public doubt about the American future that is astonishing in a nation traditionally as optimistic as ours. In the autumn of 1970, Haynes Johnson and I went out knocking on voters' doors, in the kind of pre-election survey our paper, the Washington *Post,* and others so often do. But what we found on this journey was a story so much bigger and more important than we expected that we had to start our series of reports with the dispatch headlined, quite accurately, "A Pessimistic America Questions Its Future."

Everywhere we went on that assignment, from the prosperous high-income suburbs of Boston and San Francisco, to working-class and poor neighborhoods of Cleveland, Indianapolis, Atlanta, Richmond and Los Angeles, we encountered a paradox. Most

Americans were saying things were not so bad for them personally, but they were gravely worried about the future of their country—whether it would even survive. "Typical of the overwhelming opinion voiced by Americans in all sections of the country," we wrote, was this comment by a housewife in a small town near Houston. "I don't know about the future," she said, "and I'm terrified of bringing my children up in it. I used to feel my son was going to have a future, and now I don't know any more."

Ours was an unscientific sampling, and necessarily impressionistic. But confirmation arrived in the summer of 1971 in a careful poll by Albert H. Cantril and Charles W. Roll, Jr., for a book called *The Hopes and Fears of the American People,* published by a private group called Potomac Associates. Using a technique of measurement validated in 1959 and 1964 studies, they found that, on the whole, Americans expressed just about as much sense of personal accomplishment and of optimism about their personal futures in 1971 as they did in the previous years. But, unlike the earlier studies, that of 1971 showed that those surveyed believe "their country has lost rather than gained ground over the past five years" and may "barely recover the reverses of the last half-decade" in the next five years. Late in 1971, when Johnson and I repeated our own polling, we found that a certain degree of hope had been rekindled by President Nixon's actions to limit wage and price increases, but the suspicion of government and doubt about the future remained. In the minds of many Americans, "government as usual" is simply not good enough.

The governmental system is not working because the political parties are not working. The parties have been weakened by their failure to adapt to some of the social and technological changes taking place in America. But, even more, they are suffering from simple neglect: neglect by Presidents and public officials, but, particularly, neglect by the voters. It is to remind us that the parties can be used for positive purposes that this book is written.

Some students of government who share this view of the importance of political parties in American government nonetheless think it futile to exhort readers on their behalf. Such political scientists as James L. Sundquist and Walter Dean Burnham, whose knowledge of American political history is far deeper than my own, believe we are simply in the wrong stage of the political cycle to expect anything but confused signals and weak responses from the parties.

The last major party realignment, it is generally agreed, took place in 1932, and set the stage for the New Deal policies of government intervention in the economy and the development of the welfare state. We are, these scholars argue, perhaps overdue for another realignment, but until an issue emerges which will produce one, an issue as powerful as the Great Depression, it is futile to complain that party lines are muddled and governmental action is all but paralyzed. Their judgment may be correct, but I do not find it comforting. The cyclical theory of party realignment is an easy rationalization for throwing up our hands and doing nothing. But we do not know when the realignment will take place. Some scholars have thought there was a thirty-six-year cycle, with 1896 and 1932 as the last "critical elections." But 1968, the scheduled date, on this theory, for another "critical election," has come and gone, and our drift continues.

The level of frustration in the country is terribly high—dangerously high. I do not think that we can just assume that people will bide their time and wait for relief to arrive from some new party, or some rearrangement of constituents between the Democrats and Republicans. There is clear danger that the frustrations will find expression in a political "solution" that sacrifices democratic freedoms for a degree of relief from the almost unbearable tensions and strains of today's metropolitan centers. Basically, I believe that our guarantee of self-government is no stronger than our exercise of self-government; and today the central instruments of self-government, the political parties, are being neglected or abused. We must somehow rescue them if we are to rescue ourselves.

In 1963, when James MacGregor Burns, the Williams College

political scientist and biographer of Roosevelt and Kennedy, published his analysis of the political impasse, calling it *The Deadlock of Democracy*, many of his colleagues in political science dismissed his picture of "drift, delay and devitalization" as overdrawn.

In 1965, when Lyndon Johnson rushed bill after bill through a compliant Congress, some of them argued that Burns's theory had been knocked into a cocked hat. That judgment was, to put it kindly, premature. Today the "Great Society" exists mainly on the pieces of paper collected in the Johnson Library in Austin and in the souvenir bill-signing pens gathering dust in offices on Capitol Hill. Instead of the "Great Society," what we have is a society in which discontent, disbelief, cynicism and political inertia characterize the public mood; a country whose economy suffers from severe dislocations, whose currency is endangered, where unemployment and inflation coexist, where increasing numbers of people and even giant enterprises live on the public dole; a country whose two races continue to withdraw from each other in growing physical and social isolation; a country whose major public institutions command steadily less allegiance from its citizens; whose education, transportation, law enforcement, health and sanitation systems fall far short of filling their functions; a country whose largest city is close to being ungovernable and uninhabitable; and a country still far from reconciling its international responsibilities with its unmet domestic needs.

We are in trouble. And now, unlike a decade ago, the people know it. The question is, Can we still save ourselves from deadlock without sacrificing our democracy?

Eisenhower

Responsible party government, the concept that is central to this book, requires, as a minimum, that everyone is clear which party is responsible for the policies and actions of the government. That condition is not met when different branches of the government are controlled by opposing parties. Divided government is the opposite of responsible government. And divided government is what we have had, with increasing frequency, since Dwight D. Eisenhower came onto the national scene.

In only four of the twenty-six elections from the beginning of this century until 1952 did the voters give the President's opposition a majority in *either* house of Congress. But in five of the ten elections since Eisenhower was elected in 1952, the voters have established opposition majorities in *both* houses of Congress. The new pattern of divided government, with neither party having responsibility in Washington, began in 1954, when the Democrats won Congress in the middle of Eisenhower's first term. It continued throughout his second term, despite his landslide re-election victory, and it has resumed now in the presidency of Eisenhower's Vice President, Richard M. Nixon.

The concept of responsible party government is not a complex one. Essentially, it suggests that there be a link between the voters and the elective officials of our democracy, provided by the political party to which both give their support. But aligning those three elements, voters, officials and parties, in any stable arrangement has proved to be increasingly difficult. This is true despite the fact that the major parties in America are remarkably durable institutions. The Republicans have a history of more than a century; the Democrats are almost as old as the nation. In the past hundred years, these two parties have almost monopolized the election of public officials in this country. The President, every governor, every member of the House of Representatives and all but two of the hundred sitting senators in office today were elected to office on either the Republican or Democratic ticket. While many municipal elections are nominally nonpartisan, most of the big-city mayors also play an active role in one or the other of the major parties.

These parties of ours also exert a powerful hold on the voters, or at least they did until recently. About 60 percent of the electorate think of themselves as being affiliated with one or the other of the major parties. Warren E. Miller, co-author of *The American Voter,* the classic in its field, argues that party loyalty is as durable for an individual as any value in his life except his sex and his religious identification.

Yet, for all that, we can see that there has been a weakening of responsible party government in the past generation. The legs on which it stands are being kicked out from under it, and the structure is wobbly, if it has not actually collapsed. The party activists—what the political scientists call the "cadre party"—have always been a small proportion of the general public, but even their loyalty is not what it used to be. Patronage has been reduced by civil service reforms, and the attractiveness of political jobs as an incentive to party work has been minimized by the affluence of our economy. Most of the work of the political parties is now done by volunteers, who feel free to come and go as the whim, or the issue, strikes them.

The candidates, while still seeking nomination through the parties, are far more independent of the party structure. They count on their "personal image" more than their partisan affiliation to win them votes and worry more about their television appearance than the solidity of their ties to the organization. And the voters too are demonstrating their independence. By 1970, half again as many called themselves political independents as had done so a generation earlier. In the 1968 election, more than half the voters reported splitting their tickets.

Eisenhower: The Man and the President

The start of what Walter Dean Burnham calls this process of "disaggregation," the pulling-apart of the tripod that supports responsible party government, can be seen in the Eisenhower years.

Dwight David Eisenhower came to politics and the presidency a national hero, the commander of the army that liberated Europe and defeated Hitler. He left the White House more popular, if anything, than he was on the day he was first sworn in as President. Thanks to his popularity, two-party competition became a reality in America again. After the Democrats had governed the country for a full generation, growing weary in the process, the Republicans finally found themselves a winner. Indeed, in two full generations, from 1932 to 1972, only two Republicans have been able to capture the presidency: Eisenhower and the man he chose as his running mate, Richard Nixon. That, perhaps, is distinction enough for Eisenhower. But one can also say of his presidency that it was the time when America began the long and still uncompleted tasks of negotiating a reconciliation of the two races that share this Republic and of the two nuclear-armed superstates that share this globe.

Eisenhower redeemed the most important pledge of his first campaign by ending the war in Korea and its attendant domestic controversies. He opened the explorations for détente and disarmament agreements with the Soviet Union that began to bear fruit in the terms of later Presidents. He appointed the Chief

Justice who led a unanimous Supreme Court in striking down the legal supports for a segregated society, and, without much enthusiasm, Eisenhower enforced the orders of the Court. Belatedly but effectively, he brought to bear his immense personal prestige to quash the ugly menace of McCarthyism.

Mainly, though, Eisenhower provided a breathing spell, a calming interlude, in American politics. It may have been—and likely was—a needed pause. The nation had gone through twenty years of almost unbroken tension, starting with the Great Depression, then World War II, then the sickening realization of the new conflict with Russia in the Cold War, and climaxed by the frustrating war in Korea and the revelations of scandal and treason in the too-long-entrenched Democratic Administration. It was, as the GOP slogan said, "time for a change," not simply of party but of mood. With grateful relief, Americans agreed, almost to a man, that "We like Ike," and they relaxed and enjoyed his loose-reined leadership.

Walter Lippmann, with his remarkable insight, defined "the Eisenhower mission" exactly in a column written in January, 1954, less than a year after Eisenhower took office.

His appointed role, the role for which he was chosen—the role for which he is fitted—is that of the restorer of order and peace after an age of violence and faction.

Nobody who knew Dwight Eisenhower . . . would ever have picked him to be a dynamic, progressive and crusading President of the United States. . . . To be a dynamic, progressive and crusading President calls for a knowledge and an experience of civil affairs and of American politics which General Eisenhower did not have, and could not possibly be expected to acquire at the age of sixty. . . .

Nobody who knew him, and the American scene in which he would have to work, would have turned to Eisenhower if in 1952 the times had demanded a dynamic, progressive crusade. The fact was, however, that by 1952 this country and the western world had had all the dynamism, all the innovation, all the crusading that human nature can take.

For more than twenty years the people had had more than enough upheaval in their lives, of ups and downs, of being drafted, taxed, and moved around, of excitement, of fervor and of fear and of hope, of big words and hot feelings. . . . By 1952 . . . it had become imperative that this country collect itself, that it consolidate itself, that it restore its confidence in itself, that it find a way to quiet its frayed nerves, to allay its suspicions, and that it regain its composure and its equanimity.

That was the wellspring of the Eisenhower movement. He was the man who was above party and above faction. He was the man outside the issues that were dividing the nation. He was the protector of the things on which Americans are united. He was a strong man, invulnerable to all suspicion, and of good will. He was to fill a role which in the unfolding of history needed to be filled.

The trouble was that the breathing spell lasted too long and inculcated some costly habits. One term of Eisenhower might have been necessary; a second term was an expensive self-indulgence for the country. As Richard H. Rovere has written, "By 1956, Eisenhower had achieved just about all that it was in his power to achieve. . . . The second term was anticlimax all the way."

Those last four Eisenhower years were wasted. They were a time of economic stagnation, of lost opportunities for starts on the problems of the cities and the schools and on the reinvigoration of the Federal system, problems which all but overwhelmed us in the 1960s. What seemed to many almost a halcyon period, the longest period of peace we have known as a nation in the last thirty years, and an era of muted strife and partisanship at home, was, so far as our domestic needs were concerned, an expensive holiday from responsibility.

Eisenhower and the Republicans

It was also a holiday from party responsibility, the start of this long era in which party lines have worked not to shape and discipline government action but to hobble it. And for this, too, Eisenhower bears some responsibility.

He came late, of course, to partisan politics and it is perhaps unfair to criticize him for failing to recognize the role of party in government. He speaks in his memoirs of "my isolation, from boyhood, from nearly all politics." Not until the beginning of 1952, the year in which he was elected President, did he even publicly declare his Republican affiliation. His nomination was as unpopular with the "cadre party," the traditional Republican organization men who supported Senator Robert A. Taft of Ohio, as it was popular with the country. His election depended only to a minimal degree on the support of Republican party workers; Eisenhower himself felt much closer to the "Citizens for Eisenhower," the independent-minded volunteers who joined in helping nominate and elect him.

Once elected and in office, he displayed some willingness to take up certain of the traditional duties a President acquires as head of his party, a role which his Democratic predecessors, Franklin D. Roosevelt and Harry S Truman, had played with undisguised joy. He campaigned dutifully for Republican congressional candidates in the midterm elections. By the end of his tenure, in 1959 and 1960, when his own increasing fiscal conservatism was sharply at odds with the expansionist economic policies Senate Democrats were advocating, he even began to see that some fundamental policy questions did divide on party lines. But Eisenhower never really overcame his initial distrust of partisanship and his skepticism about the role of the political party in government. "I think it is quite apparent," he told a press conference in 1954, "that I am not very much of a partisan. The times are too serious, I think, to indulge in partisanship to the extreme."

His attitude had at least three sources. For one thing, he never lost the professional soldier's distaste for the messy and sometimes sordid wheeling and dealing of backroom politics. Robert J. Donovan, in his account of the first term, *Eisenhower: The Inside Story*, reported that the new President "bitterly resented" the patronage demands of Republican party leaders and in October, 1953, "heatedly gave the Cabinet to understand that he was sick and tired of being bothered about patronage."

Second, Eisenhower was greatly concerned about keeping alive the tradition of bipartisan support for American foreign policy, in which he had been steeped during all the years he was a senior military–foreign policy figure under Democratic Presidents. "My belief," he said, "is that we must seek agreements among ourselves, with respect to foreign policy, that are not confined to any party. . . . Regardless of what party takes over, there must be a stability or there is no foreign policy." Keeping the peace and meeting America's world responsibilities were Eisenhower's main interests as President. To succeed, he believed, he needed the cooperation of Democratic leaders. And, since both Speaker of the House Sam Rayburn and Senate Majority Leader Lyndon B. Johnson were unstinting in their support of his foreign policy, the bipartisan approach seemed to him fully justified.

Finally, and this is a bit ironic, Eisenhower was a shrewd enough politician himself to recognize that his own popularity and prestige were so much greater than his adopted party's that he could only damage his own standing by letting himself be dragged into the role of a partisan. He tended to dismiss the slambang rhetoric of politicians as beneath his notice and contempt, even when it came from his own close associates. "I have my own doubts that any great partisanship displayed by members of the Executive Department is really appropriate at this day and time," he told a press conference early in the 1954 campaign year. Six months later, when asked about the speeches Vice President Nixon was giving, blaming Democratic "appeasement" for the loss of China and the wars in Korea and Indochina, Eisenhower put some distance between himself and his Number 2 man. "Each individual . . . is entitled to his own opinions and convictions," he said. "I admire and respect and like the Vice President. . . . [But] I carry administrative and executive responsibilities . . . that don't fall on some of the other individuals. . . . Now there have been from the beginning of parties intemperate statements. . . . We seem to survive them."

Party chairmen and Republican officeholders may have cursed privately as the President, time after time, airily dismissed as "partisan talk" their elaborately orchestrated attacks on the Democrats, but the public admired his independence, as Eisenhower knew full well.

As a result of this detachment from his role as party leader, and despite his oft-stated desire to make the GOP an instrument of what he called at various times "dynamic conservatism" or "modern Republicanism," the Republican party never became, in fact or in the public mind, Eisenhower's party. When he was barely three months in office and a vacancy occurred in the national chairmanship of the party, Donovan reports that Eisenhower "refused to take a position on the choice of the chairman, because he did not wish to be responsible for the latter's being marked as 'my man.'" By the time he had been in office three years and had seen leaders of the Old Guard congressional wing of the GOP repudiate the more progressive parts of his program, Eisenhower was even contemplating starting a third party of his own. He finally dismissed the idea as impractical, but the fact that he even considered it is, as Donovan says, a measure of the breach that had developed.

Eisenhower acknowledged his failure in his comment on the 1956 election, in which the voters returned a Democratic Congress despite his personal triumph over Adlai Stevenson. "From my viewpoint," he told reporters, the election returns mean that "the United States has not yet been convinced that modern Republicanism is with us and is going to be the guiding philosophy of the Republican party." It is hardly surprising, then, that the Eisenhower Administration's ranks produced very little in the way of Republican leadership for the 1960s and 1970s. Aside from Mr. Nixon, only three Cabinet-rank officials later ran for office, and all three were defeated. Even among the lower-rank officials it is difficult to find men who later emerged as winners of major office. There were John A. Volpe and Elliot L. Richardson, William W. Scranton and Nelson A. Rockefeller and that is about all.

Thus, from the viewpoint of the Republican party, and from the viewpoint of those with an interest in a healthy two-party system, the Eisenhower years were a time of lost opportunity. Given an immensely popular figure as their spokesman, Republicans failed entirely to increase their political base. The gains the party began to make in the South were offset by losses in other regions. In 1950, the last of the pre-Eisenhower elections, the Republicans elected 199 representatives, 47 senators and 25 governors. In 1960, when Eisenhower was leaving office, they elected only 174 representatives, 36 senators and 16 governors.

The conservative congressional wing of the party, rooted in the safe, one-party states and districts, fought a successful rear-guard action through the eight years of Eisenhower's tenure against his intermittent efforts to make Republicanism "modern." From the beginning, when Ways and Means Chairman Dan Reed balked at his tax and trade bills and Senators John Bricker and William F. Knowland tried to limit his treaty-making powers, they battled against the progressive internationalist tendencies of the Administration. Throughout the Eisenhower years, Nixon attempted to mediate the conflict between the two wings of the party, but with only limited success. He failed to dissuade McCarthy from his attacks on the Administration in 1953 and 1954, just as he failed, in 1960, to satisfy either the Rockefeller progressives or the congressional conservatives with the compromise platform written at the Chicago convention.

When Eisenhower and Nixon went into political retirement after the 1960 election, the congressional Republicans, led by Everett McKinley Dirksen, took back complete control of the party. Spiritual heirs of Robert Taft, but without his intellectual integrity, they became a classic party of lost causes, symbolized by Dirksen's dogged efforts to reinstate prayer in public schools over the Supreme Court's constitutional objections, and his equally futile effort to reverse the one-man-one-vote ruling, which ended rural control of the state legislatures. In 1964, the congressional conservatives staged their greatest "lost-cause" effort, the presidential campaign of Barry Goldwater. Goldwater had a particular genius for raising settled questions in a manner best designed to stir public fears. Only through his cooperation could Lyndon Johnson have gotten through the 1964 campaign by promising not to abolish social security and not to sell the Tennessee Valley Authority. Only with an opponent like Goldwater could Johnson have managed to avoid discussing the terrible policy choices required in Indochina, choices, we now know, he was secretly making even during that campaign.

The nomination of Barry Goldwater—a man enthusiastically supported only by a minority faction of a minority party—marked the final failure of Eisenhower's policy of neglect of his own political party. The futility of the General's sporadic attempts at political leadership became more evident to the public after he left office than it had been under the protective cover of the White House. Between 1961 and 1964, he gave his support to one or two abortive efforts to revive a progressive Republican "citizens movement" that would be a counterweight to the conservative congressional caucus.

I remember journeying up to Gettysburg in the summer of 1962, where a green-and-white-striped circus tent had been pitched on the General's lawn and a crowd of 150 dignitaries assembled, to hear him give his blessing to something called an All-Republican Conference. It was a brainchild of the New York *Herald Tribune's* Walter Thayer, and it was supposed to bring back the good folks who had nominated Ike in 1952. After the day it was launched, nothing was ever heard of it.

At various points in the pre-convention struggle of 1964, Eisenhower gave tentative encouragement to three separate moderate-progressive Republicans, Nixon, Scranton and George Romney, in their efforts to prevent Goldwater's nomination. But in the end he did nothing—except to make a phone call to Scranton that delayed the Pennsylvania Governor's entrance into the race.

Fittingly, but unhappily, for him, Eisenhower was present in San Francisco to see the last act played. I remember watching him from the press stand in the Cow Palace when the convention crowd erupted in cheers at the attack on "sensation-seeking columnists and commentators," which had been written into the Eisenhower speech. He delivered the line almost casually, and at first smiled with surprise and pleasure that he had said something that had ignited this extraordinary response. Then, as the shouting continued and was accompanied by fist-waving threats to the television booths and the press galleries, his expression changed to puzzlement and a frown of concern. In that moment, I think, Eisenhower sensed for the first time the mob emotions that had taken command of the Republican party in the vacuum of responsible leadership he had left behind. Before the convention week was over, there were more shocks. A niece complained to him that she had been "molested" on the convention floor. And when Goldwater declared in his acceptance speech that "extremism in the defense of liberty is no vice . . . and moderation in the pursuit of justice, no virtue," Eisenhower commented plaintively that "it would seem to say that the end always justifies the means, and the whole American system refutes that idea." It was a sad, but significant, end to his policy of neglect of his party responsibilities.

The Public and the Parties

As significant as the separation of governmental leadership from party responsibility that occurred in the Eisenhower Administration was the erosion of the public's sense of responsible partisanship that occurred in those years. The 1952 election that brought Eisenhower to power had some of the characteristics of a traditional party victory. Republicans gained control not only of the White House but of both houses of Congress. The gains were roughly proportional: between 1948 and 1952, the Republican percentage of the major-party presidential vote increased 7.8 percent; of Senate seats, 6.1 percent; and of House seats, 11.1 percent. But this shift occurred without any change in the underlying party identification of the predominantly Democratic electorate; the voters felt it was "time for a change," but most of them still considered themselves Democrats. The 1952 election study of the scholars at the University of Michigan Center for Political Studies attributed the Republican victory to "a temporary movement of normal Democrats and nonpartisans toward the Republican candidate," and noted the remarkably "high rate of ticket-splitting" among those voters. "Three out of five of those Democrats and Independents who voted for Mr. Eisenhower in 1952 were not willing to support the rest of the Republican slate," they said in their book *The American Voter.*

In 1954, despite a vigorous campaign, Eisenhower failed to hold the Republican majorities in Congress, and in 1956, even though he won by a bigger margin (57 percent) than in his first race, his party made no gain in Senate races and actually lost two more seats in the House—the first time since 1848 such a division of responsibility between Congress and the Executive had occurred in a presidential election year. Three out of four Democrats and independents who backed Eisenhower split their tickets, according to the Michigan team's survey. Once established in the Eisenhower elections, the habit of ticket splitting has spread down the ballot, even reaching relatively obscure state and local offices. Data collected by Walter DeVries and Lance Tarrance, Jr., in their recent book, *The Ticket-Splitters,* show just how rapid that trend has been. In nine presidential elections between 1920 and 1952, the proportion of congressional districts supporting a presidential candidate of one party and a representative of another party averaged 15.3 percent. In the last four elections that percentage has doubled—to slightly over 30 percent. The big increase came between 1952 and 1956, when it suddenly jumped from 19.3 percent to 29.9 percent, just about the level it has been ever since.

What explains this sudden and sizable break in the habit of party voting? In large part, is was the personal appeal of Eisenhower, an appeal which had little or nothing to do with his Republican label. It was so easy to cast an "I like Ike" vote, without worrying about what it was that Ike liked in the way of national policies. Eisenhower had the almost total confidence of the American people; he redeemed their faith by ending the war in Korea and by submerging the dissension in Washington. Thereafter, the public sensed, probably long before Eisenhower and his associates did, that the real work of his presidency was done. Yet they chose in 1956 to re-elect him with a Democratic Congress. Why?

The reason was that the public saw no sharp issues, no real policy choices to be made. Eisenhower and the Republicans had been swept into office on a wave of public opposition to the Korean war and the "corruption and Communism" charged against the Democratic Administration. By 1956 those issues had faded; indeed, they did not last even long enough to keep Republicans in control of Congress in 1954, when Mr. Nixon tried to use them again as the focus of his midterm campaign. And no new issues had emerged to replace them, in large part because the leadership of the Democratic party in Congress worked hand-in-glove with Eisenhower to see to it that they did not.

Johnson and Rayburn, as minority leaders of the Senate and House, extended full cooperation to the President on his modest legislative program in 1953 and 1954, in a Congress overshadowed by the controversy and eventual censure of Senator Joseph R. McCarthy. When Eisenhower made an uncharacteristically partisan comment at the outset of the 1954 campaign, warning that a Democratic victory might bring on "a cold war of partisan politics," Johnson and Rayburn deliberately turned the other cheek, sending the President a telegram that said, "Your statement of last night is an unwarranted and unjust attack on the many Democrats who have done so much to cooperate with your administration and to defend your program from attacks by members and leaders of your own party. . . . We assure you . . . there will be no cold war conducted against you by the Democrats when we gain control of Congress."

And there was not. The Democratic Congress approved the "Formosa resolution," authorizing American defense of that island, the reciprocal trade bill, the SEATO treaty and every other foreign policy measure the President asked. It also launched the Interstate Highway Program that was to be the major domestic monument of the Eisenhower years. Issues on which there was no bipartisan agreement, including aid to schools, health insurance and statehood for Hawaii and Alaska, were put aside.

The game in those years was legislative patty-cake. The Democratic leadership resolutely trimmed and cut their proposals to whatever pattern they thought the President would accept. There was pressure on Johnson from some liberal Democrats, and from Democratic National Committee chairman Paul Butler, to pass *Democratic* economic measures, *Democratic* health, education and welfare measures, even if they risked an Eisenhower veto. But, with their shaky legislative majorities, Johnson and Rayburn flatly refused to do so. As Rowland Evans and Robert Novak explain in their excellent political biography, *Lyndon B. Johnson: The Exercise of Power,* the two Texans believed that the strategy Butler recommended "would put the Democratic party in the untenable position of tormenting the benign and well-loved war hero in the White House, would promote discord in an era of national conciliation, and would expose the Democrats to a charge of politics for politics' sake."

In 1956, Joseph L. Rauh, chairman of Americans for Democratic Action, the voice of the party's liberal wing, complained that "under the banner of Senate Majority Leader Johnson, the congressional Democrats have become practically indistinguishable from the party they allegedly oppose." The evidence of the polls indicates they were almost indistinguishable—so far as issues were concerned—to the general public. But Johnson and Rayburn held to their course, and found vindication in the election of a Democratic Congress in 1956 while Eisenhower was achieving his second landslide.

That result, Johnson said, showed the wisdom of "responsible cooperation." If it also marked a defeat for responsible party government, Johnson was not alone in being blind to the implications of that fact. The complacency of the period was widely shared. Even James Reston, normally the least complacent of men, was impelled to write a *New York Times* column a month before the 1956 election implying that politics had become irrelevant. "The American voters are funny people," he said. "They don't listen. Once every four years they are courted and coaxed by Presidents and would-be Presidents, by Democrats and Republicans, by commentators, socialists, teetotalers, vegetarians and prohibitionists, but they don't listen. . . . They don't read. They don't vote. They don't care. But that's all right. They don't need to: never did need to. They get along. And think of the nonsense they miss every four years."

The euphoria, the smugness, of 1956 did not last long. In less than two years after Eisenhower was sworn in for his second term, the United States was caught in another recession, with unemployment far more severe than it had been in 1954; Governor Orval Faubus had set the pattern of diehard resistance to school desegregation; the Soviets had launched the first space vehicle; and Communism had established a Western Hemisphere foothold in Cuba. The issues of our lagging schools, social services, health care and defense—which had been submerged—began to surface. Prodded by the activist Democrats elected to Congress in the 1958 landslide and by Butler's Democratic Advisory Council, Johnson and Rayburn began in 1959 and 1960 to put forward identifiably Democratic programs to meet these needs. Eisenhower, recognizing belatedly that there were genuine issues between the parties, fought back with a series of vetoes and strong public condemnation of the Democratic "reckless spenders." Issues were drawn on party lines for the 1960 election.

But the heritage of the Eisenhower era has not been so easily obliterated. Once broken, the links between the public and the political parties, the government and the parties, have not mended. The fateful separation between national policy and party responsibility that began sixteen years ago continues today.

2

Kennedy

The damage to responsible party government that occurred during the Eisenhower years might have been repaired during the presidency of John F. Kennedy, but it was not. It was not repaired because Kennedy was not granted the time it would have taken for the parties to relocate themselves around the issues that emerged in the 1960s or for public opinion to readjust to their changing alignment.

Whether eight years of a Kennedy presidency, and particularly the kind of election campaign he would have fought in 1964, would have revitalized the party system is, of course, conjectural. There is much in Kennedy's pre-presidential history to indicate he was capable of being the catalyst for such a development, and there is some evidence that in his last year in office such an effort was beginning to take shape in his mind. But for most of the time he led the Democratic party, at least from his nomination through the mid-term election of 1962, Kennedy felt himself under such severe political constraints that he had little room for maneuver. So his chapter in the saga of responsible party government is an equivocal one—a tale of what might have been, not what was.

He was, himself, an equivocal political figure, part of the Democratic party structure, yet never wholly its creature. He was the model for the man of whom James Q. Wilson, the Harvard political scientist, wrote in *The Amateur Democrat:*

New political leadership in times of party crisis or organizational decay is frequently provided by young men who are politically "marginal"—who stand between two worlds, the old and the new, the ascendant and the dying, and who because of their unique position can create a new alliance which will perpetuate the political system. Typically, they have a background which symbolizes different and even competing values in the community. For example, one might be an Irish Catholic with a Harvard education and an intellectual manner.

Equivocal as Kennedy was, the political situation in which he operated was even more so. The old party lines had begun to melt during Eisenhower's tenure. Traditional party loyalties had been cast off by some voters; millions more were indicating their uncertainty by splitting their tickets. The South had shown in three consecutive elections from 1952 through 1960 that it was not afraid to vote Republican at the presidential level, but it still sent overwhelmingly Democratic delegations to Congress. Kennedy made major breakthroughs in the once-Republican suburbs, but their congressional seats remained in the hands of the GOP. Symptoms of a party realignment were beginning to become evident, but they were confused by the welter of conflicting racial, religious, economic and regional forces that were at play in 1960.

While Kennedy's election ended (temporarily) the pattern of divided party control of Congress and the presidency, there was still little symmetry between his constituency and that of the congressional Democrats. One hundred and fourteen congressional districts voted for a congressman of one party and a presidential candidate of the opposite party in 1960, just sixteen fewer than had done so in 1956.

It was, in short, a transitional time in politics, a time in which an equivocal political leader was attempting to cope with a shifting party situation and a fluid public opinion.

Kennedy's time on the national stage may be divided into three phases. The first period, which stretched from the start of his career to the time of his nomination, saw him and the "amateur Democrats," whose liberal policy views he came to accept, gain the upper hand, first in Massachusetts, and then in the national Democratic party. The second stage, which lasted from the time of his nomination until the midterm election of 1962, was essentially an effort by Kennedy to accommodate himself to existing power relationships in the party and in Congress. The final stage, cut short by his death, saw him, no longer an "outsider," try to reshape the political-governmental structure along more responsible lines.

Phase One: The Kennedy Takeover Technique

The organizational secret of Kennedy politics was so simple that it was often overlooked: it was a politics of personal involvement, on a massive scale. It was laid out publicly, at the time of John Kennedy's presidential campaign, by Lawrence F. O'Brien in the manual for Democratic precinct workers:

> Volunteers are essential to the success of any political campaign. . . . There is no such thing as having a surplus of volunteers. There are any number of ways of recruiting volunteer workers, including: asking persons who have offered their services to the candidate. Asking persons who have returned worker cards . . . indicating they will perform some specific volunteer function in the campaign. Asking college and high school students. Asking members of political, civic, church and social clubs. Asking persons who express a desire for political participation and experience. Asking persons who have worked in previous political campaigns. Asking elderly persons, who may be willing to perform light campaign chores, such as addressing envelopes. Asking members of Democratic state, city, county and town committees. Asking members of labor unions. . . . Asking the wives, husbands, sons, daughters, sisters, brothers, fathers, mothers, aunts, uncles, cousins, and friends of everyone in the preceding categories. . . .
> It is the responsibility of campaign headquarters to make certain . . . that everyone who volunteers to work is given an assignment. It is terribly discouraging to a person who has volunteered to work in a campaign not to be given something to do. More than that, it is a sure

sign of an inefficient campaign organization. There is *always* work to be done in a political campaign.

Despite O'Brien's explicitness, commentators and rival politicians kept looking elsewhere for the secret of Kennedy's success. Some said it was the family money. Some said it was his "glamour" or "charisma." Some said it was the "ruthless efficiency" of his organization. None of these considerations, obviously, is irrelevant. Had John Kennedy been a homely, tongue-tied, penniless orphan, surrounded by a gang of incompetent hacks, it is unlikely he would have become President of the United States. But in the competition for that office, which attracts mainly men of ability, strong personality and access to money and talent, what gave him his critical advantage, I believe, was his distinctive ability to make his supporters become his workers, and to utilize their efforts effectively.

I encountered this ability early in my coverage of his presidential campaign, and the forcefulness of the lesson kept me from underestimating Kennedy as much as some of my more experienced colleagues did in that spring of 1960. I was working for the Washington *Star* by then, and was assigned to do an "in-depth" study of the Kennedy-Humphrey battle in the West Virginia primary.

The time was April of 1960. Kennedy had won the Wisconsin primary over Hubert Humphrey, but in a way that was almost as damaging to his chances of nomination as to the loser's. He had carried the Catholic, urban areas of Wisconsin, but lost most of the Protestant, rural sections. He had come to West Virginia—a state that was suspicious, isolated, poor and 95 percent Protestant—against the advice of some of his advisers, fearing a defeat but seeing no way to avoid the test.

The place I chose to focus my story was Raleigh County, southeast of Charleston, a section of the state even more poor and more Protestant than average. All the political powers in the county—Senator Robert C. Byrd, United Mine Workers district chairman George Titler, Sheriff Okey Mills—were supporting Humphrey. It seemed a hopelessly stacked deck, until one looked closely. Humphrey's big-name supporters were not nearly as concerned about him as they were about the new nominees for governor and sheriff to be chosen in the same primary. The Humphrey head-quarters in Beckley, the county seat, was actually being run by one salaried secretary and two volunteers, one a retired railroad brake-man and the other an oil company salesman who said, "I haven't been too active, 'cause this is my busy season on the turnpike."

But the real surprise was to see the activity engendered for Kennedy in a county where the local Democratic "power struc-ture" apparently had him locked out. O'Brien outlined it for me on a drive down from Charleston, and he did not exaggerate its dimensions. The organization had been put together from concen-tric circles of friends, acquaintances and enlisted allies, most of them newcomers to any politics, let alone a presidential primary. The Raleigh County coordinator for Kennedy was Ben Smith, of Gloucester, Massachusetts, one of his Harvard roommates. (Smith was later to earn a footnote in history as the man who kept John Kennedy's Senate seat warm for two years, until Ted Kennedy was old enough to run for it.) Smith had help from Cecil Saunders, a Kentucky lawyer and former state senator, who had roomed with JFK at PT-boat training school, and Grant Stockdale, a Miami stockbroker and social friend of the Kennedys. Ted Kennedy was spending a good deal of time in Raleigh County himself, hand-shaking at the shift changes in the mines and lending his glamour to the volunteer efforts.

The local recruits to the Kennedy campaign were also interest-ing. The chairman was a thirty-year-old lawyer named Don Hod-son, a relative newcomer to town, who had no stake in the old-line factional battles. Mrs. David Kennedy, whose husband was pre-vented from working openly for John Kennedy because of his job as a UMW lawyer, was the women's co-chairman. A local baker, who was a Catholic, and a former sheriff, who was at odds with Okey Mills, comprised the remainder of the steering committee.

Each of them, in turn, had brought in his own friends and

associates. Mrs. Kennedy, for instance, had put together a fifty-one-woman committee to make a complete telephone canvass of the county. How had she done it? "I got most of the names from the financial statement of our church," she said. "Even a lot of my Republican friends changed their registration, so they could work and vote for the Senator." Others had recruited dozens of Beckley College students to deliver Kennedy tabloids to every house in the city and address a mailing to every rural letter-box holder. It was obvious after two or three days in the county that far more work, effort and enthusiasm were going into the Kennedy campaign than into Humphrey's. And it was having an impact. While the politicians in town (including most of the Kennedy campaign leaders) predicted unanimously that Raleigh County would go for Humphrey by a wider margin than the state as a whole, my unscientific sampling of 112 prospective voters showed Kennedy with better than a two-to-one lead.

I wrote that story for the *Star* in advance of the primary, and had the satisfaction (rare in a journalistic career marked by some monumentally bad guesses) of seeing Kennedy carry West Virginia by a three-to-two margin and take Raleigh County by a margin of two to one. What he had shown was a talent for going outside the normal political channels and enlisting, in large numbers, the energies of enthusiastic political amateurs. The amateur, as James Wilson describes him in his book, "is one who is motivated to action by the idea that politics is the channel for expressing a serious concern for determining public policies." His principal reward, Wilson says, "is the sense of having fulfilled a felt obligation to 'participate.' "

What is not well appreciated is how fearful most professional politicians are of the amateurs. The amateurs are unpredictable, emotional, unwilling to compromise and dogmatic on what they regard as principle—all traits which make a professional politician acutely nervous. A professional fears the unknown. He wants to win, but even more, he wants to control. This means he would rather lose with his own men and keep control of the organization than take the risk of bringing in a lot of strangers, who just might be able to deliver a victory but who would not be under his control.

Since most men who run for President and their principal staff assistants are professional politicians, this conflict turns up at one stage or another in almost every presidential campaign. A good many presidential campaigns fail because the "inner circle" never opens to admit the kind of outside help necessary for the cause to succeed. Kennedy did not permit this to happen. His politics was always a politics of inclusion. It may have been simply that, coming from that big family, the notion of a personal, exclusive campaign never had a chance to take root. Not only did his brothers, sisters and parents participate in a big way, but each of them brought his own friends and acquaintances along. Indeed, the keynote of the entire effort was to reach out beyond the defined limits and bring in new people: new workers, new supporters, new voters. Registration was a major emphasis of every Kennedy campaign.

Kennedy was by no means the first of the Presidents of the modern era to practice the politics of expansion and inclusion. Roosevelt significantly increased the electorate, particularly in his second-term landslide. Eisenhower did so even more dramatically. Indeed, the General, who had none of the habits or the inhibitions of the professional politician, played "reach out" politics with great success. His supporters won Texas—which proved to be the key to the nomination—by flooding the precinct caucuses, the county conventions, and finally the state convention with hordes of newly-enlisted amateurs, whose Republican credentials the Taft regulars protested in vain were nonexistent. In the general election, too, Eisenhower went outside the defined limits of politics and stirred a massive outpouring of voters. In 1948, only 48 million Americans participated in the four-way contest among Harry S Truman, Thomas E. Dewey, Henry A. Wallace and Strom Thurmond. In 1952, 61 million came out, and Eisenhower won by 6 million votes even though Stevenson drew 3 million more ballots than Truman had in winning four years before.

Kennedy had a similar, if smaller, success in 1960. The total vote increased almost 7 million from 1956. Although Nixon came within 1.5 million of matching Eisenhower's landslide figure in the previous election, he lost the election narrowly to Kennedy who attracted 8.2 million more voters than Stevenson. It is one thing, however, to pull votes for yourself—as Eisenhower and Kennedy both did—and another thing to reshape the electorate in a way that gives your party a decisive long-term advantage, which was Roosevelt's feat.

Eisenhower never managed, and only intermittently tried, to convert his immense personal strength into a broadened base of support for the Republican party. But, on the face of it, Kennedy was a far more partisan figure than Eisenhower, by both background and instinct. Both grandfathers had been successful Democratic politicians in Boston. His father was an influential figure and major official in the Roosevelt Administration, until his break with the President over American preparations for World War II.

While Kennedy always thought of himself and was considered a partisan Democrat, he held back from ever being an "organization man." When he returned to Boston after World War II to begin his political career, he turned down what would have seemed to most fledgling politicians a flattering offer. Governor Maurice Tobin invited Kennedy to come onto the 1946 ticket as his running mate for lieutenant governor. But Kennedy declined, preferring not to enmesh himself either in Tobin's own fate (he was defeated for re-election that year, as it turned out) or in the snarls of statehouse politics.

Instead, he entered the already crowded field for the 11th District House seat which James Michael Curley had vacated to return, one last time, as Mayor of Boston. Kennedy won the nomination easily in a ten-man field, exploiting the double tactics so typical of his ambivalent relationship with the party: his father used his funds and his contacts to line up as many of the organiza-tion politicians as he could reach; Kennedy and his contemporaries enlisted the amateurs and carried the campaign to voters beyond the grasp of the organization. Six years later, by the time he was ready to reach for the Senate, the "Kennedy organization" in Massachusetts, in which the professional politicians were a distinct minority to the amateurs, was so far superior to anything the fac-tion-ridden state Democratic party could muster that every other office seeker in the state was frantically grabbing for Kennedy's help and coattails.

He was not above rejecting pleas for aid made in the name of party unity. As a freshman congressman, he was the only Massa-chusetts Democrat who refused to sign a plea for executive clemency for Curley, who had been convicted of mail fraud. In 1954 and again in 1960, Kennedy did everything in his power, so obviously that it infuriated other Massachusetts Democrats, to ease his Republican colleague Leverett Saltonstall's path to re-elec-tion, even declining to endorse by name his Democratic opponent.

About the only times during his ten years as the Common-wealth's leading Democrat that he deigned to concern himself with the state Democratic organization was when he wanted something from it. In 1956, he intervened successfully in a fight over the state chairmanship in order to assure his control of the National Convention delegation. He did the same thing in 1960, on the eve of his own nomination, and, after his election, he intervened again to arrange the disposition of his Senate seat within the Kennedy family. But, for the most part, he treated the Massachusetts Democratic party as a snakepit—which is not an inaccurate description. Arthur M. Schlesinger, Jr., quotes a 1954 conversation, in which Kennedy expressed despair about his home state party: "Nothing can be done until it is beaten—badly beaten. Then there will be a chance of rebuilding. If I were knocked out of the presidential thing, I would put Bobby into the Massachusetts picture to run for Governor. It takes someone with Bobby's nerve and his investigative experience to clean up the mess in the Legislature and the Governor's Council." But John Kennedy never paused to "clean up the mess" in his home party, nor did Robert Kennedy, nor has Ted Kennedy.

On the basis of their Massachusetts experience, John Kennedy and his brothers developed a healthy contempt for most old-line organization Democratic leaders. Schlesinger quotes Kennedy as telling Stevenson on the eve of the 1960 convention, "The support of leaders is much overrated anyway; leaders aren't worth a damn." There was some braggadocio in the statement, but the fact was that he had just finished outmaneuvering most of the established leaders of the party, whose attitude toward his candidacy had been skeptical if not outright hostile. A few, including John M. Bailey of Connecticut and Charles A. Buckley of the Bronx, had thrown in with him from the start. Others, like Governors J. Millard Tawes of Maryland and Michael V. DiSalle of Ohio, had capitulated early when faced with the threat of primary fights in their home states. New York's Carmine DeSapio came along later, when Kennedy had many of the second-echelon leaders in the city and state in line; Pennsylvania's David L. Lawrence and Illinois's Richard J. Daley withheld their support until convention eve. New Jersey's Governor Robert B. Meyner refused to acknowledge the facts of political life and insisted on maintaining his favorite-son candidacy against the strong support for Kennedy in the state organization; Meyner never recovered politically from his misjudgment.

The point is that, despite his Democratic heritage, despite his personal and family links to some of the established powers in the party, Kennedy won the nomination essentially by going outside the organization, using "political amateurs," to round up votes in the primaries and thus forcing the professionals in the "cadre party" to accept him as the nominee.

As part of the price he paid for his help from the "amateurs," many of them previously Stevenson supporters, Kennedy accommodated himself to the liberal programs they espoused. As late as

1956, his liberalism had been suspect; the South backed him for Vice President against Kefauver and Humphrey, the liberal candidates. But in the next four years, Kennedy gradually shifted his voting record on such issues as farm subsidies, public power and reclamation projects and identified himself more clearly as an advocate of civil rights and welfare measures.

His shift coincided with the emergence of an "activist" Democratic bloc of liberal senators and representatives, whose ranks were swelled by the Democratic landslide of 1958. Their proposals were publicized by Democratic National Chairman Paul Butler's Democratic Advisory Council, a liberal group which Kennedy joined just before he formally launched his presidential campaign. Butler saw to it that the liberals and activists had control of the Democratic platform committee, with a Kennedy ally, Chester Bowles, as its chairman, and the nominee found the platform much to his liking.

Thus the first phase of the Kennedy period, which culminated in his nomination, is a story of mutual accommodation—his gradual, relatively easy acceptance of what came to be the program supported by the party's activist, liberal majority; and their gradual, but not so easy, acceptance of him as their legitimate leader and spokesman.

Phase Two: Playing by the Rules

As soon as he was nominated, Kennedy's focus shifted. His urgent necessity, as he saw it, was to come to terms with the powerful elements of the Democratic party that were opposed both to his nomination and to the liberal party platform. The process began immediately, with the choice of Lyndon Johnson as his running mate. Johnson was the candidate of the South, of the conservatives and of the congressional Democratic elders—the three major power groups in the party most affronted by what had taken place in Los Angeles.

The selection of Johnson has become a matter of major controversy, with many close Kennedy lieutenants asserting he never expected Johnson to accept. What is significant, however, is the rationale that caused Kennedy to make the offer, a rationale which Schlesinger and Theodore C. Sorensen, his two main biographers, agree was dictated by reasons of political prudence, relating primarily to the election of the *Democratic* ticket and secondarily to the capacity of a *Democratic* Administration and a *Democratic* Congress to furnish effective national leadership. Kennedy hoped to win as a Democrat and to govern as a Democrat, and, with his Catholicism certain to alienate some of the party faithful, he could not afford any other splits in the ranks.

In Schlesinger's version, Kennedy

came that night to a quiet decision to make the first offer to Johnson. He decided to do this because he thought it imperative to restore relations with the Senate leader. Johnson was the man whose cooperation would be essential for the success of a Kennedy legislative program, and he was in addition the representative of the section of the country which regarded Kennedy with the greatest mistrust. News of the offer, Kennedy hoped, would reunite the Democrats, please the older generation of professionals, now so resentful of the "angry young men" who had taken over their party, improve the ticket's chances in the South and lay the basis for future collaboration with Johnson.

Sorensen puts it this way:

As runner-up in the presidential balloting (409 votes compared to Kennedy's 806), as leader of the party in the Senate, as candidate of the area most opposed to Kennedy, as spokesman for a large state that would be difficult for Kennedy to carry, Johnson was the strongest potential running mate and the logical man to be given "first refusal" on the job. Al Smith, the only previous Catholic nominee, had picked a Protestant Southern Senator, Joseph Robinson; and Franklin Roosevelt had picked a Texas Congressional leader, John Garner. Johnson, Kennedy felt, would strengthen the ticket in the South. And he was less certain that the Midwest and the West, his other areas of weakness, could be carried by the Democrats in 1960 no matter whom he selected.

Throughout the general election campaign, Kennedy wrapped himself in his party cloak, and appealed for votes by parading the names and the symbols of party loyalty.

In liberal states like Michigan and New York, he cited the historical records of the two parties on social legislation, recalling, for example, that "Republicans had voted 90 percent against a minimum wage of 25 cents an hour in 1935, and 80 percent against a minimum wage of $1.25 this year."

In Hamtramck, Michigan:

I can tell you that I am a member of a party which has believed in progress, and I run against a party which has opposed every single piece of progressive legislation which this country has tried to pass in the last 25 years, minimum wage, social security, housing, housing for the aged, and all the rest. The Republican Party has said no, and we have said yes, and we are going to say yes on November 8.

Again, in the Eastgate Shopping Center, outside Detroit:

One of the reasons why I am glad to come to Michigan is because I am running with distinguished, vigorous, progressive Democrats. One of the great things about being a Democrat is you don't have to do what Mr. Nixon does, who keeps saying that parties don't mean anything. He says, "I am not really a Republican, that is, I don't think I am." Until he goes down to Arizona, and Barry Goldwater takes him in the room and puts the rubber hose to him and finally he says, "Yes, I am a Republican." But I am a Democrat every day of the year, and I run as a Democrat, and I run in the succession of Woodrow Wilson, and Franklin Roosevelt, and Harry Truman. Mr. Nixon is the intellectual heir to McKinley, Dewey, Landon, Coolidge, Harding, Taft, and the rest. [Kennedy was always careful not to put Eisenhower in the Republican lineage.] And I don't believe in 1960, the American people are going to turn over the destinies of this State and the destinies of the United States to a party and leader who stands still.

The obverse side of this appeal came in areas of the South and Southwest, where neither Kennedy himself nor the progressive platform was popular. In such areas, Kennedy coattailed shamelessly on the popularity of incumbent (and mainly conservative) Democratic congressmen. Typical is this excerpt from a speech in

Wichita Falls, Texas, home of Congressman Frank Ikard, a staunch conservative.

You have 21 Democratic Congressmen. [A reference to the Texas delegation.] You have put your confidence in a Democratic Governor. You have put your confidence in two Democratic Senators. Can you imagine if this country elects a Democratic House and a Democratic Senate, and elects Dick Nixon a Republican President of the United States? Would Lyndon Johnson and Sam Rayburn go over to meet with him as the leaders of the Congress and sit down with Dick Nixon, who in 1952 said Acheson had graduated from the College of Cowardly Communist Containment, in 1951 called Truman a traitor, in 1960 called me a liar, in 1960 called Lyndon an ignoramus. . . . Do you think Frank Ikard is going to go over and tell him about the problems of this district? I think, when the Democratic leaders of the House and Senate go over to the White House, they ought to sit down with a Democratic President. Why do you elect a Democratic Congressman? Why do you elect a Democratic Senator? Why do you elect a Democratic Governor? Because you believe the Democratic Party stands for something. Grover Cleveland said 60 years ago, "What good is a politician unless he stands for something?" What good is a party unless it stands for something? What possible use is it saying that you have confidence in your Senators, in the Speaker of the House, in your Governor, in your Congressmen, and then saying, "You go with them there, but we want a Republican President like Dick Nixon."

It was easy enough to poke holes in the logic of Kennedy's argument that the Texans' votes for Democrats at the state level proved they believed the Democratic party "stands for something," at least for something that he represented, at the national level. In plain truth, the Texas Democrats had taken the rare step of passing their own platform *after* the national convention, and it repudiated many of the liberal planks of the national platform. Their allegiance to Kennedy's program was, at best, dubious.

Clearly, what dictated Kennedy's emphasis on party labels and party loyalty in both liberal and conservative areas was not any intellectual commitment to the doctrine of responsible party government but his acute sense of his own urgent political problems. Indeed, it can be argued that Kennedy threw programmatic consistency to the winds in embracing such conservative Democrats as Ikard—even though he did not retreat from the pledges of the party platform. But he had little choice. For the first time in his political life, he found himself asking not what he could do for his party but what his party could do for him. He was visibly weaker than the local Democratic candidates in many states and districts. In part, this was because of his youth; in part, it was because of his liberal positions, particularly his advocacy of civil rights. But mainly it was because of the irrational factor of religious bias—the fear on the part of many voters, including many normally Democratic, of putting a Roman Catholic in the White House.

Kennedy's religion won him some votes in 1960 and cost him others. The University of Michigan Center for Political Studies, in an analysis challenged by Republican election statisticians, concluded that Kennedy had suffered a net loss of about 1.5 million votes because of his religion. Whatever the case, he was certainly weaker than his party. The ratio of his vote to the party's congressional vote was the lowest for any President in the century. Kennedy trailed the Democratic congressional candidate in 303 of the 437 districts. The absence of his coattails probably contributed to the oddity of the Democrats' losing twenty seats in the House and two in the Senate while they were recapturing the White House. And those facts of political life—the reduced Democratic margins and Kennedy's weak showing compared to his party's—largely determined his legislative strategy in his first two years as President.

According to Schlesinger, Kennedy was wont to quote Jefferson's maxim, "Great innovations should not be forced on slender majorities." And his were slender indeed. His popular-vote margin over Nixon was only 118,574 out of more than 68 million ballots. The nominal margins in Congress were deceptive; on paper, Democrats had a 64-to-36 advantage in the Senate, and a 263-to-174 advantage in the House. But 21 of the Democratic senators and 99 of the Democratic representatives came from the Old Confederacy, and most of them were conservatives skeptical of the program on which Kennedy had been elected.

The measure of his precarious position came early, when the Administration, with Rayburn's agreement, moved to take effective control of the House Rules Committee, the conservative coalition's favorite roadblock. In the previous Democratic Congresses, the Rules Committee, which had the power to delay (or clear) legislation for floor debate, had been made up of eight Democrats and four Republicans. But two of the Democrats were Dixie conservatives, who sided with the Republicans to block any bill too liberal for their taste. Rayburn proposed that the committee be increased to fifteen members, adding two pro-Administration Democrats and a Republican, in order to provide an 8–7 majority for most Kennedy bills. The Speaker threw his own immense prestige into the fight, closing the debate with a plea that "the House . . . be allowed to work its will . . . on the program he [Kennedy] thinks will be in the interest of . . . the American people." Kennedy used all the patronage available to a new President and even called House members himself to plead for their votes. And yet, in the end, the reform won by only five votes, 217–212, with 22 Republicans helping the Administration and 64 Democrats deserting it. The Rules Committee fight was a necessary battle, but it was an expensive one, at the outset of the term, and Kennedy was realistic when he told Sorensen the outcome was not so much a show of strength by the Administration as a measure of "what we're up against."

The Rules Committee fight was the first—and last—such battle that Kennedy risked during his first two years. He stayed silent during the fight to ease the Senate's filibuster rule. A year later, after Rayburn's death, he gave no encouragement to talk of an insurgency by younger House Democrats and accepted without a murmur the elevation of an old antagonist in Boston politics, John W. McCormack, as the new Speaker. When a personal feud between eighty-three-year-old House Appropriations Committee

Chairman Clarence Cannon and eighty-four-year-old Senate Appropriations Committee Chairman Carl Hayden blocked action on financing government agencies for months in 1962, Kennedy squirmed with displeasure, but did not intervene.

His political policies were similarly conventional and cautious in those first two years. The coalition that had elected him was essentially the old Roosevelt coalition, minus some Southerners and with extra increments of big-city Negroes and suburban Catholics, and his appointments were appropriate to that constituency. The original Cabinet, like Noah's Ark, had two of every animal: two Catholics; two Jews; two Southerners; two Republicans (it had been, remember, a very close election); two Westerners; two Midwesterners. The Cabinet was all white, but Kennedy made more appointments of blacks at other levels than any previous President, and tried to create an Urban Affairs Department as a Cabinet spot for Robert C. Weaver, who finally became the first Negro Cabinet member under Johnson. When Cabinet vacancies occurred, they went to representatives of important voting groups missed the first time around: Anothony J. Celebrezze, a big-city mayor and an Italo-American, and John A. Gronouski, an academic and a Polish-American.

Kennedy did not do badly playing the presidential game with the cards he had been dealt. O'Brien assembled the largest and most skillful White House congressional liaison staff Washington had ever seen, and, for the first time, coordinated the lobbying efforts of all the individual departments. His careful attention to the needs and interests of individual members softened the opposition of some Southern Democrats and strengthened the alliance with the handful of liberal Republicans in each chamber.

As a result, elements of the Democratic legislative program began to become law. In 1961 Congress approved many of the economic stimulants the Democrats had tried unsuccessfully to pass over Eisenhower's vetoes. The minimum wage was boosted; unemployment insurance and social security benefits improved; manpower training, housing, public works, and air- and water-pollution abatement grants increased; and a new program of aid to depressed areas finally was launched.

Kennedy also was able to redeem his campaign pledges to create the Peace Corps and the Arms Control and Disarmament Agency. He arranged a loan to the United Nations, funding for the Development Loan Fund, saw the Communications Satellite public corporation come into existence, and, in 1962, after a major effort, guided through Congress a Trade Expansion Act which represented an important step in foreign economic policy. Expenditures for a flexible defense system were significantly increased and America was launched on the journey to the moon.

By no means, then, can the Kennedy years be set down as a legislative cipher. But it is a fact that almost every measure that was passed was the result of a compromise with the opposing forces. In return for the support that key Southerners like Carl Vinson and Wilbur Mills provided for his economic recovery measures, Kennedy withheld his promised civil rights legislation for more than two years. Defense contracts, higher cotton support prices, big chunks of patronage (including the designation of Southern Federal judges) and whopping portions of all the new economic aid programs were channeled into the South to buy their passage. Even so, something was sacrificed on almost every bill. The extension of coverage of the minimum wage law, for example, was procured by continuing the exemption for laundry workers—whose plight Kennedy had cited repeatedly during the campaign—as the price for Vinson's support.

In addition to the compromises, which were dictated by the legislative realities, there were some serious defeats. Mass-transit legislation, a program to combat youth unemployment, a curb on literacy tests for voting, and five major reorganization plans for the Executive Branch all were turned down in his first two years. Most disappointing to Kennedy were the defeat of Federal aid to education, which was blocked by an 8–7 vote in the Rules Committee after efforts to compromise the question of aid to parochial schools failed, and the defeat of medicare, by a four-vote margin, in the Senate.

Phase Three: The Attempt to Alter the Balance

In the first major speech of his campaign for the Democratic nomination, Kennedy had portrayed himself as a believer in responsible party government.

Legislative leadership is not possible without party leadership. No President . . . can escape politics. He has not only been chosen by the nation—he has been chosen by his party. And if he insists that he is "President of all the people" and should therefore offend none of them —if he blurs the issues and differences between the two parties—if he neglects the party machinery and avoids his party's leadership—then he has not only weakened the political party as an instrument of the democratic process—he has dealt a blow to the democratic process itself.

In the precarious political position of his first two years, Kennedy did little to show he meant those words. But as the economy responded to the stimulus of his policy, as he shook off the effects of the Bay of Pigs fiasco and the Berlin crisis and showed a firmer grasp of international affairs, he began to strengthen his hand in politics. He kept a close watch on party affairs, through the steady stream of visitors to the Oval Office, the work of O'Brien and Kenneth O'Donnell, his appointments secretary and political lieutenant, through Robert Kennedy, and the staff of the national committee, headed by John Bailey, the earliest of the pro-Kennedy bosses.

Gradually, he began trying to alter the political atmosphere in ways that would expedite action on the Democratic agenda. As early as the fall of 1961, he campaigned personally to elect Richard J. Hughes as Governor of New Jersey and sent Johnson and a full crew of national committee operatives into Texas to help Henry B. Gonzales win a special House election. He staked out an active role for himself in the 1962 midterm campaign, aiming to upset the historical pattern of off-year losses for the party in power and, if possible, to increase his margins in Congress. In a July news conference, he explained why he thought "this election in November is a very important one."

The President: I think what the American people have to understand is that the Republican party [members], by and large, with very few exceptions, have opposed every measure that we have put forward, whether it was in agriculture, whether it was in medical care, whether it was in public works, whether it is in mass transit, whether it is in urban affairs, and they have been joined by some Democrats who, for a great many years, have opposed a good many Democratic programs. . . . If the American people are against these programs, then of course they will vote Republican, and we will have a state of where the President believes one thing and the Congress another for two years, and we will have inaction. There are those who believe that is what we should have. I do not. . . . Fortunately, the American people will have a choice. They will choose, as I have said, either to put anchor down or to sail. So we will see in November.

Question: Mr. President, do you plan any reprisal against the Democrats who have not supported you?

The President: No, I think most of the Democrats who have not supported me are in areas where—in one-party areas. What I am going to do is attempt to elect, to help elect, although I have never overstated what a President could do in these matters—I am going to help elect Democrats who support this program. The areas I will be campaigning in are seats where there will be a very clear choice between Republicans who oppose these actions, and Democrats who support them. That is where I am going to go.

And go he did, almost every weekend from then until the Cuban missile crisis erupted in October. This time, unlike 1960, he was dealing from strength; at the outset of the campaign, the Gallup Poll reported that Kennedy was approved by 69 percent of the voters, while Democrats had only a 55-to-45 advantage in the prospective vote for Congress. As he promised, Kennedy concentrated on the Northern states, where there were clear contests between supporters and opponents of his program. And he did not hesitate to indicate that his goal was to change the power alignment. In Harrisburg on September 20, he said, "I do not intend to conceal the differences between the two parties. . . . If the Democratic party is charged with disturbing the status quo, with stirring up the great interests of the country, with daring to try something new, I plead guilty."

In addition to his efforts in the general election, Kennedy intervened, on a selective basis, in some nomination battles. In two districts in Texas, three in Tennessee and one in Georgia, there was evidence of covert assistance from the White House or the Democratic National Committee for supporters of the President's legislative program who challenged incumbent, conservative Democrats. According to those involved, there were another seven or eight districts scattered through the South where similar efforts went undetected.

In these campaigns, the White House worked closely with organized labor and with the civil rights groups just beginning to emerge as a new political force in the South. One major motivation for the effort, participants say, was to encourage Negro voting registration and to lock the rising Southern black vote into the Democratic party, looking ahead to Kennedy's own race in 1964. A second purpose was to prod Southern Democratic congressmen into closer alignment with the national party program. O'Brien calculated that his combination of diplomacy-and-patronage had reduced the hard-core Southern Democratic opposition in the House from ninety votes to about half that number. The aim in encouraging selective primary-election challenges to some of the hard-core opposition was to show their brethren that the South was changing.

In only two of the six known instances did the White House–backed challenger make it through the primary and general election and into Congress: Richard Fulton replaced J. Carlton Loser in Nashville and Charles L. Weltner beat James C. Davis in Atlanta. But, as a trial run, the project was deemed a success. So was the overall 1962 strategy. The Democrats held the GOP to a two-seat gain in the House, and actually added four seats in the Senate. Financial assistance steered to Democratic challengers in key races—with some nonincumbent Senate candidates receiving as much as $30,000 from White House sources—played a significant part in the outcome.

The successful defensive battle in 1962 put Kennedy in a strong position to attempt to reshape the party and the Congress along national Democratic lines in 1964, his re-election year. In the spring of 1963, representatives of the White House and the Democratic National Committee attended a series of regional conferences sponsored by the AFL-CIO Committee on Political Education, where "target districts" were discussed and plans made to recruit, finance and assist challengers to conservative Democratic and Republican incumbents. The intervention went so far that the White House even supplied covert financial help for a referendum campaign aimed at blocking a legislative reapportionment plan in Ohio that would have jeopardized Democratic chances for future gains in that state's congressional seats.

The evidence that Kennedy would have followed through on these plans, had Oswald not intervened, seems persuasive. Schlesinger quotes him as counseling patience when, in the autumn of 1962, James MacGregor Burns was complaining about the laggard performance of Congress. "We can make loyalty to the ticket the test in 1964, and then we can deal with those who failed to support the ticket," Kennedy said.

Kennedy expected to be in a strong position to help reshape the party in 1964. Sorensen says that in 1963 Kennedy privately "predicted—and fervently hoped—that Barry Goldwater would be nominated." Kennedy was proved right, for Goldwater was nominated, notwithstanding the fact that his "Southern strategy" had even less chance of success against Lyndon Johnson than it would have had against Kennedy. In the last Gallup Poll trial heat before his death, Kennedy held a 54 to 40 percent lead over Goldwater, and Sorensen writes:

There was no doubt in his [Kennedy's] own mind that he would win, despite defections over the issue of civil rights. He expected to carry at least all the states he had carried when religion was a handicap in

1960—with the possible exception of a few more southern states—and to carry as well California, Ohio, Wisconsin and others. In his two races in Massachusetts, he had moved from a squeaker to a landslide, and he hoped to duplicate that pattern nationally. The growing urban majorities, the civil rights movement and his new "peace" commitment might even have led to a fundamental realignment and a new and stronger majority party.

Obviously it is necessary to underline the word "might" in Sorensen's last sentence; yet the possibility seems anything but remote. The tax reform bill and the civil rights program Kennedy put to Congress in his last year were well designed to attract new elements to the Democratic coalition, while medicare offered a powerful incentive to the older constituency. On the other hand, Goldwater would probably have run even stronger in the white South and in the rural Midwest and West against Kennedy than he actually did against Johnson. A realignment, certainly less lopsided but possibly more durable than what actually occurred in 1964, might well have been possible, had Kennedy lived.

In addition to his bolder legislative and political tactics, Kennedy late in his tenure began moving toward some of the fundamental structural reforms that are needed to give cohesion, discipline and responsibility to our political parties. In 1962, he endorsed the report of a presidential commission on campaign costs, calling for income tax credits and deductions for small political contributions, and sent Congress legislation to carry out its recommendations. Kennedy recognized that the existing system of dependence on wealthy candidates and big contributors was not only an invitation to scandal but a source of fundamental irresponsibility in the political-governmental system. He achieved a degree of success, despite the protest of many congressional Democrats, in centralizing the party's fund raising in the Democratic National Committee and using those campaign funds as a tool of executive leadership in behalf of candidates committed to the party program. Had he lived, he seems certain to have carried on his effort to cope with the problem of money in politics—the least-disciplined, least-responsible element in it today.

Second, Kennedy addressed himself to the question of television and politics—a second major wild card in the present political deck. Having won the presidency with a great boost from the televised debates with Nixon, he had publicly accepted his obligation as an incumbent to participate in a similar set of meetings with Goldwater or any other challenger in 1964. He had asked Congress to repeal the "equal time" provision to make such debates possible. Johnson later balked at such a confrontation and the legislation was allowed to expire. Thus, a precedent for what can, in my judgment, be the most responsible use of the electronic medium was lost.

Third, according to Sorensen, Kennedy had started to tackle the problem of reforming and improving that vital institution of responsible party government, the political convention. Sorensen writes that in the planning sessions for the 1964 convention, Kennedy asserted that "he favored a reapportionment of convention delegates to reflect actual Democratic strength, a liberalizing influence comparable in importance and timing to Roosevelt's abolition of the two-thirds rule in 1936." That project, too, was aborted by his death, only to be taken up again years later by Democratic reformers in the wake of the disastrous convention in Chicago in 1968.

How far we would have moved toward responsible party government had Kennedy lived we can never know. But much was lost that afternoon in Dallas. A political leader of magnificent potential, one almost uniquely fitted to provide the kind of redirection needed, as Wilson said, "in times of party crisis or organizational decay," was struck down. The hope he represented, including the hope for a responsible party and governmental system, has not been recaptured. I was in the motorcade in Dallas that terrible Friday afternoon, and, in the shock of the moment, I barely remember hearing the shots fired. But all of us have felt their impact ever since.

3

Johnson

Unlike his predecessors, Dwight Eisenhower and John Kennedy, Lyndon B. Johnson had ample time and opportunity to make responsible party government work. For the first three of his five years in the White House, at least, he had the mandate, the majorities, the program and the power to demonstrate the capacity of the American government to act on the nation's problems. There was action aplenty, sometimes rapid and public, at other times slow and secretive. But the net effect of the Johnson era was not to build public confidence in the capacity and integrity of our political-governmental system but to erode it. The tragedy of Lyndon Johnson's presidency lies in part in the personal destruction of the dreams and reputation of a remarkable political leader. But the greater tragedy is the fact that what might have been, in the hands of another man, a time of glorious vindication for the American political system became, instead, a time of shame. The symbol of Johnson's failure is, of course, Vietnam—the war he entered by stealth, failed to win and let continue until it had fearfully divided the American people.

The complex tale of American policy in Vietnam is outside the scope of this book, but the qualities Johnson displayed in his management of the war are crucial to understand, for they lie at the root of his failure—and the failure of the opportunity for responsible party government.

Less than a week after Johnson succeeded Kennedy in the White House, I went to interview James H. Rowe, Jr., the Washington lawyer who had been his close friend since Johnson arrived in Washington as a freshman Congressman a quarter century before. We talked about the strength and skill the new President had displayed in the traumatic week of Kennedy's death, the genius for maneuver he had acquired in the rough survival course of Texas politics and Capitol Hill. Rowe predicted, with accuracy, that Johnson's talents would have immediate effect in moving some of the stalled Kennedy legislation. He also predicted that the new President, a man he called "the last Populist," would produce a domestic program of his own outstripping anything seen since the New Deal. "Instinctively," Rowe said, "he's a helluva lot more liberal than Kennedy."

Then the talk turned to the problems Johnson would face as President and the liabilities he brought to the office. Rowe mentioned the difficulty anyone would have in following a President who, if controversial in his lifetime, had become a martyred national hero with his death. He spoke of Johnson's feeling that he had been looked down on, subtly (and not so subtly) patronized by the Kennedy men who were now the nucleus of his White House staff. Rowe mentioned what seemed to him Johnson's foolishly parochial fear and dislike of the snobbish Easterners, who dominated Washington's social-political-journalistic Establishment.

And then he said something that riveted me: "Lyndon's main problem is that there haven't been very many people in his whole life he's ever really trusted, and most of them are dead." He mentioned Roosevelt and Rayburn and several Texas politicians of an earlier generation. And then he repeated: "The few men Lyndon ever really trusted, they're mostly dead and gone."

Seven years later, George Reedy, the scholarly ex-newsman who served as Johnson's press secretary, wrote a book called *The Twilight of the Presidency,* in which he reflected on what he had seen. "The environment of deference, approaching sycophancy," in which a President lives, Reedy said, "helps to foster another insidious factor . . . a belief that the President and a few of his most trusted advisers are possessed of a special knowledge which must be closely held within a small group lest the plans and the designs of the United States be anticipated and frustrated by enemies."

Secretive and suspicious, Johnson was also enormously active, creative and visionary, ambitious, not only for himself, but for his country. He wanted to use the power of government to make this a "Great Society," one that shared its riches widely, and particularly one that dealt justly with the poor and the blacks whose treatment through history shamed our national honor. It was a noble dream, and the central one of Johnson's presidency, but it was flawed by its paternalism, the sense that the benefits were to be handed down from above, not won by the exercise of the recipients' own power.

Johnson was not insincere when he wrote in the preface to the collection of his 1964 speeches, *My Hope for America,* that his highest purpose was to satisfy "the simple wants of the people." As a young Congressman, he took great pride in bringing REA power and electric lights to the farms and ranches of the Texas hill country. As a presidential candidate in 1964, he cried out to his audiences, "Vote Democratic. Vote for yourselves. Vote for Molly and the babies."

Journalist Jack Bell, in his book *The Johnson Treatment,* recalls a speech Johnson made in Jacksonville, Illinois, fifteen months before he became President, in which he lamented that "there had been 'no concentrated effort toward improving our national life at home' since Roosevelt had lived." What Johnson seemingly did not realize was that the demands had changed since Roosevelt's time. As the controversy over the poverty program was to show, the poor wanted a share of power, not just of benefits, "a piece of the action, not just a piece of the pie." That involved conflict Johnson was loath to admit existed.

"When Americans aren't talking politics," Johnson said in the Jacksonville speech, "there is very little difference between us about the kind of life we want for all of our people. We don't want slums and sweatshops. We don't want poorhouses and potters' fields. We may not want the other fellow to be richer than we are, but we don't really want anyone to be poor or sick or unemployed or denied justice and opportunity because of his color and creed."

And so, when Johnson had the political opportunity to pursue his goals, his primary purpose was to provide all the tangible benefits that Federal initiative could devise and Federal money buy. There was no pause to consider how each of the new Federal programs meshed with all the others, or whether the function was one the national government could most appropriately undertake. Nor was there much serious consideration of the structure of government through which all these services were to flow. As James Reston said of Johnson, "He does not concentrate on thinking programs through but on getting them through."

When the choice came, Johnson was willing to sacrifice quality for quantity in the legislation that was designed to build the Great Society. And, in the rush to construct that monument to his liberalism in 1965 and 1966, he also sacrificed public support for his critical foreign policy venture in Vietnam.

As William V. Shannon has written in the *New York Times:*

His ambition was to put through a big domestic program and be remembered as a social reformer as great as his hero, Franklin Roosevelt. If in the fall of 1964 or the spring of 1965, he had taken what seems in retrospect would have been the logical, straightforward course, he would have asked Congress for a declaration of war or its legal equivalent, mobilized the National Guard, asked for a "victory tax" to pay for the war, and imposed wage and price controls.

There is little doubt that he could have gotten such a program through Congress at that time. But it would have distracted the attention of Congress and the public from medicare, aid to education, the voting rights act of 1965, the war on poverty and all his other social programs. . . . Johnson sacrificed candor in foreign affairs for the sake of driving through his domestic program.

The result of this mistaken decision was not merely the destruction of his magnificent if grandiloquent hope of building a Great Society at home. It was not merely the personal and political humiliation he suffered in being driven from office four years after achieving one of the great political mandates of American history. Even more serious and far-reaching in its consequences was the damage the "good faith and credit" of the American government suffered in the eyes of its own citizens—a damage whose ultimate cost we still cannot reckon.

Thus, the period of 1964–66 becomes a crucial period for understanding, not only the later destruction of Johnson's hopes, but the lost opportunity for vindicating the good name of responsible party government in the United States.

What Kind of Mandate?

Lyndon Johnson inherited his original program from John Kennedy—in the form of the 1960 platform and the legislative proposals Kennedy had made before his death. Many of those proposals, including the major tax cut Kennedy had urged as a long-term economic stimulus and the sweeping civil rights program he had sent Congress in 1963, were stymied. But Johnson, with skill and eloquence, converted the shock of Kennedy's murder into a strong public mandate for the passage of his program. In 1964, he added legislation of his own, notably the basic authorization for a "war on poverty," and stamped it with his personal label by calling it a design for a "Great Society." In the election year, he saw Congress approve the tax bill, the civil rights bill, the antipoverty measure, a start on Federal aid to mass transit, a permanent food stamp program for the needy, major expansion of the national defense education act and hospital construction aid, creation of a program of legal services for the poor, and establishment of a National Wilderness System, long sought by conservationists.

In a bit of exaggerated rhetoric at a White House reception for congressmen in August, 1964, Johnson, with pardonable pride, called it "a year without precedent" in executive-congressional cooperation. "This session of Congress," he said, "has enacted more major legislation, met more national needs, disposed of more national issues than any other session of this century or the last."

But it was to be merely a prelude to the 89th Congress, the Congress Johnson would call "The Great Congress." Johnson's landslide victory over Goldwater in 1964 produced the heaviest Democratic margins in Congress since 1936—a 295-to-140 advantage in the House and a 68-to-32 advantage in the Senate. The new members, particularly in the House, came from non-Southern districts, effectively ending the power of the "conservative coalition" of Republicans and Southern Democrats to block or delay legislation. Johnson, unlike Kennedy, showed enormous political muscle, the kind of muscle no congressman could ignore. He rolled up the biggest popular-vote margin in history, carried 44 of the 50 states and 375 of the 435 congressional districts, running ahead of the Democratic nominee in 274 of them. Never was there a more emphatic mandate to a President and a party.

Just what that mandate consisted of was a little vague, however. The Democratic platform devoted three times as much space to reciting the accomplishments of the previous four years as to listing the promises for the next four. The catalogue of new programs was vaguely worded, except for the handful of measures, like Federal aid to education and medicare, which Congress had not yet passed. Johnson himself probably summed it up accurately when he told one audience in the campaign, "We're in favor of a lot of things, and we're against mighty few."

In view of what came later, his failure to use the campaign period to develop both public and party support for his program was to limit the extent to which the building of the Great Society could be called an exercise in responsible party government. Even at the time, the absence of content in the Johnson campaign was a subject of comment. John Bartlow Martin, a journalist and Democratic speechwriter, wrote that "the 1964 election was supposed to raise the most fundamental issues of American policy—war and peace in the nuclear age and the proper role of government in a free society—but it turned out to be one of the silliest, most empty and most boring campaigns in the nation's history."

In a dispatch I filed to the Washington *Evening Star* after following, breathless, on a ten-thousand-mile, week-long swing late in the campaign, I commented on the same fact:

Some Democrats fretted before the campaign began that Johnson was so eager to woo Republicans and independents for himself that he would not plug hard for other Democratic candidates. Those fears were needless. In Johnson's world, one can be nonpartisan, bipartisan and super-partisan all in the same speech. . . .

Others worried that the President would stress the accomplishments of the past and neglect the need for policies of the future. They were right.

Johnson the politician has been so busy for 30 years dealing with the problems of the moment that he has hardly had time to look ahead.

He can dwell at length on the battle for the 25-cent minimum wage or list in detail the 51 "major bills" that passed the Senate this year.

But he is notably vague about his plans for the future. Last night he made a speech about education which entirely skirted any mention of Federal aid for classroom construction. He has been equally silent on Vietnam, NATO and a host of other problems.

But the President's great good fortune is in having an opponent who has raised fundamental questions about the decisions of the past and provided few clues to his own policies for the future.

In any election in the past 20 years, a Democrat who campaigned in Tennessee primarily on the promise that "I will not sell TVA" would have been laughed off the platform. But Goldwater did propose such a thing, so Johnson drew cheers in Nashville for affirming the obvious.

And in Denver last night, while fuzzing his own program for meeting education needs, he drew enthusiastic cheers by taking a forthright stand against Goldwater's 1960 statement that "the child has no right to an education. In most cases, the children will get along very well without it."

In fact, Johnson has been able to get by this campaign by doing little more than defending the policies that have been at the root of American policy since the establishment of the United Nations, the passage of the first foreign aid bill and the enactment of the Full Employment Act in the 1940s.

The reasons for Johnson's deliberate imprecision on his future plans were twofold. His campaign strategy was to make Goldwater the issue—not his own program. By keeping the focus on his opponent, Johnson could, and did, win support from millions of Republicans and independents, many of whom might have had trouble swallowing parts or all of the Great Society program. Second, his penchant for secrecy was already evident. The framing of the program was being done by White House task forces—most of whose membership and existence were kept secret—and Johnson wanted to wait until after the election to review their handiwork.

While the basic approach of his program was at least as old as the New Deal, while many of the specific ideas had been lying dormant on Capitol Hill in one bill or another, and while Johnson was realistic enough to know that Congress would not hesitate to tamper with his handiwork, he was also determined that the Great Society bills would have his stamp on them.

Thus, if his 1965 legislative program was something more than a set of personal ideas, which it certainly was, it was also considerably less than a well-discussed, well-articulated package of proposals, understood by his party and mandated by the voters in the election.

What the voters did mandate was a Congress with inflated Democratic majorities, and Johnson lost no time in using them. As Evans and Novak report in *Exercise of Power*, Johnson, in January, 1965, assembled the congressional liaison men from all the departments—the Administration lobbyists—in the Fish Room of the White House, and laid out the rationale for his strategy. "I have watched the Congress from either the inside or the outside, man and boy, for more than 40 years," the President said, "and I've never seen a Congress that didn't eventually take the measure of the President it was dealing with." He recited Wilson's frustration by the Senate, Harding's humiliation by the Teapot Dome investigators, the partisan warfare between the Democratic Congress and Herbert Hoover in the last two years of his term, and, of course, Roosevelt's defeat on the Supreme Court packing plan by a Democratic Congress in 1937, the year Johnson himself came to Congress. Speaking of that last incident, he said, "Here was a man who had just been elected by the biggest landslide in history and had the Congress slap him down."

Then Johnson turned to his own situation:

I was just elected President by the biggest popular margin in the history of the country, 15 million votes. Just by the natural way people think and because Barry Goldwater scared the hell out of them, I have already lost two of those fifteen and am probably getting down to thirteen. If I get in any fight with Congress, I will lose another couple of million, and if I have to send any more of our boys into Vietnam, I may be down to eight million by the end of the summer.

The conclusion was obvious: The time to pass the Great Society program was now. All of it. Right away. And so the work began. On the opening day of the 89th Congress, the Democratic majority in the House put through three rules changes designed to remove any roadblock to swift enactment of the forthcoming program: The most important of these gave committee chairmen authority to call up for a floor vote any bill the Rules Committee had held for twenty-one days. These procedural changes were underlined by a bit of political discipline that made it evident the Democrats would not tolerate too much dissent in their own ranks. Two Southern congressmen, Mississippi's John Bell Williams and South Carolina's Albert W. Watson, who had endorsed Goldwater over Johnson the previous fall, were summarily censured and stripped of their seniority by the party caucus.

On the night of January 4, 1965, Johnson went before the Congress to report on the State of the Union, and in a speech that included only four brief paragraphs on Vietnam, the President declared, "We are only at the beginning of the road to the Great Society," and then outlined how far he planned to march:

I propose that we begin a program in education to ensure every American child the fullest development of his mind and skills. I propose that we begin a massive attack on crippling and killing diseases. I propose we launch a national effort to make the American city a better and more stimulating place to live. I propose we increase the beauty of America and end the poisoning of our rivers and the air that we breathe. I propose we carry out a new program to develop regions of our country that are now suffering from distress and depression. I propose we make new efforts to control crime and delinquency. I propose we eliminate every remaining obstacle to the right and the opportunity to vote. I propose we honor and support the achievements of thought and the creations of art. I propose that we make an all-out campaign against waste and inefficiency.

The agenda had been set.

The Great Society Congress

The next nine and a half months, the gestation period of the Great Society, are unique in the politics of this era. To recount what happened is to play the record of a half-mad, half-drunk Texas square dance, with Johnson, the fiddler and caller, steadily increasing the tempo, speeding up the beat—his music and his call punctuated, but never interrupted, by the offstage explosion of crises from Vietnam to the Dominican Republic and the rising clamor of riots in the cities of America.

The flow of messages begins:

January 7—medicare and health.
January 12—education.
January 13—overhaul of the immigration law.
January 14—foreign aid.
January 15—space.
January 18—defense, cut back several hundred million dollars from the previous year.

There is a brief intermission for the inaugural ceremony, and then immediately come the Budget Message and the Economic Report. The congressional committees organize quickly, and by February 1 the Senate has repassed two measures—the Appalachia aid and water pollution bills—it had passed the previous year but the House had failed to enact.

February 5. A House education subcommittee clears the massive elementary and secondary school aid bill, 6–0, with Republican members boycotting in protest of the "hasty and superficial" consideration given the measure.

February 7. An offstage explosion. Following Communist attacks in South Vietnam, Johnson orders evacuation of American dependents and the start of retaliatory air strikes against North Vietnam.

February 8. The fiddle is going again. He sends Congress his ambitious program to "beautify" the cities, the countryside and the highways.

February 10. The House Public Works Committee clears the Appalachia aid bill, with Republicans complaining of "steamroller tactics."

March 3. The Appalachia aid bill passes the House exactly as it came from the Senate, after Democrats defeat seventeen Republican amendments, causing one disgruntled GOP member to say, "It now looks like we have the great stampede, rather than the Great Society."

In early March, there is another explosion. Demonstrators in Selma, Alabama, led by the Reverend Dr. Martin Luther King, Jr., are set upon by police dogs, fire hoses and club-wielding police while protesting obstacles to voter registration. On March 15, Johnson, in a televised address to a joint session of Congress, offers a sweeping voting rights bill, and says, "This time, on this issue, there must be no delay, or no hesitation, or no compromise with our purpose."

March 24. Medicare passes the Ways and Means Committee for the first time in history, on a strict party-line vote.

March 26. The House passes the landmark general education bill, after defeating nineteen Republican amendments, each given five minutes of consideration. Johnson hails it as "the greatest breakthrough in the advance of education since the Constitution was written."

April 8. The House passes medicare under a closed rule, barring any amendments.

April 9. The Senate passes the general education bill exactly as it came from the House, after three days of debate and rejection of all eleven Republican amendments.

April 11. Johnson signs the education bill into law outside the one-room schoolhouse in Stonewall, Texas, where he began his own education. That same day, both houses of Congress approve a compromise version of the Manpower Act, and the Senate Judiciary Committee, formerly the graveyard of civil rights legislation, clears a voting rights bill even stronger than Johnson had proposed.

By the end of his "first hundred days," on April 13, an exhilarated President tells his Cabinet the 89th Congress has "a record of major accomplishments without equal or close parallel in the present era." Two weeks later, however, he is forced to send Marines to the Dominican Republic to prevent what he calls the threat of a Communist takeover. And on May 4 there is another disturbance in the wings. Johnson summons congressional leaders to the White House and announces he needs an emergency $700 million appropriation to meet the rising costs of the Vietnam war. Exactly fifty-three hours later, with only seven representatives and three senators dissenting, the money is voted. Reassured, Johnson resumes his pattern of sending Congress two new requests in return for each bill it passes.

May 17. He asks for a $4 billion excise tax cut in order to stimulate what is rapidly becoming a wartime economy.

May 18. He asks repeal of Section 14b of the Taft-Hartley Act, the "right-to-work" authorization despised by his labor union backers.

May 26. The Senate passes the voting rights bill.

June 2. The House passes the excise tax cut over opposition protests of the "headlong speed" of action.

June 17. The excise cut becomes law—exactly a month after it was requested.

June 24. Medicare clears the Senate Finance Committee.

June 28. The Senate passes a bill to build regional medical centers to fight major diseases.

June 30. The House passes the housing bill, including the controversial rent-supplements program.

July 9. The Senate passes medicare and the House approves the voting rights bill.

July 15. The Senate passes the housing bill.

July 22. The House passes the poverty bill, more than doubling its funds, and the Senate approves home rule for the District of Columbia.

But, at a press conference on July 28, once again those offstage explosions are heard. Johnson announces he is increasing the troop level in Vietnam from 75,000 to 125,000 men, with more men to be sent in later, and is doubling monthly draft calls. He also makes another fateful decision: Arthur Goldberg will leave the Supreme Court to replace the late Adlai E. Stevenson at the United Nations, and Goldberg's place will be taken by Johnson's old friend and adviser, Washington lawyer Abe Fortas.

Ironically, that same day is a day of legislative triumph. The right-to-work repealer, brought to the floor of the House under the twenty-one-day rule, passes by an eighteen-vote margin. On the same day, the Senate completes congressional action on the final version of medicare, ending a thirty-year legislative struggle. On July 30, Johnson flies to Independence, Missouri, to sign the medicare bill into law in the presence of Harry Truman, who led an unsuccessful fight for national health insurance when he was President. A week later, the President signs the Voting Rights Act in the President's Room of the Capitol, where Lincoln had signed the Emancipation Proclamation.

Bill signing now becomes as frantic as the legislative schedule. There are major health bills on three consecutive days in August, part of "the greatest record in our nation's history in the health field." On August 10, he signs the housing act, calling it "the single most important breakthrough in the last 40 years." As if on cue, the next day rioting breaks out in the Watts section of Los Angeles, triggering what will prove to be three successive summers of civil disturbance in the black ghettos. Johnson, his eyes on another, more visionary future, signs a measure authorizing research on ways to convert the oceans into fresh water for man's use.

Through the dog days of the Washington summer, Congress labors on. In August, the Senate sends the President a $3.25 billion Economic Development Act, a vast expansion of the depressed-areas bill passed in Kennedy's time. The House passes the farm bill and the Senate approves doubling the antipoverty funds. The lawmakers are visibly weary now after eight months in session, with little time off for visiting their home districts, but Johnson on August 24 hands the legislative leaders a list of a dozen more major bills he wants passed before adjournment. They go back up the Hill to labor some more.

August 26. The House passes the higher education bill.

August 31. Both chambers complete action on a bill creating the Department of Housing and Urban Development.

September 2. The higher education bill clears the Senate. .

September 3. After intense White House pressure, the necessary 218 signatures are obtained on a discharge petition in the House, freeing the home rule bill for the District of Columbia from the Southern-dominated District Committee.

There are now clear signs of restiveness, even among freshman Democrats who have voted almost 100 percent with Johnson on every bill. The chairman of their informal group, Representative Lee Hamilton of Indiana, writes Johnson on September 10 requesting "a pause" in the hectic legislative schedule. "We are completing one of the most productive sessions of the Congress in the history of our nation," he says, but the freshmen hope "we may look forward to a more deliberate pace of legislation in 1966."

Overriding this and other warnings, Johnson pushes for more action. On September 14, the House is kept in session past midnight, and, in the course of the stormy twelve-hour session, the twenty-one-day rule is used to bypass the Rules Committee and pass four controversial bills, including a Johnson favorite, the bill to create National Foundations for the Arts and Humanities. The next day, the House rebels and, handing Johnson his first serious setback of the year, rejects the conference report on the poverty bill and insists on retaining the provision that gives governors veto power over certain programs in their states. Unfazed, Johnson announces the next day that he is commissioning a task force study of "a broad and long-range plan of worldwide educational endeavor," part of a program he will give Congress in January "to show that this nation's dream of a Great Society does not stop at the water's edge." Groaning under the burden of attempting to make the United States alone a Great Society, Congress labors on.

September 16. The Senate sends the President the Arts and Humanities bill and, on the same day, passes "the Ladybird bill"—the highway beautification measure, including five amendments sent over from the White House just before final passage.

September 21. Congress finishes action on the "clean water" bill, part of the environmental package.

September 22. The Senate passes the immigration bill, ending the system of national-origin quotas.

September 23. The House accepts a compromise on the poverty bill, retaining the governors' veto right but giving the administrator the power to override.

September 24. The House passes the "clean air" and solid wastes disposal research bill and the Senate completes action on the poverty bill.

September 30. The Senate sends the President the regional medical centers bill. But the House, increasingly fractious, rebels against the District of Columbia home rule bill, and with substantial defections among pro-Administration Democrats, defeats it by fifty-three votes.

By the end of September, the warnings are coming thick and fast. Representative Sam Stratton of New York, a Johnson loyalist, says, "The natives are getting restless and want to go home. If something doesn't happen soon, there could be an explosion." Senate Republican Leader Dirksen chimes in: "If I were the President, I'd have carefully considered when it was time to quit."

But Johnson wants more. His doctors have told him he must enter Bethesda Naval Hospital on October 8 to have his gall bladder removed, and the President wants the next seven days to bring the Great Society legislation to fruition.

On September 30, he signs the bill authorizing a pilot project in high-speed rail transportation; on October 1, the air pollution and solid wastes disposal bill; on October 2, the water pollution bill; on October 3, at the Statue of Liberty in New York Harbor, the new immigration law. On October 4, prodded by the President, the Senate takes up the right-to-work repealer, despite threats of a filibuster. On October 6, Johnson signs the regional medical centers law. The grand climax is planned for the next night, October 7, a "Salute to Congress" celebration at the White House, immediately after which the President will enter the hospital for his surgery. Johnson prepares a speech for the occasion to put it all in historic perspective:

There haven't been many times in our history when the President could stand before Congress at the end of a session and express the gratitude and the pride that I feel tonight. There were many Congresses which weren't too interested in hearing what the President had to say. All too often, the relations between the executive and the legislative branches have been marred by bitterness. George Washington warned that his legislature would "form the worst government on earth" if some means were not found to stem its corruption. A great Republican, President Theodore Roosevelt, once wished he could turn loose 16 lions on his Congress. When someone pointed out that the lions might make a mistake, he replied, "Not if they stayed there long enough." We all remember the time Harry Truman named the 80th Congress "the second worst Congress in the history of the United States." I can bring this up without fear of hurting anyone's feelings here tonight, because I was a member of that Congress, too.

Well, now we are going to balance the ledger. Tonight, the President of the United States is going on record as naming this session of Congress the greatest in American history. . . . From your committees and both your houses have come the greatest outpouring of creative legislation in the history of the nation. You passed legislation to fulfill the century-old promise of emancipation. Today, where once men were afraid, they now walk proudly to the polling place. You passed legislation to ease the burden of sickness and want for older Americans. Today, though millions must face old age, they are no longer dependent on kin folks for their medical care. You passed legislation that should brighten every classroom in America. Once the children of poverty began life on the hopeless road toward despair. Today they have a new chance to hope and to achieve. You have promised to millions of American families better housing and better homes, and a rebirth for our cities.

You passed a poverty program so that poor families can train and work. You passed a bill that will meet head-on the nation's top murderers—cancer, heart disease and stroke. You told our cities and our industries they must stop polluting our water and poisoning our air. You passed legislation to dam our rivers—to prevent floods—to produce power—and to provide beaches and playgrounds for our children.

You gave us blueprints for a rapid rail system to carry our commuters of tomorrow. You passed a farm bill that puts more income in the farmer's pocket and at the same time allows him to compete at home and abroad. You passed an immigration bill that no longer asks a man "where do you come from?" but "what can you do?" You have given local officials the tools to restore law and order on our streets.

You passed the excise tax reduction. In a little over 20 months, at current income levels, taxes have been cut a little over $20 billion.

And tonight you served notice on the spoilers of our landscape that we will battle with all we have to preserve the bounty of our land and the beauty of our countryside.

At this point in the text, Johnson takes time to rebut a story I had written for the *New York Times*. A month earlier, when the American Political Science Association was meeting in Washington, I had interviewed several of the visiting scholars and reported they were considerably less dazzled by Congress's performance than most in Washington. One of them, Nelson Polsby, then of Wesleyan University and now of the University of California, was quoted as saying, "All you really have is a swollen congressional majority, that Barry Goldwater handed the Democrats, passing programs that have been kicking around since New Deal and Fair Deal days."

It is this thesis that causes Johnson to take umbrage. "I read criticism in one newspaper not long ago," he says, "that there was nothing new about what you have done. I read that you have simply enacted programs that have been 'kicking around since New Deal days.'" To rebut any notion that the Great Society is not as original as it is massive, he goes back over the record again, citing examples of bills that "had their beginnings and their end in the 89th Congress."

And then comes the prepared peroration:

This has been the fabulous 89th Congress. . . . An inspired group of dedicated Americans, representing a sense of the national purpose, have written for the United States a new chapter in greatness. I want to say to every member of the 89th Congress—Democrat or Republican—who wrote and supported this record: Your people will revere you, and the Nation will honor you long after you are gone.

It was a magnificent salute. Unfortunately, the speech was never delivered. The night Johnson had planned as the climax of his legislative achievement turned into a fiasco and marked, instead of his triumph, the clear signal of the unraveling of his entire strategy.

The problem was that paragraph in the prepared text which began, "And tonight you served notice on the spoilers of our landscape. . . ." When the speech was drafted, the House had not yet passed Ladybird's highway beautification bill. It came up for consideration on the afternoon of Johnson's party. At cocktail time, with debate continuing and many amendments still to be voted on, the House leaders asked the White House if they could adjourn and pass the bill the following day. The word came back quickly: Johnson wants it for Ladybird, and he wants it tonight.

Furious at being forced to leap through one more hoop before receiving their reward, Republicans forced time-consuming quorum calls and insisted on teller votes on every amendment. All evening the acrimonious struggle continued, while members' wives, dressed in their White House party finery, watched with dismay from the gallery. Finally, fifty-one minutes after midnight, the bill was passed. But by then Johnson was on his way to the hospital, his tribute undelivered. From that point on, his relations with Congress went steadily downhill. Before final adjournment, Congress finished work on a few more bills—higher education aid, farm legislation, and, of course, highway beautification. But the Senate refused to cut off the filibuster against the right-to-work repealer, and the House refused funds to start the rent supplement program Johnson had pushed through Congress with such effort.

Thus, the most notable session of Congress in the last two decades ended on a distinctly sour note. While the volume of legislation had been great, so was the cost, not just in frayed tempers and impaired relations between the branches of government, but in the public credibility of the entire governmental process. In the breakneck pace of 1965, little time was taken to develop public support and public understanding of the enormous new ventures which were beginning. Indeed, many programs whipped through Congress so fast that few of the lawmakers themselves comprehended what was being done. Inevitably, many of those hastily written laws have failed.

It is easy, and in important respects, accurate, to place the blame on Johnson for this abuse of the legislative opportunity which the 1964 election provided. His impatience, his egotism, his autocratic manner demeaned the legislative process. But we should not forget that what goaded him to this frenzied pace, what kept him whipping Congress on, was his belief that he had only a narrow span of time in which action would be possible. His assumption—expressed to the liaison men at the beginning of the year—was that the political balance would soon shift and the conditions of governmental stalemate return.

So long as any President thinks he has only an occasional chance to move on the national agenda, the likelihood is he will over-react—as Johnson did—when that opportunity comes along. What 1965 shows us is that the price we pay for an absence of responsible party government is not just long periods of impasse. There is also a risk of "overkill," of hasty, ill-considered, profligate action when leaders try to seize the few moments for initiative they are granted.

Johnson and the Democrats

When Congress returned in 1966, Johnson's political position had worsened. His former protégé, Bobby Baker, had just been indicted for income tax evasion. The troop level in Vietnam was approaching the 200,000 mark and heavy fighting had resumed following the Christmas–New Year bombing halt and "peace offensive." A sober President told Congress and the country "the brutal and bitter conflict in Vietnam . . . just must be the center of our concerns." With inflation threatening, he asked for postponement of the excise tax cuts that had gone into effect just twelve days before. But to the despair of his own congressional leaders, who had promised a short session devoted to what Senate Majority Leader Mike Mansfield called "the perfection, the elaboration and the refinement of the basic legislation" written with such haste in the previous year, the President came in with a list of requests almost as long, if not as sweeping, as his 1965 agenda.

"This nation is mighty enough," he told the skeptical lawmakers, "to pursue our goals in the rest of the world while still building a Great Society at home." Congress went back to work, but the whipcracking days of 1965 were over. The Senate spent a month debating right-to-work and finally conceded the votes were not there to break the filibuster. When Congress recessed for Easter, only five major bills had passed, all but one of them closely related to the war.

Throughout the spring, Johnson faced rising demands from his own Democrats that he negotiate a halt to the Vietnam war—or at least explain where his policy of escalation was leading. Republicans, backed by most economists, demanded that the President raise taxes or cut spending to avoid the war-induced inflation that was becoming more acute every day.

The President satisfied neither set of critics, but insisted doggedly that if Congress just followed his direction everything would be all right. In press conference after press conference he denied the evidence of growing public dissatisfaction, saying his polls showed incumbents of both parties doing well and arguing that those who cooperated with him would find there would not "be any great difficulty this year" in being re-elected.

The summer saw worse fighting in Vietnam, and the spread of riots to New York, Chicago, Cleveland, Jacksonville, South Bend, Milwaukee, Atlanta and many smaller cities. The breach between President and Congress and that between Johnson and his party widened steadily. Angered by criticisms of his war policies from more and more Democratic senators, Johnson lashed out at the "nervous nellies" in his own party. He angered many Democrats by calling on Congress to order striking airline machinists back to work, after his own efforts to mediate the dispute had failed. And in the fall, reacting belatedly to the fiscal and budgetary problems caused by his own unwillingness to seek higher taxes to finance the war, he began publicly criticizing Congress for the "add-ons" to his own domestic programs.

The session that finally ended on October 23, giving the members less than three weeks to campaign for re-election, was not without legislative accomplishment. The minimum wage was raised to $1.60 and extended to an additional eight million workers; strong auto and highway safety laws were passed; education programs broadened; rent supplements funded; a program of "model city" development launched; air and water pollution laws strengthened; and a Cabinet-level Transportation Department created.

But the momentum of progress on civil rights, probably Johnson's proudest achievement, was halted when the Senate failed to cut off a Dirksen-led filibuster against the open housing bill. Right-to-work repeal and home rule for the District were rejected again, as were a variety of consumer bills, overhaul of the unemployment compensation program, and the package of political financing reforms the President had sought.

It was a nervous and unhappy band of Democrats who went home to face the voters in the 1966 election. Twenty months earlier, when the 89th Congress began, Johnson had been lavish in his political assistance to the congressmen who "went along" with his program. Particularly was he solicitous of the seventy-one freshman Democrats his coattails had carried to victory in normally-Republican districts—the men whose votes provided his winning margin on roll call after roll call in the House.

Early in 1965, Johnson ordered the executive agencies to help the freshmen on projects for their districts. In small groups, they were brought to the Democratic National Committee for private sessions with representatives of the White House and the domestic departments. Before the meeting, each congressman was given a list of pending projects for his district and encouraged to make his choice from the "shopping list." Delivery was prompt. Lee Hamilton, the freshman class chairman, for example, got thirteen post offices and three major public works projects for his constituents.

Johnson not only furnished the goods for his freshmen, he helped them brag to the home folks about them. Instead of dismantling the National Committee's publicity machine after the presidential campaign, the President kept it functioning, on a slightly reduced scale, for the benefit of the freshmen. Long-distance telephone lines and expensive recording equipment were used to feed the members' comments on the day's work in Congress, or announcements of project grants, to radio stations in their districts. A similar teletype service carried their press releases into the newsrooms of their local papers, all at the party's expense. Production assistance, subsidies and big-name Administration guests were provided for their "public service" television programs. An elaborate computer, renting for $5,000 a month and staffed by fifteen attendants, was brought into the National Committee to process the Congressmen's mailings to their constituents. Those who were tongue-tied could avail themselves of help from a six-man speech and news-release writing team, carried on the national committee's payroll.

There was political backup in the districts, as well. Field men from Washington, working with a coalition of organizations with a big stake in the Great Society legislation—the AFL–CIO, the National Farmers Union, the National Association of Rural Electric Co-operatives, the National Education Association, the Co-operative League of the U.S.A., the National Association of Land Grant Colleges and the National Council of Senior Citizens—set up informal "advisory committees" in the freshmen's districts. By arranging speaking invitations that provided air fare home for a weekend, by giving them audiences and access to volunteer workers, and by contributions, they helped the freshmen get a head start on their re-election campaigns. In the autumn of 1965, these "voter education committees," as they were called, scheduled a series of sixty-five theater parties, premiering unreleased films (obtained by Arthur Krim of United Artists, chief fund raiser for Johnson and the Democratic National Committee), which were expected to net at least $1 million. Another $1 million was expected from the sale of ads, at $15,000-a-page, for the program book to be distributed at the premieres.

It was the program book that caused the whole scheme to come apart and marked the end of Johnson's brief experiment as a proponent of party organization activity. When the slick-paper volume appeared, it was stuffed with ads from airlines, truckers, railroads, public utilities and other regulated industries, from big defense contractors and from firms whose executives were prominent Democratic contributors. The blatancy of this device (if not its originality, for similar program books had been used by both parties before) for channeling tax-deductible corporate contributions into Democratic campaigns caused a public furor. Senator John J. Williams of Delaware pushed through an amendment to the tax code to close the loophole that permitted such deductions. Johnson, reportedly furious at the uproar, ordered the program book proceeds put into escrow and the remainder of the planned movie parties canceled. Immediately thereafter, he demanded an audit of the National Committee's finances, which disclosed an unexpected debt of more than $2 million from the 1964 campaign. This was followed within weeks by the resignation of party treasurer Richard Maguire, a Boston lawyer who was a holdover from the Kennedy days. To replace him, Johnson named one of his long-time Texas aides, Clifton C. Carter. Carter, at Johnson's orders, immediately slashed the committee's payroll by a third, laying off several top Kennedy operatives and even John Bailey's chauffeur. The layoffs continued through 1966, until only forty-five remained of the staff of one hundred, only ten of them Kennedy holdovers. The voter registration section, a keystone of the Kennedy operation, vanished entirely. The budget for services to the freshman congressmen was slashed from $1 million in 1965 to

$400,000 in 1966; three of the four WATS lines used to relay their message to home town stations were given up.

A reporter visiting the National Committee in mid-1966, when campaign preparations should have been at a peak, found Carter, the operating head, shuffling through a large stack of wedding invitations received by the President. "My job," he explained with some chagrin, "seems to include telling the social secretary which of these couples deserve greetings from Mr. and Mrs. Johnson." Shortly afterward, he resigned.

Paralleling the cutback in the National Committee's services was Johnson's gradual withdrawal from personal involvement in the midterm campaign. Between July and Labor Day, he visited fifteen states on four "nonpolitical" weekend swings, accompanied by the local lawmakers. Those were his last such trips, except for brief, desultory visits to New York, New Jersey and Delaware in early October.

At the height of the campaign, in mid-October, he left the country for two weeks, ostensibly to attend a conference of Asian leaders in Manila. The conference produced nothing tangible, and on his return Johnson compounded his party's problems by a flagrant misrepresentation. Reporters traveling with him in Asia were told the President planned a last-minute campaign blitz, covering at least ten states with key Senate and House races. Instead, he went straight to his Texas ranch, announcing that he would rest in preparation for minor surgery. When newsmen reported he had canceled his campaign plans, Johnson angrily denied the plans had ever been formulated. Television news programs carried his denial, along with photographs of the dismantling of the stands that had been erected for his speeches in Portland, Chicago and other cities. In the end, Johnson left the freshman Democrats the task of combating his credibility gap, the rising public apprehension over inflation and the war—and an unanswered barrage of Republican attacks, led by Richard Nixon, on the "rubber-stamp" Democratic Congress.

The results were what might have been expected. Democrats lost forty-seven seats in the House, three seats in the Senate and eight governorships—more than wiping out their gains of 1964, and taking the power balance in the House back to the precarious state it had been in when Kennedy came to office.

Two days before the election, Johnson had said, "I expect us really to hold our own or pick up seats in the Senate. If we do suffer any losses in the House, they will be minimal."

Now he attempted to pass off his disappointment, conceding to reporters at the ranch on November 10 that the results would make it "more difficult for any new legislation we might propose," but saying, "I do not think any President should be too unhappy after he has had the results we have had in 1963, 1964, 1965 and 1966. . . . As a good American, I think we are all glad to see a healthy two-party system."

Other Democrats had a far more critical reaction. Caucusing in White Sulphur Springs, West Virginia, a month after the election, the Democratic governors issued a particularly blunt appraisal of the election results. Their spokesman, Iowa's Harold E. Hughes, who was later to be a leader in the dump-Johnson movement, said they had agreed the election reflected "an anti-administration trend," which, he said, would give the President "a very rough race" if he sought re-election. The governors criticized Johnson for the glut of legislation written, they said, with minimal consultation with the state and local officials who would have to administer the hundreds of new Federal aid programs. Even Johnson's closest political ally, Texas Governor John B. Connally, said the new programs had come so fast and in such profusion it was "extremely difficult, if not impossible, for people to understand them and for the government to provide intelligent and effective administration for all of them."

The Origins of Consensus Politics

The seeds of the conflict that was to drive Johnson from office in 1968 were planted in 1966. And if his turnabout in that year—the self-destruction of the relationship he had created with his own fellow partisans—seems astonishing in its abruptness, one should remember what Johnson's background and historic attitude toward the Democratic party had been.

Unique among the modern Presidents, Johnson is the product of a one-party state. Texas has voted Republican in two of the last five presidential races and one of its senators is from the GOP. But, despite those facts, its affairs—both in Austin and in Washington—have essentially been handled by Democrats, and its real power struggles have taken place not between the parties, but within the Democratic party. Normally, the pressures of nominating convention and electoral college politics give the advantage to men from the swing states with fierce two-party competition: Dewey and Roosevelt of New York, Stevenson of Illinois, Kennedy of Massachusetts, Nixon of California, Humphrey of Minnesota.

The one-party Texas background shaped Johnson's conception of national leadership in several important ways. For one thing, it made him skeptical of party organization, as citizen-soldier Eisenhower had been. The Democratic party in Texas consisted, quite simply, of the officeholders and the lawyers, lobbyists and money men who surrounded them. Party organization as such was nonexistent. Registration was made deliberately difficult, to exclude Negroes and Mexicans from voting, so there was no need for an army of precinct workers to haul voters to the polls. Some politicians had personal organizations; of Johnson it was rightly said, "Lyndon doesn't have an organization; he uses everybody else's." By tradition, the Governor picked the chairman of the State Democratic Executive Committee, who was, typically, an Austin lawyer. He ran the party from his law office, took his orders from the Governor, tried to remain on friendly terms with the senators, and saw to it that the big contributors (who often became his law clients) got what they wanted from the legislature. No wonder Johnson told Cliff Carter in 1965, "I'm damned if I can see why one guy and a couple of secretaries can't run that thing [the National Committee]." The notion of the cadre party or the party chairman as a political force, independent of the elected officeholders, is absolutely alien to Texas. When Paul Butler attempted in the late 1950s to make the Democratic National Committee a liberal counterforce to the conservative Democratic congressional leadership, Johnson's and Rayburn's shock was both genuine and understandable.

But the Texas background had a second—and deeper—influence on Johnson's attitude toward his party, for it was at the root of his idea of "consensus politics," the fundamental and distinctive concept he brought to the presidency. The Texas Democratic party, during Johnson's political lifetime, included most of the same elements found in the national Democratic party: labor, Negroes, Mexican-Americans, small farmers, small businessmen and the less-affluent portions of the middle class. But, in addition to those groups, the Texas Democrats also drew support from, and effectively represented, big businessmen, whether in oil and gas, insurance or banking; big ranchers and cotton growers; and most of the educated, the wealthy and the well-born.

For a time, those latter groups were welded in by the same "brass collar" tradition that kept other Confederate states Democratic. But as the industrial and commercial revolution swept Texas in the 1940s, 1950s and 1960s, bringing in thousands of Yankee Republicans and uprooting thousands of rural Texans from their Democratic roots, it took brilliant, ruthless maneuvering by Johnson and the state's Democratic Establishment to suppress the emergence of a genuine two-party system.

One device for doing that was deliberately to obscure even the vaguest notions of party ideology, party program or party loyalty —anything that might be a barrier to keeping everyone inside the fold. I remember my surprise when I attended my first Democratic State Convention in Austin in the spring of 1960. The business of the convention was to endorse Johnson as the favorite-son candidate for President. But that did not inhibit the members of the Dallas County delegation from wearing their Nixon-for-President buttons. *And no one challenged their right to be there.* Indeed, when Johnson finally ran for President in 1964, many of those same Nixon Democrats worked for him and helped him carry Dallas.

As President, Johnson was being true to his Texas heritage when he talked, as he so often did, of making the Democratic party "a great big tent." "We are going to build it [the Great Society]," he told a crowd in Minneapolis during the 1964 campaign, "by uniting our people, by bringing our capital and our management and our labor and our farmers all under one great Democratic tent, and saying to all of them, 'Contribute your part, do your share, and you will share in the fruits that are ours.'"

He made room in his party for both Henry Ford II and Walter Reuther, for John Connally and former ADA chairman John Roche. Indeed, Johnson never hesitated to include Republicans in his consensus. As minority leader of the Senate in 1953–54, he had discovered that he could often snag Republican votes away from the slow-witted majority leader, William F. Knowland of California, and thereby take effective control of the chamber. His skill in trading across the center aisle was sharpened between 1955 and 1958, when he was working with only a one- or two-vote majority, and he needed to forage for Republican votes to offset inevitable defections from one flank or the other of the Democratic party. He developed a close personal friendship and a profitable political arrangement with Knowland's successor, Everett Dirksen, which continued and was strengthened after Johnson became President. Johnson felt far more affinity for the cynical, showboating opposition leader—who was always ready to cut a deal—than he did for the prim, proper and painfully honest majority leader, Mike Mansfield. It was Dirksen who was endlessly flattered and courted and allowed to take credit for such measures as the civil rights bills of 1964 and 1965. On the other hand, the House Republican Leader, Gerald R. Ford, Jr., of Michigan, whom Johnson thought rigid and not-quite-bright, was often the target of presidential criticism.

But there was more than just personal whim in this. Fundamentally, as a consensus President, Johnson regarded excess partisanship, like Ford's, as a danger. On the few trips he made during the early part of the 1966 campaign period, it was hard to tell which party he supported. In Burlington, Vermont, Johnson beamed as Democratic Governor Philip Hoff led the crowd in singing "Happy Birthday" to Republican Senator George Aiken. In Maine, on that same August trip, the Republican incumbents, Senator Margaret Chase Smith and Governor John Reed, drew warm public praise from the President, while their Democratic challengers, who were also on the platform, rated only the briefest of introductions.

In Ellenville, New York, an earlier stop on that swing, Johnson lauded Congress and said: "I don't say just the Democrats—I say the Democrats, the Republicans, the independents and the what-nots—all of them—this has been the best Congress. And I say that with full knowledge that if some Democrat starts breathing down a Republican Congressman's neck, he's going to quote that—and I expect him to."

His decimation of his own party organization in 1966 was not accidental; it was the expression not only of his Texas background but also of his belief that partisanship is the enemy, not the servant, of responsible government.

In the best-known statement of his political philosophy, written for the *Texas Quarterly* in 1959, Johnson made it very clear where he ranked party loyalty. "I am," he wrote, "a free man, an American, a United States Senator and a Democrat—in that order." He went on in that piece to defy anyone to categorize his thinking: "I am also a liberal, a conservative, a Texan, a taxpayer, a rancher, a businessman, a consumer, a parent, a voter, and not as young as I used to be nor as old as I expect to be—and I am all these things in no fixed order." Being all things in no fixed order was the key to his approach to leadership. Sitting in the White House on the eve of the 1964 Democratic convention, he gleefully took two visitors on a tour through his state-by-state polls.

"You see," he said, pointing out one chart from his Wisconsin study, "right here's the reason I'm going to win this thing so big. You ask a voter who classifies himself as a liberal what he thinks I am, and he says 'a liberal.' You ask a voter who calls himself a conservative what I am, and he says 'a conservative.' You ask a voter who calls himself a middle-roader, and that's what he calls me. They all think I'm on their side."

Johnson's concept of leadership in a democratic society was not to define issues but to obliterate them. In a 1964 speech at the University of Texas, cited by Jack Bell in his biography of Johnson, the President declared "the real voice of America" is one of unified purpose. "It is one of the great tests of political leadership to make our people aware of this voice, aware that they share a fundamental unity of interest, purpose and belief," he said. "I am going to try to do this. And on the basis of this unity, I intend to try and achieve a broad national consensus which can end obstruction and paralysis, and can liberate the energies of the nation for the future. I want a happy nation, not a harassed people."

The Characteristics of Consensus Politics

As practiced by Johnson during his presidency, consensus politics had at least four distinctive characteristics in addition to the suppression of partisanship.

First, since the consensus was dependent on support for the President from diverse (and sometimes antagonistic) elements of the electorate, Johnson had to shape his program to include incentives and rewards to each of the elements in his wide-ranging constituency. This fact, as much as the unique opportunity afforded by the 1964 landslide, explains why Johnson offered such an incredible array of programs, rather than concentrating on a few fundamental reforms, in his design for a Great Society. Not all the programs were of great importance to him, obviously, but each had practical or symbolic value for some element of his constituency. As Samuel Lubell wrote, "The instrument that Johnson wielded with truly revolutionary political impact was the federal budget. No previous budget had ever been so contrived to 'do something' for every major economic interest in the nation—medi-

care for the pensioners, tax rebates for business, loosened production controls and a subsidy boost for farmers, antipoverty grants
for Appalachia and for Negro slums, educational aids for a generally school-conscious public." Even in 1966, when the necessity
for selectivity was becoming clear in the face of mounting war
costs, Johnson kept so many irons in the fire, as one congressman
remarked, "he damn near put the fire out." A consensus President
must be a prodigal President; to set priorities is to see his consensus shatter.

A second characteristic of consensus politics is that it is highly
personal. It depends for its success almost entirely on the negotiating skill, the persuasiveness and the creative compromising ability
of the President. This was Johnson's forte; indeed, his genius. The
talent for political compromise—for discovering the formula that
men and groups who thought themselves antagonists could come
to "live with"—that had powered Johnson's rise in Texas politics
had been refined in his years as Senate leader. Between 1955 and
1960, he transformed that often-balky institution, repeatedly
achieving agreement, through endless cloakroom negotiations and
strong doses of personal salesmanship, where senators and Senate
observers thought no agreement was possible.

Translated to the broader realm of the presidency, the technique
put tremendous demands on Johnson. He had to know how far
each affected party could be pushed, how much a civil rights bill
had to be softened to prevent a successful Southern filibuster, how
strong it had to be to keep Martin Luther King from leading
another demonstration. He had to know whether the Joint Chiefs
wanted a particular weapon system badly enough to make a
public fight if it was dropped from the budget, whether Protestant
reaction to a personal emissary to the Pope would be serious
enough to endanger the compromise on parochial school aid in the
general education bill. And he had to know all these things himself, directly, by face-to-face talks with those involved, because
only he was in touch with all the diverse elements of the constituency. It became, as the Associated Press's Saul Pett wrote at

the time, and press secretary George Reedy later confirmed in his book, "the most personalized presidency in our history."

A third, closely related characteristic of Johnson's style of leadership was that relationships with group leaders became much more important than his relationship to the general public. Johnson rarely dealt with The Public; he dealt with many little publics, and he dealt with them through their established leaders.

In the first weeks of his presidency, there was a veritable parade of such personages through the White House. First came the foreign rulers who attended Kennedy's funeral. Then came the domestic monarchs: congressional leaders, governors, labor union heads, top businessmen, civil rights spokesmen, and, not least, clergymen. Everyone with a recognizable constituency was invited in, and few were ever asked to leave, so long as they commanded a segment of opinion important to Johnson's consensus.

Johnson made it perfectly clear he would do business with anyone. Partly for that reason, he commanded deep-felt attachment from almost no one. That lack of public support—the deep, personal attachment millions felt for Roosevelt, Eisenhower and Kennedy—was ultimately to cost him dearly. But for a time, at least, he showed how far he could go by courting the group leaders and counting on them to keep their constituents in line. As an example of his technique, Johnson told a group of state legislative leaders how evangelist Billy Graham played a crucial role in the period of delicate negotiations that finally broke the long deadlock over parochial school aid and led to passage of the general education bill.

Johnson said he had ironed out an agreement between the National Education Association, most important of the public school lobbies, and the National Catholic Welfare Conference, and

just about the time I had it all put together, one of my Baptist friends called up and said that he wanted me to know that the Pope had taken over Washington and the Baptists wouldn't go along with that bill.

One of my secretaries told him that I couldn't talk then. He said, "Why?" She said, "He is swimming with Dr. Graham."

He said, "You don't mean he is swimming in the middle of the day?"
She said, "Yes, he is swimming before lunch."
"Who did you say he was swimming with?"
"Dr. Graham."
He said, "Our Billy?"
The fact that Dr. Graham was here—"our Billy" was here at that time
—helped us to put those factions together. Because the B'nai B'rith and
the Catholic organizations . . . and Dr. Graham and the Baptists and
others finally agreed on the elementary school bill—it had never been
done before—we have over a billion dollars this year going to the needs
of children.

One reason that Johnson could pass such a "liberal" program
was that these group leaders understood perfectly well that at
heart he was an Establishment man. He would not think, as
Roosevelt did, that he could appeal to the mine workers over the
head of John L. Lewis. He dealt with the leaders, even when, as in
the case of the machinists' strike against the airlines, they turned
out to be unrepresentative of their own rank-and-file. Basically,
Johnson recognized as legitimate other men's claims to authority
on their own turf. The proposals he made were designed to permit
them to preserve their prestige and power base, as he preserved
his own. He was protective of their status and interests, as he
expected them to be of his.

When mayors of both parties complained, for example, that
community action groups created by Johnson's antipoverty program were developing into independent political organizations
that posed a threat to City Hall, Johnson sided with the mayors
against some of his own administrators. This decision was dictated
by the requirements of a consensus presidency, but it produced
understandable resentment among many of the poor and the black
Johnson had thought of as the primary beneficiaries of the Great
Society.

Fourth and finally, Johnson's leadership emphasized decision
making by private negotiation, not public debate. As Philip L.
Geyelin said in his book *Lyndon B. Johnson and the World,* one of
the prime tenets of "Lyndon Johnson's Common Law" was: "The

proper time for public debate about a presidential decision is after the decision has been made."

From his years as Senate leader, Johnson had derived a strong belief in withholding his own judgment until all other points of view had been expressed and their support gauged, and also in the value of the surprise tactic in resolving a controversy. Public debate, Johnson felt, only aroused strong feelings and tended to lock people into antagonistic positions. Like partisanship, it was the enemy of consensus. In his time as majority leader, he managed to a remarkable degree to extinguish debate in a chamber that had long prided itself on being the last arena of unlimited debate.

He brought the technique with him to the White House. Politicians and pundits, congressmen and commentators who sought to question the direction Johnson was heading found themselves summoned to the executive mansion for "the treatment." "The treatment" consisted of two approximately equal parts. One was the fervid assurance that the recipient and his advice were cherished by the President and that the presidential ear would always be open to any suggestion one might care to make; the second was the mournful warning that those few benighted creatures who could not understand this, who insisted on "agitating" or "jumping up and down, trying to attract attention" with their views, were, unwittingly or not, hurting the cause of unity, hurting their country, delaying the day of peace in Vietnam and the birth of the Great Society at home. All this, delivered nose to nose, with the earthy forcefulness Johnson commanded, and in the setting of the Oval Office, had a powerfully restraining effect on many incipient dissenters.

But Johnson did not rely on his persuasiveness alone. Equally important to him was the blanket of secrecy which cloaked his intentions. What was not known to the public could not become the center of debate, he reasoned. Elaborate steps were taken to restrict the flow of news from the Administration; Cabinet officers and White House aides were warned in blunt terms to make no unauthorized disclosures; violations were punished, often, by discipline of the offender or cancellation of the project he was promoting.

Inevitably, this penchant for secrecy brought Johnson into conflict with the White House press corps, a far less complaisant group than he had been accustomed to either in Texas or on Capitol Hill. But the conflict was not well understood. What was important was not the petty sniping between a President who declined to give the reporters advance notice of his schedule, and a press corps which retaliated by inventing derogatory nicknames or printing unflattering photos. What was important was the fact that the President basically saw no constructive role for public debate in the formulation of national policy, and therefore systematically shut down public access to the plans he was making.

The Failure of Consensus Politics

As we all know too well, Johnson's system of consensus leadership fell apart on the issue of the Vietnam war. In his final two years in office, Congress passed a few more bills, notably a package of consumer and conservation legislation and the open housing law. But funds for Great Society programs were restricted and many recommendations defeated by what Johnson called "the old coalition of standpatters and nay-sayers."

The root of the problem was not in Congress but in the White House, and the system of artificial consensus Johnson had tried to impose on the country. After long denying it, Johnson was forced in late 1966 to concede that war costs were eating into the funds necessary for his Great Society programs. The consensus President was required to take the politically fateful step of assigning priorities. The businessman who did not care what Johnson "squandered" on social programs as long as profits were high and taxes declining now began to complain about the billions going into the poverty program. The young father who was happy to see medicare relieve him of his parents' hospital bills was considerably less happy when Johnson asked him to pay a 10 percent surtax to help finance the war.

The President who had tried to keep his finger on every important pulse found himself increasingly preoccupied with managing the tactical details of an ever-larger war. Group leaders trying to interest him in their domestic concerns found him less accessible, and, if they chanced to oppose him on the war, they found he was not available at all. Those men stopped being satellites of the President and resumed being independent political agents, playing their own game with the Kennedys or the Republicans, as the case might be, and making their own deals.

The President who had counted on those leaders to defend him to their constituents found he had shockingly little support of his own, when they began to desert. As early as 1966, the Gallup Poll showed Johnson a second choice to Robert F. Kennedy in the presidential preference of Democratic voters. Engaged by then in a bitter feud with the press, Johnson found he could not appeal directly to the public, no matter how many variations he tried in the formats of his public speeches and press conferences. Increasingly, he withdrew within the shell of the White House.

Finally, the public debate Johnson had tried to suppress burst forth in the Senate Foreign Relations Committee, on college campuses and in political forums. The war provoked massive public demonstrations, some of them violent, which, along with the continuing Negro riots, presented a frightening picture of a society shaken by internal dissension. As the debate mounted, becoming more shrill and personal, some of the facts and the decisions Johnson had sought to keep secret became public, and his own credibility became as much of an issue as the war itself.

For a man who had said only four years before, "I want a happy nation, not a harassed people," it was a tragic ending, when on March 31, 1968, he announced he would step aside and not seek another term. It would be easy to say that but for the mischance of Vietnam—a war that was already old when he became President— it all might have ended differently. But what I have suggested in this chapter is that the root of Johnson's failure was not in Vietnam but in his own flawed concept of presidential leadership and party responsibility in a democracy. Consensus government cannot work —because there are real choices to be made, choices of goals, choices of means, choices of values.

Because Johnson did not recognize this, he damaged the public credibility of the presidency, demeaned the Congress and brought the shadow of corruption to the Supreme Court. The conflict-of-interest charges which led his appointee, Abe Fortas, to resign from the High Court when the Senate balked at confirming him for Chief Justice were symptomatic of the moral blind spots which flawed Johnson's concept of government as well. In their world, as Johnson's speeches made clear, there was no sharp line between private and public interests, any more than there was a division of responsibilities inside the government. It seemed proper to both of them that Fortas should continue to operate as a White House insider and a private adviser to the President even after he was sitting as a Justice of the Supreme Court. And it seemed proper to Fortas that even after he was on the bench he should continue to receive a substantial fee from a private foundation whose head, a former law client, continued to consult with the Justice on his legal problems with the government.

Just as Johnson's concept of government was fatally flawed, so was his method of governing. It was, in fact, the very opposite of responsible party government. Johnson saw government, not as the *end product* of a wide-ranging process of discussion, debate and political action that defined the goals of the nation and allocated the costs of reaching them, but rather as the *source* of those benefits and services determined by its leaders to be appropriate for a Great Society. It was hand-me-down government carried to its ultimate expression, with bounties, benefits, and, of course, directions issuing from the top.

He did not see political parties as necessary vehicles for communicating the often inchoate preferences of the voters to those in power. Nor did he see the parties as instruments for disciplining the whims of the elected leaders and holding them accountable for their actions. Instead, he saw them as unwanted intruders on the process of consensus government.

Philip Geyelin, in his study of Johnson, says his slogan might well have been "We shall overwhelm." That captures the essential failure of his approach to the presidency. He did not so much try to run the government as to smother it. Leadership to Johnson meant the monopolization of power. Vietnam was his most evident failure, and he left behind him a country divided, bitter, suspicious of its government and distrustful of anyone who even employed the rhetoric of strong leadership. It was a sad legacy.

4

Nixon

It is significant that, among all his predecessors as President, the man Richard M. Nixon most often quotes and cites as a model is Woodrow Wilson, the man who, among his other distinctions, really introduced the idea of responsible party government into both academic and practical discussion of American politics. President Nixon is an advocate of party responsibility in government; what is not clear at this time, and what concerns us in this chapter, is whether he will have an opportunity to put his belief into practice.

For differing reasons, none of his three predecessors did so. Dwight D. Eisenhower arrived at the presidency quite innocent of any notion of how his party could help him govern. Before he discovered the relevance of politics to government—if, in fact, he ever did—the voters had stripped the Republicans of control of Congress, thus effectively ending any hope for responsible party government in his time.

John F. Kennedy, on the other hand, was a President with a clear concept of party responsibility and an activist approach to government, both of which Eisenhower lacked. But the narrowness of his victory, the constraints he felt upon his leadership, and the deep divisions he confronted within the Democratic party limited his success in putting the concept to work. Only in the last year of his life did Kennedy begin to fit practice to theory, and the effort was cut short before its potential for success became clear.

The frustration of responsible party government under Lyndon B. Johnson had yet another source. In 1964, Johnson and the Democrats won an emphatic mandate for government, but Johnson lacked the understanding of responsible partisanship to make proper use of the opportunity. What might have been this era's great period of responsible party government became instead a fiasco, and one which damaged the public credibility of both the political process and government itself.

On the face of it, Richard Nixon's situation resembles Eisenhower's. He is a Republican President confronting a Democratic Congress—a situation that defies party responsibility. But, in other important respects, the comparison to Kennedy is closer. Nixon is operating from a narrow personal mandate. His party base, in Congress and the country, is even weaker than Kennedy's. But, like Kennedy, he knows where he wants to go and his long-term strategy for achieving the conditions that permit responsible *Republican* government is, if anything, better defined than Kennedy's plan for responsible Democratic government.

What remains very much in doubt at this point, however, is whether Nixon and his associates have the talent and the skill to achieve their goal. To answer this question—at least as well as it can be answered two-thirds of the way through his first term—we have to consider, first, Nixon's present political situation, then his long-term strategy, and finally his Administration's tactical capability for accomplishing what it has set out to do.

Nixon's Mangled Mandate

Richard Nixon got to be President of the United States by being more durable than any of his political rivals—not by being brighter, more attractive, wittier or more eloquent. He is not the best-loved politician of his time, only the most familiar.

In personal terms, his recovery from his defeats for President in 1960 and for Governor of California in 1962 is a remarkable human saga. Written off as a "burned-out case" after his second defeat, he rehabilitated himself, first in the eyes of his party and then in the eyes of his country. Considering the cost in personal terms of the rigorous, exhausting, disciplined course that led from his "last press conference" in November, 1962, to the Inaugural Stand on the East Front of the Capitol in January, 1969, no one would have blamed Nixon for exulting in his moment of triumph. Instead, he was never more modest and sobersided than on the day when he was, at long last, sworn in as President, and chose to remind a nation still reeling from Lyndon Johnson's version of the Great Society that "greatness comes in simple trappings."

"To lower our voices would be a simple thing," Nixon said. The clear implication that Americans should also lower their expectations and demands was spelled out a few moments later when he added, "We are approaching the limits of what government alone can do."

"In these difficult years," the new President said, "America has suffered from a fever of words; from inflated rhetoric that promises more than it can deliver; from angry rhetoric that fans discontents into hatreds; from bombastic rhetoric that postures instead of persuading. We cannot learn from one another until we stop shouting at one another—until we speak quietly enough so that our words can be heard as well as our voices."

The tone of the Inaugural Address seemed right for a nation sorely anguished, rattled, and in need of calming reassurance. The previous four years had brought war, severe inflation, riots, assassinations and sweeping social change disturbing to millions. As Nixon said, "We have endured a long night of the American spirit."

But, if the President's words that January noon were appropriately calm and modest, it was also true they were spoken by a man who, in political terms, had a great deal to be modest about. He had been elected with 43.4 percent of the popular vote in a three-way race, the lowest percentage for a winning candidate since Woodrow Wilson in 1912. Nixon had the unenviable distinction of being the first President in 120 years to begin his White House tenure with an opposition-controlled Congress.

The narrowness of his victory is the more remarkable when one understands that the potential was there for a much greater personal and party sweep. Walter Dean Burnham, a political scientist who specializes in studies of presidential elections, has called 1968 the year of "the abortive landslide," commenting that "while the magnitude of the gross Democratic decline can only be compared with the Republican collapse of 1932, the Republican gain over 1964 was so small that Nixon was barely able to win."

The team of scholars from the University of Michigan Center for Political Studies has underlined the same point. Noting that the Democratic proportion of the vote dropped from more than 61 percent in 1964 to just over 43 percent in 1968, they said, "It is likely that the proportion of voters casting presidential ballots for the same party in these two successive elections was lower than at any time in recent American history. Among whites who voted in both elections, a full third switched their party." They compare the "massive drain from the Democratic ranks" with that of 1952, the year of Eisenhower's election, "for in both cases an electorate professing to be of Democratic allegiance by a considerable majority, had arrived at a sufficient accumulation of grievances with a Democratic administration to wish it out of office."

The obvious question, then, is why Nixon and the Republicans did not win a victory comparable to that of 1952. Such an outcome seemed possible as late as October 10, when Nixon led Democratic nominee Hubert H. Humphrey 44 percent to 29 percent in the Gallup Poll, with George Wallace in third place with 20 percent of the vote. At that point, Humphrey was without campaign funds and the Democratic organization was a shambles. Nixon, on the other hand, seemed supremely confident, with ample financing, a campaign team tested in the spring primaries, and an indelible stamp on the three great issues of the year. He had pledged to end the war in Vietnam (and, somewhat equivocally, "to win the peace"), to halt the rampaging inflation and restore balanced growth to the economy, and to take stern measures, including the appointment of "strict constructionist" judges and a tough Attorney General, to curb the rising rate of crime and disorder.

Yet, less than a month later, Mr. Nixon limped in by only half-a-million votes. Republicans gained five seats in the Senate and only five in the House, leaving the Democrats with a sixteen-vote margin in the upper body and a fifty-one-vote advantage in the lower. What happened to the landslide?

Part of the problem was Wallace, the Alabama segregationist who drew more popular votes than any third-party nominee since 1924 and more electoral votes than any minor candidate in a century—9.9 million and 46, respectively. His vote was heaviest in the South, where Humphrey was able to win only Texas. Of the five states whose electoral votes Wallace carried—Alabama, Arkansas, Georgia, Louisiana and Mississippi—all but Arkansas had been Republican in 1964 and likely would have been so again had Wallace not been in the race. Surveys taken during and after the election showed that while most Wallace voters were nominally Democrats, they favored Nixon over Humphrey by a ratio of roughly 5 to 4. If Wallace had not run and all of them had voted, Nixon's plurality might have tripled to about 1.5 million votes, tipping several more states into his column. So Wallace's presence in the race hurt Nixon and the GOP.

Nixon was also hurt by Humphrey's rather spectacular October recovery. Once he managed belatedly to separate himself from the war policies of the lame-duck Johnson Administration, by publicly advocating a bombing halt, both his support from dissident Democratic "doves" and his financial contributions picked up. Organized labor unleashed an extraordinary, expensive propaganda campaign on its own members, which succeeded not merely in detaching many of them from their original preference for Wallace, but in bringing them back to the Democratic party. This latter development was largely unforeseen by Nixon's campaign manager, John Mitchell. Mitchell and his personal public opinion analyst, Kevin Phillips, had assumed that in the late stages of the campaign many Wallace supporters would begin to realize the unlikelihood of his winning and feel the urge to "make their vote count." They assumed most of them would move into the Nixon column. Nixon had carefully positioned himself to catch the Wallace dropouts. He echoed Wallace's themes—if not the extravagance of the Governor's rhetoric—in his hard line on law-and-order and in his opposition to school busing and suburban rezoning for the purpose of racial integration. Time and again, he told his audiences that a vote for Wallace was a vote for Humphrey, the old civil rights champion, who only recently had told an audience that, if he were a Negro, "I might have led a pretty good riot myself."

In the South and Border States, the strategy worked as planned. But in the North, where September surveys found one out of every six Wallace voters a member of a union family, the union propaganda assault on Wallace as a low-wage, antilabor Governor brought those straying Democrats back to their traditional political home.

But, when all due credit is given Wallace and Humphrey for their showing, it remains clear that it was Nixon himself and his campaign tactics that made the final results surprisingly close. He had 43 percent of the vote in the polls when the nominations were made and that is exactly what he had at the end of the general election campaign. This outcome was hardly surprising, considering the "no-risk" holding-operation kind of campaign Nixon chose to run. It was, as Jules Witcover says in *The Resurrection of Richard Nixon*, an "exercise in letting sleeping dogs lie." Confident from the outset that Humphrey would find his personal difficulties and his party's rifts insuperable, Nixon sought mainly to avoid any error. The thought of debates with the other two candidates was rigidly excluded. Encounters with the press, as Witcover describes so well, were severely restricted. The focus of his own and his advisers' efforts was on his television appearances, particularly the contrived and well-controlled "panel shows" with selected citizen-interrogators, which gave a semblance of direct dialogue with the voters without the risk of genuine give-and-take.

Nixon was equally careful about his use of issues. While position papers came off his mimeograph machine in profusion and radio talks (with tiny audiences) dealt with a variety of national concerns, his personal campaigning and his television ads hammered relentlessly on the three main issues—Vietnam, inflation, crime and disorder.

From the beginning of his political career, it has been Nixon's fate to run as a Republican, and a clearly partisan Republican, at that, in constituencies predominantly Democratic in their makeup. That was true of his congressional district in southern California, where he ousted a ten-year Democratic incumbent. It was true of the state of California, where he ran for the Senate and the governorship. And it has been true of the United States in every one of his four national campaigns.

Throughout his career, Nixon's technique has been to attempt to split off a section of that nominally Democratic electorate by aggressive exploitation of some conservative issue. In the early part of his career, the issue was the danger of Communism, domestic and foreign. It helped him defeat Jerry Voorhis for the House and Helen Gahagan Douglas for the Senate; his identification with the Hiss case helped him win a place on the national ticket in 1952.

The Communist issue failed him in 1960 and 1962, when he ran his two losing campaigns, but in 1968 Nixon found an effective substitute in the trio of Vietnam, crime and inflation. But even on these, where public opinion was massively in his corner, Nixon was wary not to become too specific. Despite all efforts to draw him out, he declined to go into the nature of his oft-referred-to "plan" to end the war. When pressed on that or any other subject, he would fall back on the assertion, which was true enough, that the Johnson Administration having failed to resolve the problem, it was time for "new policies," "new leadership" or "a new road."

The opportunity that might have been used by a favored candidate to employ the campaign period to develop public understanding and support of his program was not so used by Nixon. Neither did he use the fall of 1968 to expand his own constituency. Nixon had defined that constituency with precision. It was suburban and rural, not urban. It was middle-aged and elderly, not young. It was middle and upper class, not poor. And, most definitely, it was white. This definition came through clearly in the concept of the "forgotten Americans" to whom Nixon addressed his acceptance speech, and, indeed, his entire campaign. It dictated his schedule and his itinerary. Much time was spent stumping the suburbs of Philadelphia and Chicago and the "Outer City" areas from Los Angeles and Orange counties, California, to Bergen County, New Jersey. One whole day was spent whistle-stopping through rural Ohio, but in the whole campaign, he addressed only two predominantly black audiences, both tiny.

The results were as sharply demarcated as the campaign had been. The CBS sample precinct analysis showed Nixon led Humphrey by 15 points among high-income voters, trailed him by 9 points among low-income voters. The same analysis gave Nixon an 11-point margin in suburban precincts, but showed him losing in the big cities by 25 points. Gallup's post-election survey showed Nixon with a 6-point advantage among voters over 50, but a 9-point deficit among those under thirty. The sharpest polarization was racial: Nixon received 47 percent of the white votes in the three-way race but only 12 percent of the black.

As a result of the campaign he conducted, Richard Nixon entered office with serious disadvantages for the task of governing. Like John Kennedy, he came to the presidency with neither a majority nor a mandate, but, unlike Kennedy, he lacked party control of Congress. What most men achieve en route to the White House he has had to strive to build after he was in office. In one of the radio addresses during his campaign, more thoughtful by far than his stump talks or television spots, he discussed the nature of presidential leadership and remarked that a President must "take hold of America before he can move it forward." Nixon took office with only the shakiest grip on his country.

The Republican Planners

The weakness of his political position might have been a less serious problem had Nixon shared Eisenhower's notion of a passive presidency or had Eisenhower's narrow goals for his Administration. But, despite the restrained rhetoric of his inaugural, Nixon had ambitious plans. It took the Washington press corps—and the country—some time to awaken to the existence of these long-range designs. Most Presidents improvise, even if they are Democrats and talk the rhetoric of social planning. Republican Presidents are just assumed to be essentially *laissez faire* in their approach; administrators, not innovators. In Nixon's case, that assumption has proven to be dangerously misleading. Indeed, I think the case can be made that there has been more serious, long-term planning at the high levels of the government, actively supported by the interest of the President, in the Nixon Administration than in any of its Democratic predecessors. Certainly there has been more attention to the process and structure of government itself.

Nixon's objectives are obviously not identical to those of his Democratic predecessors. His priorities are not theirs, but neither is his constituency. Nixon was elected in a popular reaction against the central tendencies of the Johnson Administration; that reaction was centered in the white suburbs and the South. For the millions of Americans who were on the losing side of the 1968 election, who may believe that the test of any administration is the extent to which it succors the poor, the ill and the aged, the compassion with which it deals with the blacks, the Indians, the Chicanos and the other victims of segregation and discrimination, Nixon's vision and Nixon's goals may seem fundamentally, even morally, flawed.

There is no doubt that Nixon is marching to a different drummer. The voices he heeds are those of the middle-class and upper-class whites who put him in office. He has not satisfied them wholly; indeed, the most conservative of his constituents were probably more outraged by his policies toward China and the Soviet Union, his turnabout on the economy and his acceptance of deficit spending, than any liberals were by his Supreme Court appointments or pronouncements on racial issues.

But for now it may be worthwhile to put aside the ideological criticisms of Nixon's record and the many failings of the Administration's day-to-day operations and remark on the largely unnoticed fact that Nixon has made a serious effort at planning America's future according to a rational design.

It was the Nixon Administration which began the first five-year projections of Federal finances—outlining in the Budget and Economic Report its estimates of future governmental revenues and the foreseeable demands upon them, as an aid to rational planning. It was President Nixon who reorganized the White House staff and the executive office to facilitate such planning—linking budget and central management functions in an expanded Budget Bureau called the Office of Management and Budget. It was he who regrouped (and expanded) the White House staff into functional units—a Domestic Policy Council, a Council on International Economic Policy, as well as the existing National Security Council and Council of Economic Advisers.

It was Nixon who recommended to Congress a similar reorganization and consolidation of Cabinet departments along functional lines. He set up the Environmental Quality Council and the Environmental Protection Agency to coordinate long-range government efforts against pollution. He standardized the regional units of the domestic agencies and consolidated their field headquarters, risking the inevitable political outcry that had deterred his predecessors from such action. It was on his recommendation that Congress created a Commission on Population Growth to remedy what the President rightly called "the greatest single failure of foresight—at all levels of government—over the past generation." He also proposed a major reform of the welfare system, which, among its many ramifications, moved us significantly closer to a national system of income maintenance.

In these and other areas, Nixon has not hesitated to assert and expand the role of the national government in centralized planning and administration. Many of his other reforms, however, are aimed at dispersing power from Washington and moving the control of programs into local government or private hands. That is the thrust of his proposal for revenue sharing with the states and cities and for shifting Federal aid from narrow categorical grants to broader channels, with increased local options on the use of the funds, another step his predecessor had studied but declined to take. It is Nixon's Administration which has finally seen the long-discussed reorganization of the patronage-ridden Post Office Department into a professionalized public corporation called the U.S. Postal Service.

There were hints in Nixon's campaign speeches that his administration would usher in what he chose to call "an age of reform," and much in the intellectual climate of the late 1960s made it altogether likely this would occur whoever became President. The Johnson Administration had marked the utmost extension of the problem-solving approach developed two generations earlier by Roosevelt's New Deal. The Great Society programs not only used up the stockpile of unenacted proposals from earlier years, they also consumed most of the remaining public confidence in Washington's capacity to devise and manage solutions for all these problems. Disillusionment with the discernible results of the flood of Johnson programs was widespread. Correctly or not, much of public opinion linked the plethora of new Federal programs in the late 1960s with the upsurge of social disorder and violence in that same period, as cause and effect. When New Haven, which had received more Federal aid per capita than any other city, had its riot in 1967, the reaction of many was, "Well, that proves how much good all these programs do." The logic of that syllogism was certainly open to question, but serious practitioners of government did not dispute that the crush of new legislation had all but overwhelmed the existing bureaucratic structure.

As it happened, occupying a crucial position on Nixon's staff, as his counselor on domestic affairs, was an exponent of the "new skepticism," Daniel Patrick Moynihan. Moynihan, a sociologist and Kennedy Democrat, had seen the growth of the new programs as a Labor Department official in the years the Great Society was born. Then, from his academic berth at the Harvard-M.I.T. Joint Center for Urban Studies, he had written about the failures of the anti-poverty program and its companion measures. He came back to government, despite the many risks of being tagged as Nixon's "house Democrat," to advise the new Administration, as Edmund Burke had said, "to consider the wisdom of a timely reform." It was Moynihan who sold the President on welfare reform, who interested him and educated the staff on the importance of long-term demographic, economic and social trends, and who gave the early Cabinet meetings the classroom air that Washington found so unexpected in a Republican Administration.

But the President's interest in long-range planning was not confined to Moynihan's area of social reforms. It also distinguished his approach to each of his top-priority problems—the war, the economy and national unrest.

Vietnam was the bottleneck in the foreign policy situation he inherited. Nixon had supported the American commitment to the independence of South Vietnam under four Presidents, but he recognized the political imperative of ending the combat role of American GIs. His problem, then, was to arrange the withdrawal at a pace fast enough to satisfy domestic public opinion but deliberate enough to avoid the impression of a rout and to protect, so far as possible, the survival chances of a non-Communist government in Saigon.

The instrument of this "wriggle-out" policy was the Vietnamization program—a staged American withdrawal linked to intensified training and equipping of the South Vietnamese army. But, even as he began this policy in 1969, Nixon was sketching his plans for a post-Vietnam foreign policy. First outlined in mid-1969 and for-malized in early 1970, the "Nixon Doctrine" has as its central thesis the view "that the United States will participate in the defense and development of allies and friends, but America . . . cannot undertake all the defense of the free nations of the world." The policy acknowledges the adverse public reaction to the Vietnam intervention, but it also recognizes a more fundamental change. As Nixon said in his 1970 foreign policy message, "the postwar period in international relations has ended," the world has evolved be-yond the cold war between two superpowers, Russia and the United States, into a complex and potentially less-dangerous rela-tionship involving many powers—Japan, China, the economically integrated European countries and the emerging nations.

Surprising to many who had thought of him as a reflexive anti-Communist cold warrior, Nixon began deliberately to work for long-term changes and improvements in all these relationships, fulfilling his inaugural pledge to make this "an era of negotiation." He reopened diplomatic talks with China, eased trade restrictions, ended American opposition to its seating in the United Nations and—in the most stunning diplomatic coup of his presidency—sent his foreign policy adviser, Henry Kissinger, on a secret mission to Peking to arrange a presidential visit to that capital.

He negotiated the return of Okinawa to Japan, signaling its full partnership in the security of the Pacific. Deliberately, he let Western European leaders take over from the United States the negotiation of improved trade and diplomatic relationships with Eastern Europe, looking ahead to the prospect of a resolution of the long Berlin dispute and a negotiated, balanced reduction of military forces on both sides of the no-longer-impervious Iron Curtain.

He secured ratification of the nuclear nonproliferation treaty and continued the long, complex negotiations with Russia on strategic arms limitations, which, as he has repeatedly said, hold the key to the future security of both countries and relief from the ever-mounting cost of new weapons systems and defenses.

Finally, he involved the United States deeply in the peace-keeping effort in the Middle East, recognizing the Arab-Israeli dispute as one which could not be ignored without risk of world war. In all these ways, Nixon spoke and acted so as to indicate his long-term purposes in foreign policy.

There was a similar design in economic policy. As in Vietnam, the immediate options available to the President were very restricted. Inflation was rampant; in the year before he took office, the consumer price index rose 6 percent. The political imperative to curb rising prices was clear. But, again as in Vietnam, Nixon saw dangers in sudden, severe action to meet the short-term problem. Just as he rejected the option of immediate withdrawal from Vietnam, so he rejected the option of boosting taxes and cutting government spending, which might have ended inflation but only at the risk of plunging the country into a recession. Instead, he chose the domestic version of a Vietnamization policy, gradually reducing the growth of government expenditures and gradually applying the brakes to the economy's expansion.

Again, as in foreign policy, the short-term measures were accompanied by the outline of a long-term design that offered promise of far more attractive vistas. The Budget and Economic Report issued in 1970—the first year in which Mr. Nixon had control of its preparation—contained "a strategy for the seventies . . . placing heavy emphasis"—and overdue emphasis, it might be added—"on the long-range implications of current decisions."

"We must," Nixon said, "become increasingly aware that small decisions today often lead to large cash outlays in the future. Past failure to recognize this fact is responsible for much of the current budgetary inflexibility, hampering our present progress."

To guide long-term planning, to provide a rationale for necessary reductions in marginal programs and a basis for assigning priorities among the many claimants for Federal support, Nixon's economic and budget advisers made five-year projections of the resources of the Federal government and the demands on it. Their projections indicated that with the built-in cost increases of existing programs (beyond whatever economies and cutbacks could be achieved) and the new programs to which the Administration had already committed itself, like revenue sharing and welfare reform, there would be little, if any, margin of uncommitted funds through 1972. But a significant $22 billion "nest egg" was visible by fiscal 1975—the middle of what might be a second Nixon term. Only then, they suggested, could major new funds be allocated to improve the environment, housing, transportation, health care, education and the like.

It was hardly a glowing picture, but, as in the Nixon Doctrine for foreign policy, it offered a rational, long-term design that could serve as a guide to policy planning.

There were similar, if less publicly stated, Administration designs in other vital areas. With the appointment in 1969 of Warren Burger, a judicial conservative with respectable credentials, as Chief Justice, to succeed liberal Earl Warren, Nixon began the process of reshaping the Supreme Court and the Federal judiciary to the "strict constructionist" model he had set forth in the campaign. He also put into motion programs for expanding Federal financing of local law-enforcement and correctional services and offered a package of stiff laws, using the District of Columbia as his pilot laboratory, to reduce street crime, as he had promised.

Nixon also evolved a "communications strategy" aimed at avoiding the credibility problem the Johnson Administration had encountered. The number of publicity men in government was markedly expanded and Herbert G. Klein, Nixon's long-time press spokesman, installed in the new post of "communications director" to orchestrate their efforts. As in the campaign, newspapermen were given help in publicizing the programs and views Nixon wanted discussed, but were severely restricted in their direct access to the President. In his first two years in office, Nixon held only fourteen press conferences and granted no private interviews to newspapermen covering the White House. Meantime, as in the campaign, television was exploited fully, under controlled circumstances, to get the President's message to the public, with minimum "interference" from news representatives. He appeared on prime-time television about once a month, and when the Administration began to suspect that the comments of television newsmen after these appearances were interfering with the President's "clear channel" to his constituents, Vice President Agnew was sent out to attack the "small band of network commentators and self-appointed analysts, the majority of whom expressed in one way or another their hostility to what he [Nixon] had to say."

Nixon's Political Strategy

In all of these areas—governmental reform, foreign policy, economics, law enforcement, communications—Nixon has been acutely conscious that he lacks the political weapons to bring his ambitious targets within range. More aware than anyone else of the narrowness of his political base, he has set out systematically to expand it. He campaigned personally for the pro-Nixon Republican candidates in the two gubernatorial elections in 1969 and saw them take control of the statehouses of Virginia and New Jersey, both critical states for his own re-election. But his goal is really more ambitious than his own second-term victory. More than most Presidents, Nixon thinks of himself as a partisan, and he believes in the idea of responsible party government. His goal, often stated to associates, is to use his presidency to make the Republican party the majority party, the governing party, in America.

That means several things. So far as popular support is concerned, it implies a continuous effort to expand the Republican vote base, particularly in those areas of shifting political allegiance, the South and the suburbs. One goal is to eliminate, or significantly reduce, the potential of a George Wallace candidacy to divert votes from the Republican column again in 1972. To this end, it is important that the Nixon Administration be perceived as the friend of the South—the white South. Nixon has appointed a Southerner to the Supreme Court, has tried to weaken the Voting Rights Act, to delay school desegregation deadlines and to shift the burden of enforcing desegregation plans from the Administration to the courts. He and Agnew have made frequent appearances in the South and Nixon has warmed Confederate hearts by assailing "the double hypocritical standard of Northerners who look at the South and point the finger and say, 'Why don't those Southerners do something about their race problem?' "

What is often described as the Administration's "Southern strategy" is, in fact, only half of its long-term political plan. The other half is the "suburban strategy," whose goal is to extend the Republican base in the outer cities and rings of commuter towns. The suburbs are, if anything, even more important to Nixon's success than the South. Whereas Wallace held the key to 9.9 million votes and the electoral votes of perhaps half a dozen, mainly small Southern states, the suburbs of the thirty-five largest metropolitan areas alone cast 17.4 million votes (half again as many as the central cities of those areas) and control the electoral votes of most of the major states.

In the 1950s, when the mass movement to the suburbs was just gaining momentum, most politicians assumed that Republicans would benefit almost automatically from the population shift. The idea was that when the family quit the apartment in the city, joined the crabgrass set, and learned that with their enhanced status came a mortgage and high property taxes, why, they would just naturally start voting Republican. In fact, what happened was that many of the families carried their Democratic voting habits with them to the suburbs. As Richard M. Scammon and Ben J. Wattenberg said in *The Real Majority,*

There is no evidence that Democratic-oriented voters switch parties simply because they move from the cities or become more affluent. The "old affluent" are traditionally Republican; the new suburbanite is neither so affluent nor so Republican. In fact there is evidence that many suburbs once solidly Republican are now tossups between Democrats and Republicans, or, in some instances, already solidly Democratic.

Indeed, the Republican National Committee's 1968 election analysis showed Mr. Nixon managed only a 1.1 million plurality over Humphrey among the suburban voters in the thirty-five major metropolitan areas. The suburbs of Buffalo, Detroit, Pittsburgh and St. Louis actually went Democratic.

What Mr. Nixon has set out to do, then, is to expand the Republican suburban strength from the areas of settled affluence to the newer, middle-class suburban tracts that are the main battleground of contemporary politics.

As Scammon and Wattenberg describe them, the residents of the new suburbs "are plumbers . . . foremen . . . airplane mechanics . . . small merchants . . . union workers in an automobile plant . . . telephone repairmen with a second job or with wives who work."

They share certain interests and certain prejudices with the white Southerners, and Nixon has played to those interests and prejudices as President. Neither the Southerners nor the suburbanites like "welfare chiselers," so Nixon has loaded his speeches on welfare reform with rhetoric that minimizes its minimum-income guarantee and emphasizes, instead, its work requirements and its somewhat dubious promise to "move people off welfare rolls and onto payrolls." Defending his proposal to the nation's governors in 1971, the President said, "I advocate a system that will encourage people to take work, and that means whatever work is available. . . . Scrubbing floors, emptying bedpans—my mother used to do that—it's not enjoyable work, but a lot of people do it. And there is as much dignity in that as there is in any other work to be done in this country, including my own." That line went down well in the South and the suburbs.

Again, Southerners and suburbanites are particularly vehement in their opposition to busing. So Nixon has repeated again and again, "I have consistently opposed the busing of our nation's school children to achieve a racial balance," even undercutting his own Administration's efforts to enforce court-ordered integration in order to preserve his political stance. Both groups oppose "forced integration" of neighborhoods, and Mr. Nixon has repeatedly declared that "for the Federal government to go further than the law, to force integration in the suburbs, I think is unrealistic . . . counterproductive and not in the interest of better race relations."

With these essential components in mind, Nixon developed a long-term strategy aimed not just at his own re-election but at making the Republicans the dominant party at all levels of government. In 1970, he hoped to achieve a Republican majority in the Senate and to maintain the strong GOP position in the state capitals. Then in 1972, with his own coattails and a Republican redistricting of House seats to help, he had hoped to see the GOP recapture control of the House of Representatives.

The President worked hard at the project. He actively recruited candidates for Senate races, persuading a dozen able, veteran House members to give up safe seats in 1970 to help in the all-out bid for control of the Senate. He spurred his party to its greatest off-year fund-raising effort, with a reported $20 million being collected in 1969 and 1970 by national GOP organizations, and he reserved hundreds of thousands of dollars in a special fund for White House assistance to men in key races. Agnew was given a full-time assignment of campaigning for the Republican hopefuls and Nixon himself traveled to twenty-three states on their behalf.

Trouble with the Tactics

This, then, was the long-range Nixon strategy: Careful extrication from Vietnam, leading to a period of negotiation with hostile powers and reallocation of defense burdens with prospering allies. A gradual braking of inflation, cushioned to avoid severe recession or prolonged unemployment. A firm discipline on government spending until we reach a period in the later 1970s when sustained, real economic growth will produce a steady increase in Federal revenues, at lower tax rates, to finance programs to meet the nation's domestic needs. A restructuring of the Supreme Court and the criminal justice system to balance the "permissive" policies of the 1960s and end public fear of crime and disorder. A policy of candor (real or seeming), keyed to presidential use of television, that will close the credibility gap and reverse rising public distrust of government. And a series of elections that will move the Republicans from a shaky, tentative grip on the White House to firm command of the presidency, Congress and state government. Then, and only then, Nixon felt, would he have achieved the conditions that would make possible responsible party government.

Simply to state these objectives is to made clear how far Nixon has fallen short of his aspirations. And what must be said is that the frustration of those designs has resulted not so much from adverse external circumstances, but from the shortcomings of the Administration's own performance.

The problem was well defined by *Life* magazine's Hugh Sidey, a close and sympathetic observer of the Nixon White House, in August, 1971:

In his two and a half years, the President has spotted and defined with remarkable accuracy the problems of our society. He and his staff have held the necessary meetings, written the pertinent memos, drawn up the correct flow charts and issued the right press releases. But almost every major effort requiring domestic change has faltered there.

The President and his men have not sweated the long hours with obstreperous congressmen. They have refused to let dissidents intrude on their tidy schedules. They have mistaken memos for human meaning and flawless, close-order bureaucratic drill for real government. They have in an odd way managed to be lazy even while putting in all that work. By avoiding the tiring, bewildering battles of men and ideas and taking refuge in their executive privileges and organization tables, they have shown their smug conviction that big desks and cool, calm offices set the national mood.

In other words, the Nixon Administration has turned out to have a very limited understanding of what is involved in governing. Particularly, it has had difficulty in relating its day-to-day tactics to its grand strategies. That shortcoming is apparent even in the way it has defined its goals.

The President's own major policy statements, read with an

unbiased eye, are, generally speaking, straightforward, substantive and, on occasion, eloquent. But, as Pat Moynihan said when he took his leave after two years, the Administration has suffered "because his initial thrusts" have not been "followed up with a sustained, reasoned, reliable second and third order of advocacy." Those who should have been expounding Mr. Nixon's themes to congressional committees, to audiences of opinion makers around the country, have done their job poorly or not at all. "The impression was allowed to arise with respect to the widest range of Presidential initiatives that the President wasn't really behind them," Moynihan said. "The prime consequence . . . is that the people in the nation who take these matters seriously have never been required to take us seriously."

Moynihan did not explore why this should have been the case but the answer lies in large part with the kind of people Mr. Nixon has chosen to staff the White House and the upper echelons of his Administration.

A few have been very competent but not very articulate. Dr. Kissinger, the national security adviser, is a man of enormous intelligence, a gifted teacher who can expound brilliantly to an audience of any size. But, self-conscious about his German accent and inhibited to some extent by his advisory role, he has not been of much value to the Administration as a public spokesman. His counterpart on the domestic side of government, George Shultz, a University of Chicago economist who moved up from Secretary of Labor to head the Office of Management and Budget, is a superb bureaucrat, but one even more reticent than is common for the breed. Shultz has been of little value as an exponent of the domestic programs he understands so well.

Most of the Cabinet members, with the notable exceptions of John Mitchell and John Connally, have been too far removed from the center of power to have much credibility as advocates for the President. The key members of his White House staff—H. R. Bob Haldeman and John Ehrlichman—think of themselves as technicians and appear to lack any notion that their constituency is broader than the one man they serve. When one compares them with their predecessors in the posts of appointments secretary and chief of staff, one is struck by their failure either to recognize or to practice a public role commensurate with their private responsibilities to the President.

If there is anything that has characterized Nixon's inner circle it is not the "large vision," which Moynihan said was needed by those who serve in such posts, but the relentless small-mindedness of its members. Though lacking in Washington experience, they have become accomplished bureaucrats, constantly fiddling with their organization charts. They have also learned the art of empire building, expanding the White House staff to the largest size in its history. They pride themselves on being practical, hard-boiled operators, but they retain the psychology of their days as advance men on the Nixon campaign. Their responsibility, as they see it, is to deliver things on schedule and not to let outside pressures interfere.

In practice, this has meant isolating the President from people he does not wish to see. The Nixon White House, as the *New York Times*'s Robert Semple wrote, has been "dominated by . . . a passion for order and a passion for solitude." Within a few months of Nixon's taking office, Washington was filled with complaints about his inaccessibility. Members of Congress, including his own party's top leaders, found they could not get by the palace guard to see the President. Members of the Cabinet soon began to voice the same complaint. By May of 1970, Secretary of Interior Walter J. Hickel decided to make public a letter to the President in which he said: "Permit me to suggest that you consider meeting on an individual and conversational basis with members of your Cabinet. Perhaps through such conversations, we can gain greater insight into the problems confronting us all." A few months later, Hickel was fired.

The failures in internal communications have often led to the impression that the Administration does not know what direction it is heading. Kevin Phillips, Mitchell's former aide, who left to write a newspaper column, complained in 1971 that the Administration "has changed policies and directions so often and sometimes so erratically, that his image is one of opportunism rather than vision."

Ambitious projects have been announced with enormous fanfare, and then allowed to die, unattended, while some new extravaganza takes the stage. The "New Federalism" was unveiled in 1969, and allowed to languish through 1970. It was brought back, in refurbished and even more gaudy garb in January, 1970, as the "New American Revolution." Then, it too was supplanted by the "New Economic Policy."

The twists and turns of policy and the ineptitude of performance have damaged almost all Nixon's long-term strategies. Even in the area of his greatest success, foreign policy, he has incurred unnecessary costs. The lack of preparation of public and congressional opinion for the allied invasion of Cambodia in 1970 triggered massive protests, and the American-directed raid by South Vietnamese forces into Laos, nine months later, severely damaged Nixon's credibility. The White House seemed genuinely surprised that a Congress and a country which had been told repeatedly that the President was "winding down" the war would react with shock to such events.

The reaction undercut Secretary of State William Rogers' patient efforts to restore bipartisanship to our foreign policy and reinflamed the feud between the Senate Foreign Relations Committee and the White House, almost to the point it had reached in the Johnson Administration.

In the mass protests which led to the tragic deaths at Kent State and Jackson State, the President who had pleaded for reasonable discourse found himself the target of the shouted obscenities of the largest antiwar demonstrations in history. Though he was, in fact, ending the war, he was forced to bear the political burden of seeming to prolong and expand it. In turn, he allowed and encouraged Vice President Agnew to intensify his vituperative attacks on the dissidents, the demonstrators and the press, thus making his own Administration a party to the kind of angry debate he had vowed to end.

There were worse errors in seeking his other major objectives. The economic "game plan" may have been sound, but Nixon and his advisers bungled two key elements that were necessary to give it time to succeed. For thirty-two months they adamantly refused to use any form of White House influence to restrain price and wage hikes, even on a short-term basis. And, because their liaison with Capitol Hill was so faulty that they were ill-prepared to resist the irresponsible tax cut of 1969, they lost control of fiscal policy. Had the Administration been more sensitive to the psychology of business, labor and Congress, the economic plan might have had a chance to work. Instead, Nixon was forced to jettison it with dramatic suddenness in August, 1971, and take a series of drastic measures, including a wage-price freeze, in an attempt to avert catastrophe.

The third major effort—the design to reshape the judiciary—was botched unnecessarily by the Supreme Court appointments of Clement F. Haynsworth and G. Harrold Carswell. In the case of Haynsworth, none of the three top Republican leaders of the Senate found themselves able to support the nominee. The Carswell nomination again divided the President's party and caused Senator Margaret Chase Smith of Maine to issue a public denunciation of the President's chief of congressional liaison. When thirty-eight Democrats and thirteen Republicans voted against Carswell, Nixon issued an incredible statement, accusing the Senators of "malicious character assassination," "vicious assaults," "hypocrisy," and bias against men of Southern birth. And in the autumn of 1971, when two more vacancies occurred on the Supreme Court, Nixon bungled again, putting forward two nominees so unqualified they failed to pass the screening committee of the American Bar Association, before recanting and sending the Senate the names of two other conservatives with acceptable credentials. As a result, his relations with major elements of his own party and of Congress and his public credibility were again damaged.

The task of congressional liaison was botched in so many ways in the first two years of the Administration that Clark MacGregor, who took over the responsibility in 1971, was reduced to employing such gimmicks as giving White House staff members buttons reading, "I Care About Congress." Senators and Representatives had reason to doubt it. Too often they had found the Nixon White House disinterested in their political needs and in their legislative ideas. At the end of the 1969 tax bill fight, Senate Republican Leader Hugh Scott of Pennsylvania pointedly remarked that "I hope that the responsible people in the Treasury, in my own Administration, will listen the next time we try to advise them that legislatively we understand more about tactics and strategy than they do."

Early in the Administration, the White House managed to alienate Chairman Wilbur Mills of the House Ways and Means Committee, a normally nonpartisan legislator, to the point where for the first time in his political life, he became an avowed, partisan battler, inside and outside Congress, even stumping the country in 1971 to denounce Nixon's economic policies and domestic programs. Since the most important of those programs had to originate in Mills's committee, it was not surprising that not one major segment of "New Federalism" or the "New American Revolution" had become law two-thirds of the way through Nixon's term.

Similarly victimized was his whole long-term political strategy. The damage from the Cambodian invasion to the Administration's credibility; the divisiveness of the congressional fights to the cause of Republican unity; and, most of all, the costliness of the economic tactics, which brought a combination of continuing inflation and rapidly rising unemployment in the fall of 1970—all these undermined the Nixon strategy for capturing the Senate and controlling the statehouses in that election. (Ironically, rejected Supreme Court nominee Carswell created more political problems by running for the Republican Senate nomination in Florida; he lost in the primary, but the intraparty wounds helped the Democrats win a Senate seat Nixon had counted on the GOP gaining.)

In the end, Republicans fell 5 seats short of a majority in the Senate, lost 9 seats in the House, and, most damaging to the long-term strategy, took a net loss of 11 governorships and 244 legislative seats, thus vitiating their bright hopes of controlling redistricting of the House for the next decade.

It is easy to say, as Moynihan did, that in these various areas, Nixon was a man victimized by his associates. But that overlooks the fact that those who made the greatest errors, who caused the greatest irritation and controversy, were the men Nixon had chosen to elevate—former Secretary of Treasury David M. Kennedy, who bungled the tax bill; former Secretary of Health, Education and Welfare Robert H. Finch, who lost the welfare reform bill by the weakness of his presentation to the Senate Finance Committee; Attorney General John Mitchell, who recommended Haynsworth and Carswell; Spiro Agnew; Bob Haldeman —all were Nixon's own choices, and, in most instances, old and trusted associates.

As he moved into the last year before he would face the voters again, Nixon had failed to advance the prospects for a return to responsible party government under the Republicans. And that failure raised fundamental questions not only about the tactics of his presidency but about his concept of America and the kind of leadership it needs.

Throughout his long career, Richard Nixon has been known as a particularly manipulative politician. He has a remarkable grasp of the mechanics of politics, from the technique of a sixty-second television commercial to the factional structure of an Ohio congressional district.

What has been lacking, for most of that long period, is the larger vision, the theme, that would give his tactics coherence. In the early months of his presidency, and particularly in the Inaugural Address, he seemed to have discovered his theme—"Bring Us

Together." But if that was a goal, and not just a slogan, it has been submerged in the shifting day-to-day stratagems that have characterized the Nixon Administration.

What is not clear, even now, is whether Nixon understands that tactics must be shaped by that larger vision or they will destroy it. His record in the presidency is full of contradictions that suggest he has not yet found an integrated philosophy of leadership. In October of 1969 and September of 1970, he could argue that the "exceptional circumstances" of divided government made "a working partnership" between the Democratic Congress and the Republican Administration "imperative." But in between he ignored the members of Congress when he was not assailing their actions and denouncing their motives.

He could call for "an age of reform," and then use his veto power to delay meaningful reforms of campaign spending laws, because they might inconvenience his own re-election campaign. He could stump the country in the fall of 1970, depicting Democrats as enemies of law and order, in a wholly negative campaign, and then two months later present an extraordinarily positive, ambitious program of basic government restructuring, which had no chance for success because he had built no base of support for it in either Congress or the country.

He could propose a progressive and innovative welfare program, and then attempt to sell it in the rhetoric of the Poor Laws. He could for two-and-a-half years reject wage-price controls as unfair, unworkable, impractical and inequitable, and then turn around and appeal to his country to accept those controls as the only way to save itself from economic ruin. Worst of all, he could play fast and loose with the fragile loyalties of the young and the black and the others who had most cause to distrust his purposes and priorities. He could ask the educated youths to trust the government, and then send his Vice President out to denigrate the students' concern for their country. He could ask Negroes to judge him by his actions, and then turn around and sanction and participate in efforts to weaken the guarantees of their voting rights, to slow their integration into schools and neighborhoods, and to fill the Supreme Court with men whose records showed their lack of sympathy for the cause of equal rights.

Because of these personal failings, because of the ineptitude of too many of his close associates, the actions of the Nixon Administration have more often contradicted than advanced the President's professed goals and long-term designs. As a result, his leadership has lacked a sense of coherence or even of integrity. The prospects of America achieving responsible party government under Richard Nixon appear remote. The country has not been brought together. And time is running out.

5

Opinion

In mid-1971, the typical, put-upon, middle-aged American male who is the hero of the Washington *Star* cartoon strip called "The Small Society" indulged in a soliloquy. "Two things worry me these days," he said. "One, that things may never get back to normal. And the other," he added, scratching his head, "that they already have."

Normalcy for most Americans in this time of the nation's life means a state of anxiety. In addition to the ancient burdens of man—war and death, age and illness, poverty, hunger, personal tragedies—Americans live with frustrations peculiar to an affluent, urbanized, industrial society.

Traffic jams, smog, pollution, crime, inflation and a dozen other problems measure the failure of the government to anticipate, to identify and to remedy the unwanted side effects of America's prosperity and growth. Most Americans now recognize they have been let down by their public institutions. Individually, most of us have prospered in the past sixteen years. But, as a nation, we have floundered. We spend increasing portions of our time and temper trying to cope with public services that do not work: schools that do not teach, courts and police that do not preserve order, transportation systems that do not permit free movement.

A major reason for the national frustration is the paralysis of government that has resulted from the breakdown of a responsible party system. For the past generation at least, under four quite different Presidents, America has been denied responsible party government.

Because of that impasse, we have not made the commitment of funds and resources needed to sustain essential public services. Because of the impasse, we have not repaired the gaping flaws in our public institutions. Because of the impasse, America's morale has been sapped. The last result is perhaps the most serious. If public opinion has been so damaged and distorted by the long frustration of our political and governmental processes, it will not matter that we possess the resources and ingenuity to meet the challenge to our society. If the will to act is lacking, nothing can be done. And, unfortunately, the national will has been impaired by the failings of our politics in the past generation.

Every observer who has traveled in the United States in recent years has remarked on a paradox. In a time of record affluence, personal discontent seems undiminished. In a time of almost revolutionary change in almost every phase of life, many Americans describe themselves as feeling trapped in circumstances they cannot control. In a time of increasing education and easier communication, we seem less able to discover and articulate what holds us together as a community. In a time of easy mobility, many Americans seem not to expand their reach and vision but to withdraw into their own concerns. Even our response to our frustration is paradoxical and unpredictable. Moods of rebellion alternate with long periods of resignation. Anger is sporadic; apathy, prevalent.

Richard Lemon sums it up well in his 1970 book, *The Troubled American:*

The people themselves suddenly seem to be consumed with an aimless, puzzled, pervasive discontent. Sometimes they are angry. . . . Sometimes they talk sadly of beliefs that are passing. . . . Sometimes they talk about needing a good dictator. . . . Often they say they don't know who to turn to or where the way out lies. . . . And most often of all, they pass a frightening judgment. They say that what is wrong is not just this or that, but the whole country, everybody, everything. "Everything is dirty and indecent." "Everything is getting uglier and uglier." "We just seem to be headed toward a collapse of everything."

Albert H. Cantril and Charles W. Roll, Jr., found this same thing in their 1971 polling for the book *The Hopes and Fears of the American People*. They reported that 47 percent of those they talked to felt the unrest in America is serious enough so that "it is likely to lead to a real breakdown in this country," while only 38 percent think it "likely to blow over soon." A Gallup survey of working-class whites, done for *Newsweek* in the fall of 1969, showed that section of the populace even more pessimistic. While 46 percent said the country had changed for the worse in the previous decade (compared to 36 percent who thought it had improved), 58 percent said they expected things to get even worse in the *next* five years.

Any journalist who spent time crisscrossing America could supply his own set of anecdotes illustrating these fears. The Washington *Post*'s Haynes Johnson told of the Sterling, Kansas, department store manager who remarked, "My wife and I often talk about what's happening today, and we ask ourselves if we had to start out all over again, whether we'd even have children today. And we don't know if we would."

In 1970, Bill Moyers, who was President Johnson's assistant for domestic affairs, took a trip around the nation he had helped govern, and reported in *Listening to America:*

People are more anxious and bewildered than alarmed. They don't know what to make of it all: of long hair and endless war, of their children deserting their country, of congestion on their highways and overflowing crowds in their national parks; of art that does not uplift and movies that do not reach conclusions; of intransigence in government and violence; of politicians who come and go while problems plague and persist; of being lonely surrounded by people, and bored with so many possessions; of the failure of organizations to keep the air breathable, the water drinkable, and man peaceable; of being poor. . . .

There is a myth that the decent thing has almost always prevailed in America when the issues were clearly put to people. It may not always happen. I found among people an impatience, an intemperance, an isolation which invites opportunists who promise too much and castigate too many. And I came back with questions. Can the country be wise if it hears no wisdom? Can it be tolerant if it sees no tolerance? Can the people I met escape their isolation if no one listens?

That such doubts and despair should have been so common as the new decade began would have seemed not just paradoxical but perverse to the proverbial visitor from Mars. For this country has been blessed beyond comparison with the goods men have sought through the centuries. By whatever yardstick one uses— housing, education, income, possessions—the 1950s and 1960s saw the greatest advance in living standards for Americans in the nation's history. Moreover, that advance was widely, if not equally, shared, with a sharp reduction in the ranks of the poor and a greater proportionate improvement for blacks than for whites. Between 1950 and 1970, the average family saw its real income (discounting inflation) increase 85 percent. Its members had three more years' education, on the average, than their counterparts a generation earlier. The family added a room to its house, acquired a washing machine and a television set and moved from the central city to the suburbs, thus achieving, in at least a small way, the old dream of knowledge, wealth and land. And yet the apprehensions endure.

This is the paradox we must probe in order to understand the climate of opinion in which political choices will be made in this decade. Two groups are particularly important for this purpose— the college-educated young, who will provide much of the emerging political leadership, and the Middle Americans (to use Joseph Kraft's phrase), the working-class families whose votes and predispositions will determine which leaders and policies the nation follows.

At first glance, the Middle Americans and the college students, particularly the more politically activist students, appear to be at opposite extremes of American society. The former, for all their dissatisfactions, are the fiercest defenders of traditional values; the latter, the most convinced and dedicated apostles of fundamental change. At times, as when the "hard hats" fought the antiwar student demonstrators in New York, they have carried their disagreement to the point of violence.

Yet they are alike in two ways, both crucial to the future of politics in this country. They are both distrustful of government and cynical about the possibility they can make political processes work for their ends. At a deeper level, both groups show signs of abandoning any hope of "solving" their problems in the community. Instead, they are both seeking, with some desperation, for individual avenues of escape. Unless we can overcome the cynicism about politics and government, unless we can turn these two groups back toward society and away from their individual retreat, it is going to be very difficult to repair the damage America has suffered from its long period of political and governmental stagnation.

The Disaffected Young

A higher proportion of young Americans complete a high school education now than ever before in our history. More of the high school graduates, almost 60 percent, now go on to college. More of those who enter college complete the four years for graduation, and more of the college graduates continue on to graduate and professional schools.

In a real sense, this democratization of education can be regarded as one of America's proudest achievements. And yet, since the mid-1960s, American college students have been at the center of the protest demonstrations which have most puzzled and disturbed this country—"an aberration from the moral order of American society," as the President's Commission on Campus Unrest said in characterizing the public view of the situation.

The commission was created by President Nixon at the height of the campus disturbances in 1970 and was headed by William W. Scranton, a former Governor of Pennsylvania. Its report argued that, while the targets of the demonstrations were the war in Vietnam, racial discrimination, and unpopular college regulations, the underlying cause of the student protest was something else. The cause was the emergence of a "new youth culture," which the commission said

took its bearings from the notion of the autonomous, self-determining individual whose goal was to live with authenticity, or in harmony with his inner penchants and instincts. It also found its identity in a rejection of the work ethic, materialism, and conventional social norms and pieties. Indeed, it rejected all institutional disciplines externally imposed upon the individual, and this set it at odds with much in American society.

Some critics of the Scranton Commission report think its description of the "generation gap" both exaggerated and oversimplified the situation. Public opinion analyst Daniel Yankelovich, in studies for CBS, emphasized that the conflict of values divided members of the younger generation along class lines even more sharply than it divided parents and children. Or, as Richard Scammon put it, "The working-class kid from the Italian-American half of Cambridge whose father is a fry cook in the White Tower Restaurant, and the Harvard undergraduate son of a Scarsdale physician have less in common with each other than either does with his own parents."

Yet even Yankelovich acknowledged there is a "true generation gap" in three crucial areas: sexual morality, the importance of religion, and faith in the democratic process. Young people *as a whole* are notably more tolerant of premarital and extramarital sexual relations, significantly less inclined to believe in the importance of organized religion. They have notably less confidence in the democratic process than do their parents (by a ratio of 3 to 1, in their own judgment.). While Yankelovich himself stressed the areas of agreement between the generations (including belief in hard work, saving, competition, private property, compromise, etc.), it would be hard to think of three more significant areas of disagreement than sex and the family, the church and the democratic system.

Also, Yankelovich pointed to a sizable segment of college students who do think of themselves as being basically at odds with adult society. He called them the "forerunners." They are the students who value their education, not primarily for its economic or career benefits, but for the skills and vision it gives them for the task of reshaping society. They tend to cluster in the humanities and the social sciences, and their ideas differ sharply from those of both their noncollege contemporaries and their practical-minded fellow students in business or engineering. Only 12 percent of them say they find it easy to abide by laws they do not agree with; only 10 percent think the American way of life superior, and only 6 percent say that civil disobedience is never justified. Important as a measure of their alienation, only 24 percent of these college students think their personal point of view and values are shared by most Americans.

Yankelovich made the point that the "forerunners" represent only 43 percent of the college students and only 12 percent of all young adults. But, unless our pattern of leadership recruitment changes, they represent a very high proportion of the future national political leaders, just as they have provided the hard core of the activist student movement in recent years.

The "forerunners'" relationship with government has been brief and unhappy. Sam Brown, one of the leaders of the generation, wrote in 1970 that "a young person in this country has seen little but war, the draft, riots, racism, assassinations, pollution and government ineptness since he came into political awareness." Those in college in the 1970s became politically aware *after* the death of John F. Kennedy. They have known only two Presidents—Lyndon Johnson and Richard Nixon. My own conversations with juniors and seniors at Harvard during the 1969–70 school year convinced me that their perception of Johnson did not extend back even to the 1964 campaign, when he won his overwhelming victory against Barry Goldwater. To them, Johnson was simply and solely (and probably unfairly) the man who got us into Vietnam, and Nixon (equally unfairly) the man who kept us there. They tend to regard government as being either indifferent or hostile to their goals. Few of them seem aware that their education is publicly subsidized. Their experiences with government and politics have left them unimpressed. If they have dealt with any government official, it is likely to have been a draft board clerk or a policeman "hassling" them about their clothes, their language, their actions or their smoking materials. If they have participated in a presidential campaign (and more of them have than their counterparts in any previous generation), it is likely that they have seen their candidate defeated or killed.

Even if they are willing to concede that the fates played as large a part in the 1968 election as any inequities in "the system," they still argue that conventional politics is too slow to respond and will not achieve the goals they seek. A Gallup Poll of college students in late 1970 found 79 percent believe the American political system does not respond quickly enough to meet the needs of the people. The students I knew at Harvard argued that old-fashioned coalition politics might yield a 25-cent increase in the minimum wage every few years, or an extra $5 per month in social security benefits, but it would never go to the root of what they see as the basic problems of America: the inequitable distribution of wealth and income; the endemic racism in all aspects of our private and civic life; and the economic-military forces that distort our foreign policy. Although they make sporadic, short-term efforts to change governmental policy, they do not really expect politics to work for them. For five years, they tried canvassing, marching, demonstrating, striking and protesting. Nothing has seemed to work. In short, they have been turned off by politics.

The Blue-Collar Blues

The Middle Americans have been turned off, too, for different reasons. Their experience is longer but no less disillusioning. They provided the votes that elected every Democratic President from Roosevelt through Johnson, and yet they have felt abandoned and neglected by the Democratic party at a time when their needs are greater, not less, than they have been in the past. Some of them responded to Richard Nixon's overtures to the "Forgotten Americans," noting that he at least was talking about their greatest concerns—the war, inflation and crime. But their experience with him in his first two and a half years as President was disillusioning. The old complaints were not relieved and, what was worse, they found, as they had before, that when a Republican was President, millions more of them were out of work. As a result, you can find the same kind of disillusionment with politics and government in blue-collar neighborhoods as you hear expressed on college campuses.

The most basic measure of political participation is a vote. Voting turnout was lower in the 1968 presidential election than it was in 1964. It was lower in 1970 than it had been in the previous midterm election of 1966. Traveling the country in the 1970 campaign, I was told, time and again, in terms of cold fury or hot rage, that voting was a waste of time, because the politicians could not be trusted to keep their promises. A Norfolk shipyard worker said he would go back to voting when a law was passed to "horsewhip any candidate who doesn't do what he says." Until then, he said, he'd stay home.

The reasons for the Middle Americans' bitterness are both economic and social. In a time of general prosperity, many blue-collar workers have found themselves on a treadmill to frustration. Fully 40 percent of American families have an income between $5,000 and $10,000 a year. In 1970, a task force headed by Assistant Secretary of Labor Jerome M. Rosow reported on the problems facing the blue-collar workers who head most of those families.

It is precisely when their children reach their teens and family budget costs are at their peak that two things happen to the bulk of such male breadwinners. They reach a plateau in their capacity to earn by promotion or advancement . . . [and] their expenses continue to rise, as the last family members are born, as they become home owners, as car and home equipment pressures mount, as their children become ready for college, or support is needed for aging parents.

As Rosow noted, most industrial workers find they reach a job ceiling while still in their thirties, and after that there are no added benefits for them. Faced with heavier financial demands, the typical factory employee can do one of three things. He can encourage his wife to work—and the proportion of craftsmen and operatives with wives in the labor force rose from 32 to 44 percent in the 1960s, despite the difficulties this undoubtedly caused in many family lives.

He can moonlight himself—and millions of blue-collar workers do just that. Peter Schrag, in a *Harper's Magazine* article on "The Forgotten Americans," quotes Teamster official Nicholas Kisburg: "I don't think anybody has a single job any more. All the cops are moonlighting, and the teachers, and there's a million guys who are hustling, guys with phony social security numbers, who are hiding part of what they make so they don't get kicked out of a housing project, or guys who work as guards at sports events and get free meals that they don't want to pay taxes on. Every one of them is cheating."

The third alternative is to pressure for wage increases, but inflation has made this course self-defeating since 1965. Between 1955 and 1965, the blue-collar families stayed a little ahead in the race against inflation. In that decade, the real net spendable earnings of the average nonfarm worker (discounting inflation and deducting Federal taxes) increased from $79.06 to $91.32. After 1965, the rate of inflation was so great that despite impressive-looking contract settlements, the real earnings declined, dropping to $89.95 in 1970. Not until mid-1971 did they regain the 1965 level. (All figures are in constant 1967 dollars.)

If the private economy has been indifferent to the blue-collar workers' plight, the government has been no less so. The Middle Americans pay more than their share in taxes and get back less in public services. In the 1960s, as Federal income tax rates were cut and exemptions increased, while payroll, sales and property taxes soared, the overall tax system became markedly less progressive. As a result, the Tax Foundation in 1970 estimated, families earning under $10,000 a year paid 28.6 percent of their income in taxes, while those with incomes of $1 million or more paid only 28.4 percent.

Barbara Mikulski of the Southeast Community Organization in Baltimore summed up the complaint when she said the blue-collar worker "pays the bill for every major government program and gets nothing or little in the way of return." He is too well off to qualify for public housing, and inflation has put most homes beyond the reach of government-subsidized mortgage assistance for him. His wife is ineligible—because of his paycheck—to use the day care centers the government provides for the children of the working poor. Despite increases in college attendance, his child is less likely to have the grades and the money to attend the state university his taxes support than the child from a white-collar family. Pat Moynihan said in 1968, "We have established a Job Corps for the dropout and a Peace Corps for the college graduate, but the plain fellow with a high school diploma, and his parents, have little to show from either the New Frontier or the Great Society." Three years later, the same thing could be said of Nixon's New American Revolution.

Along with this economic frustration, the Middle American suffers from what Rosow called "the social squeeze." As Gus Tyler of the International Ladies Garment Workers' Union put it, "Once, being in the middle was an honorable estate, suggesting that he was on the climb out of the lower depths. Today, being in the middle is to be boxed in, caught in a squeeze between a top and a bottom that appear often to be in some unspoken conspiracy against Mr. In-Between."

In studies of blue-collar families, sociologists have found they suffer from a sense of "relative deprivation," not only in regard to the upper class but toward those beneath them in the social scale, particularly Negroes. A poll which the Gallup organization took in 1969 for *Newsweek's* study of the "Forgotten Americans" gave dramatic evidence on that point: It asked the working-class whites whether they thought Negroes had a better, a worse or the same chance as they did to obtain certain things, and got these results:

| | Negroes' Chance | | |
	Better	Worse	Same
Good housing at reasonable cost	39.4%	25.3%	26.8%
Good education for their children	46.2	11.8	38.9
Good-paying jobs	48.7	18.0	29.3
Financial help from government when they are out of work	68.5	2.6	20.1

"Don't Knows" eliminated; rows don't add to 100%.

The answers are striking in two respects. First, in every instance, the white working-class respondents *thought* it was an advantage to be black, even though by objective measurement the blacks were actually at a disadvantage compared to whites in the housing, education and job markets. Second, the biggest advantage the whites saw—by far—was the edge they credited the Negroes with having when it came to getting help from the government. Many of the Middle Americans blame the wealthy, educated elite for encouraging the blacks to encroach on their jobs, their schools and their neighborhoods.

George Wallace in 1968 tried to make himself the voice of the Middles' complaints against the Uppers. Wallace addressed himself to "the average man in the street, the man in the textile mill, the man in the steel mill, the barber, the beautician, the policeman on the beat." And he identified as his enemies, and theirs, "the top politicians, the heads of those big foundations, the bureaucrats, the pointy-headed professors, federal judges playing God, the press and the national news media who are going to get some of those liberal smiles knocked off their faces," and the whole army of do-good dilettantes "who don't know how to park their bicycles straight."

A year later, the same complaint was directed against John Lindsay and the "limousine liberals" of New York by Democrat Mario Procaccino in the mayoral campaign. "I charge that John Lindsay and his Manhattan Arrangement have been guilty of moral arrogance," Procaccino said.

They have commanded instead of persuaded. They have dismissed the feelings of the working people of this city, people who work two hours of every eight-hour day just to pay federal, state and city taxes, people who must then return to find themselves prisoners in their own homes. What do the select few know about the pressure of having to send your son to college on an income eaten up by inflation? What do they know about the heat and discomfort in our crowded subways and buses?

Like the students, the Middle Americans have been frustrated in finding political expression for their feelings. Procaccino and Wallace both lost, and so have most of the others who echoed their appeal. So the Middle Americans, like the students, have demonstrated, taken their grievances into the streets. In defense of their homes and their neighborhoods, they have battled with blacks who were seeking to escape from the ghetto. In defense of their country and their flag, they have fought with antiwar demonstrators. For all of this they have been condemned, much as the student demonstrators were. What none of the warring groups— the blacks, the students, the Middle Americans—seems able to understand is that they have a common complaint: American society is not living up to its ideals. Our political, governmental and public institutions are malfunctioning so badly that the results have become, for millions of Americans, quite literally intolerable.

The Scranton Commission described the disillusionment of the students, as they view their country:

Human life is all; but women and children are being killed in Vietnam by American forces. All living things are sacred; but American industry and technology are polluting the air and the streams and killing the birds and the fish. The individual should stand as an individual; but American society is organized into vast structures of unions, corporations, multiversities, and government bureaucracies. Personal regard for each human being and for the absolute equality of every human soul is a categorical imperative; but American society continues to be characterized by racial injustice and discrimination. The senses and the instincts are to be trusted first; but American technology and its consequences are a monument to rationalism. Life should be lived in communion with others, and each day's sunrise and sunset enjoyed to the fullest; American society extols competition, the accumulation of goods, and the work ethic. Each man should be free to lead his own life in his own way; American organizations and statute books are filled with regulations governing dress, sex, consumption, and the accreditation of study and of work, and many of these are enforced by armed police.

On the other side, Peter Brennan, head of the New York construction workers' union, explained why his men had taken to the streets against the students:

You people in the newspapers say we are bums and hoodlums. You beat our brains out. But our people are decent people. They work in the church and the synagogue and the Little League and the Boy Scouts. They would tear up their union cards before they would do anything to hurt this country. We build this country. We build these beautiful buildings and churches and highways and bridges and schools. We love this country. We were afraid it was going down the drain and nobody was doing anything about it. That's why we marched.

The Retreat from Society

Seeing their country "going down the drain," believing no one in authority is doing anything about it, doubting they have the capacity themselves to "turn America around," millions of Americans, young, middle-aged and old, have turned away from society and are seeking solutions, such as they are, for themselves. This is the tendency that poses perhaps the greatest challenge to our politics in the 1970s.

The retreat into self-concern was most dramatic, and least predictable, among the college students. For all that they enshrined the individual as the center of their value system, their culture was highly social in its expression. It gave us the "Woodstock Nation," thousands of "communes," and a succession of political causes operating under the generic name of "The Movement." Charles Reich, the Yale professor who romanticized the new culture in his 1970 book, *The Greening of America,* suggested that for true believers the whole world is a community. "People all belong to the same family, whether they have met each other or not," he wrote. "Hitchhikers smile at approaching cars, people smile at each other on the street, the human race rediscovers its need for each other."

No sooner were those words in print than the campus scene of which Reich wrote was profoundly altered. Instead of leaping forward into Reich's Consciousness III, the students seemed to be heading back to the 1950s and the individuality and anomie of what was called "the silent generation" on the campuses. No longer was there *a* song, or *a* movie or *a* political slogan which "everyone" on campus was singing, seeing or shouting. Instead, individuals pursued their own interests, and some even went back to their studies. Political action—particularly mass meetings, marches and movements—lost its appeal. Returning in November, 1970, after being away from Harvard only five months, I reported to my paper on the "startling return of squareness to Harvard Square," which had been torn apart by antiwar protestors during the Cambodia-invasion demonstrations the previous spring.

There are candles on the tables at Dunster House and talk of restoring the Junior Prom. Campus bulletin boards advertise more concerts and poetry readings than political meetings. The Harvard Dramatic Club is performing "The Three Musketeers," of all things, and the fence around the construction site near the law school, which last year bore the flaming red exhortation, "Off the Pigs!," now advertises "Funny Girl" at the Agassiz.

What had happened? Kenneth Keniston, the Yale psychiatrist who has made a specialty of the youth culture, speculated that "the genuine agony of the student movement" was a reaction to "a new awareness that violence lies not only within the rest of American society but within the student movement itself." I think he is right in saying there was a profound reaction against the bombings of campus buildings and even the increasing violence of the rhetoric of the antiwar movement. But there was also, among my student friends, a great feeling of chagrin at their own behavior. One young man remarked that he began to have doubts after Harvard was closed by a student strike against the Cambodia invasion in the spring of 1970. The shutdown of classes was supposed to free the students for intensive lobbying against the war. "Most of us," he said, "just stayed around here and tossed frisbees."

Having students toss frisbees may seem more attractive to many college administrators and many parents than having them out demonstrating in the streets; it is certainly preferable to tossing bombs. But if the sudden turn to individual pursuits, both frivolous and academic, represents, as some students think, a further retreat from involvement with society, then it is an expensive way to purchase calm on the campuses. The students have shown themselves mercurial, however, and no one can tell with certainty when—or in what form—they will be back.

More disturbing is the long-continuing retreat of adult Americans, a withdrawal process that also seems to have reached its peak at the beginning of this decade. When I came back to my political beat on the *Post* from the nine-month sabbatical at Harvard, I went to see Mrs. Elly Peterson, then the assistant chairman of the Republican National Committee, and one of the wisest political leaders I have ever known. I asked her to tell me what I could expect to find when I resumed my political travels. She said, "I have never seen people more involved with their personal concerns than this year. They are simply not thinking about anything but their family, their neighborhood and their own problems. If they have a son in Vietnam, or one who might go, they are worried about the war. If they or their neighbors have been out of work, they're worried about the economy. If there is a problem with drugs in their school, they're worried about that. If not, forget it. They don't want to hear about anyone else's problems, and they don't want to take any responsibility for them."

Her description was confirmed time and again in my own reporting and interviewing that fall. And the withdrawal she described is going to be harder to reverse, because it has such deep roots. It is both geographical and psychological.

The demographic phenomenon of the 1960s was the flight to the suburbs. Some 15.5 million whites were added to the suburban population, while the center cities from which they moved became increasingly black. The "common trait" of the suburbs, John Herbers of the *New York Times* said in 1971, is "a turning inward, a determination to shut out the decay and social upheavals of the central city, a lack of concern about the spreading agony and distress only a few miles away."

Herbers quoted an Atlanta legislator as remarking: "The suburbanite says to himself, 'The reason I worked for so many years was to get away from pollution, bad schools, and crime, and I'll be damned if I'll see it all follow me.' " But follow it does. Crime rates, drug arrests, pollution, traffic congestion all are rising more rapidly in the suburbs, though they still have not reached the absolute levels of the city. But the suburbanite is ready to flee again. Time and again in our 1970 travels, Haynes Johnson and I heard parents say, "We're ready to move anywhere to get our kids out of this, but where can we go?" The Gallup Poll in May, 1971, reported that 12 percent of those interviewed said they would like to move to some other country—twice as high as the proportion in 1959.

But the flight is as much psychological as geographical, for the Middle Americans, like the college students, have come to trust no one's judgment, motives or actions but their own.

As Haynes Johnson said in summing up the findings of his travels in the first six months of 1971, "Americans may still believe in themselves, but they have lost faith in most everything else. They do not believe in their President. They do not believe in their politicians. They do not believe in their press. They do not, indeed, seem to believe in any institution. This is a sweeping generalization, but in my experience it is the simple truth."

Samuel Lubell told the Republican Governors' Conference in December, 1970, that the great conflict in American politics is that between "militant individualism" and the fear of social breakdown. "Not since the 1930s," he said, "have fears of social breakdown been more widely spread in this country than today. Not since the same 1930s, has the surge of self-centered individualism been as strong."

What will the outcome be? What do people do when they can retreat no further, when they see their country "going down the drain," when they see the values that are important to their personal security eroding, when they no longer know how to cope with the forces that seem to be abroad in the land? What do they do when they no longer trust those who are governing them and no longer trust the democratic system to change government? I do not know, but I am struck by the fact that in their search for security Americans have created a boom market for two kinds of commodities: drugs and guns. Neither, of course, offers a solution. To think we can escape our problems by temporarily obliterating our consciousness, or that we can find security by arming ourselves against all strangers, is madness.

But, because the social, political and governmental institutions have provided no better solutions in the past two decades and have offered little but frustration to their hopes, Americans have retreated into such futile stratagems as these. The climate of opinion in America today is the most serious symptom of our political malaise. And it is also the most serious barrier to effective public action on our problems.

6

Needs

In the spring of 1971, with the American economy operating at the level of one trillion dollars a year—a measure of wealth almost literally beyond human comprehension—the mayors of seventeen of the nation's largest cities decided to join in what they called a "road show."

To Baltimore, San Francisco, Seattle, New York, Milwaukee and their other cities they went. At each stop, the routine was the traditional mixture for a political tour—a press conference, a lunch, a tour of the host city, sometimes a banquet. But this was no ordinary junket. For the stark, simple message the mayors were trying to drive home was that their cities were on the brink of bankruptcy and collapse. One by one, they would stand and give their testimony:

Kenneth Gibson of Newark: "I say wherever the American cities are going, Newark will get there first. Of our 400,000 people, 60 percent are black and 10 percent Puerto Rican. Newark has probably the worst quality of life of any major city. Unemployment is 11 percent. We have the highest TB rate, the highest infant mortality rate, the highest crime rate in the country. Our deficit this year is $70 million in a $200 million budget. If we had bubonic plague, the government would move in with everything it's got to save us. But our cities are afflicted with social and financial illness, and it looks like we're going to let them die."

Moon Landrieu, New Orleans: "It is appalling to believe this country would let a city like New Orleans go down the pipe, but if you're going to save it, you better save it now, because two or three years from now may be too late. We are a city of 600,000. In the last decade we lost 125,000 people—mostly white and affluent —moving out to the suburbs, and in their place, 90,000, mostly poor and black, moved in. We provide the transportation facilities, the parks, the zoo, the airport, the cultural facilities for a metropolitan area of 1.1 million. And we get nothing back from the suburbs. We don't even get the sales tax, because they have their own shopping centers. We don't have enough money even to put a coat of paint on our problems. We tax everything that moves, and everything that stands still, and if it moves, we tax it again."

Thomas J. D'Alesandro, Baltimore: "The population of Baltimore is 905,000. Of that number, 305,000 pay a state income tax. Of those, 187,000 pay on an income below $3,000 a year. That leaves 118,000 substantial taxpayers as my base. The more I hit them with increased real estate taxes, the more of them move out—and the more Baltimore becomes a repository for the poor."

Carl Stokes, Cleveland: "We've pushed our taxes as far as we can. With the recession, our income is down $25 million this year. We have already laid off 1,500 employees—health aides, city planners, people in public works, community relations. Sixty percent of the money I have left goes for police and fire protection."

Sam Massell, Jr., Atlanta: "I'm a newcomer to the group, but since I've been mayor we've had a 40 percent increase in our ad valorem tax; our police budget is up 60 percent; I've asked for increases in the sales tax, the income tax, the hotel tax, the liquor tax and the cigarette tax. We've had a police slowdown to force higher wages and we've been through a 37-day strike by the garbage men, and yet mine is one of the healthiest cities represented here today."

Harry G. Haskell, Wilmington, Delaware: "We had national guard troops in Wilmington for nine months to prevent a riot, the longest occupation of an American city since the Revolutionary War. I took them out the day I was sworn in. Our schools are 80 percent black, and they are not doing the job. We depend on the property tax, but property is no longer the basis of wealth in our city; income is. We won't go bankrupt; we'll just shrivel; that's what's happening now."

Peter F. Flaherty, Pittsburgh: "I've learned how lonely it is to be a mayor. I found that three-fourths of our zoo visitors were suburbanites. So I asked the county commissioners to pay half of the million-dollar budget. . . . They just looked out the window."

Roman S. Gribbs, Detroit: "Right now, in our current fiscal year, we face a $25 million deficit; we have raised every tax to the legal limit; the state can't help us because it has a $100 million deficit. I need $43 million more next year just to stand still, with the wage package we've negotiated with our employees. If we don't get more money, I've told the people we will have to cut every city service. I'll close 15 to 31 recreation centers, and 31 firehouses . . . and if you see those cutbacks, you'll see blowups of some kind."

Kevin H. White, Boston: "We as mayors are expendable, but our cities are not. My fear is that the public is getting bored with hearing about the 'crisis of the cities.' But we have to go on talking, because soon the time for speeches will be gone. Boston is a tinderbox. The fact is, it's an armed camp. We are faced with the possibility of a psychological collapse over racial enmities."

Wesley C. Uhlman, Seattle: "In some ways, we are better off than New York or the older cities of the East. Our racial and environmental problems are not as insoluble as theirs, but we still have the exodus of the affluent. We have 12.7 percent unemployment in Seattle—100,000 trained and educated people out of work, engineers and technicians in aerospace and other things. It's a whole new class of unemployed and no one knows how to deal with it. It's cut our revenues. We are talking about laying off a whole class of police cadets. We've cut our downtown street-cleaning from three times a week to once. We have cried wolf in the past, but the wolf is here."

By the time the mayors had finished their recital, no one who heard them had any doubt that the crisis of which they spoke was genuine. And that was the point of the whole exercise—to combat the notion that the problem was unique to San Francisco or St. Louis or Philadelphia.

So long as the problem was thought of as local, scapegoating would be easy. In the late 1960s, a whole generation of men who had been considered models of urban leadership gave up and quit trying to run their cities: New Haven's Dick Lee, Atlanta's Ivan Allen, Detroit's Jerome Cavanagh, Philadelphia's Dick Dilworth, Boston's John Collins, Minneapolis's Art Naftalin, and more. Their successors and their counterparts clung together in hopes that they too would not be picked off one by one.

Just as the mayors tried to dramatize the crisis in city government, other leaders have tried to make the same point about their realms of responsibility, using all the tools of modern public relations—conferences, task forces, white papers, foundation studies, press releases, television specials.

Doctors have announced a breakdown in health care delivery systems; judges (from the Chief Justice on down) have warned of the crisis of the overburdened courts; governors have sent forth urgent appeals for Federal help for the states; cardinals have warned that the parochial schools are closing at the rate of one a day; bus line owners have said they need higher subsidies to avoid still further fare hikes; college presidents have pleaded with alumni and with foundations to help them meet their deficits; police chiefs have asked for more men and modern equipment to cope with the upsurge of crime; medical researchers have told dramatic tales of progress against mankind's deadliest killers being delayed by cutbacks in their grants; penologists have warned that ancient, overcrowded facilities and lack of trained staffs have made the jails jungles of homosexuality, which turn out more criminals than they rehabilitate; railroad men have said their equipment and roadbeds will continue to deteriorate and their service to decline unless they receive higher subsidies from the government; hospital administrators have said the cost of care will continue to rise unless the government builds new facilities for outpatient care; and, now and then, a general or admiral tries to make his voice heard over the clamor of competing domestic claims to say that we are skimping dangerously on the national defense.

What few men in public life and few citizens want to acknowledge is that the fiscal crunch is not just the problem of a single city or of the cities as a group, not just the problem of the education system, the transportation system, the health system, the law enforcement system or the national defense system.

The dirty little secret of American politics in the 1970s is that every single essential service we depend on some public agency to provide is seriously underfinanced. In an era of general affluence, we are simply not paying enough in taxes to maintain the necessary basic community services.

Promises We Have Yet to Keep

Most people feel they are too highly taxed already. A Gallup Poll in October, 1969, found almost 78 percent of the people saying Federal taxes are too high and 59.3 percent declaring local levies exorbitant.

Obviously, taxes have increased. Between fiscal 1955, the year the narrative of this book begins, and fiscal 1971, total national, state and local tax collections rose from $87.9 billion to $273.9 billion. And yet, in those years, Federal spending has exceeded revenues by $96.5 billion and the debt of state and local government has increased by $101.9 billion. In that whole span of years, during two-thirds of which we have been at peace and during virtually all of which we have been prosperous, we have fallen $198.4 billion short of paying our governmental bills.

We have fallen ever farther short of meeting our promises to ourselves and to our country—a fact which may not be unrelated to the disillusionment discussed in the last chapter. Joseph A. Califano, Jr., who succeeded Bill Moyers as President Johnson's assistant for domestic affairs, noted in a 1970 speech how consistently we have failed to achieve the specific goals written into law by Congress and approved by our Presidents:

The Housing Act of 1949 declared that the "general welfare and security of the nation require the elimination of substandard and other inadequate housing through the clearance of slums and blighted areas, and the realization . . . of a decent home and suitable living environment for every American family. . . ." In the 1968 Housing and Urban Development Act, Congress recognized that for 20 years the promise had not been kept, noted the failure as "a matter of grave national concern," and rededicated itself to "the elimination of all substandard housing in a decade." Yet what has been done to fulfill that commitment to the 26 million Americans who still live in housing unfit for human habitation?

The 1966 Model Cities legislation affirmed that "improving the quality of urban life is the most critical domestic problem facing the United States. . . ." Its stated purpose was to provide "financial and technical assistance to enable cities of all sizes . . . to plan, develop and carry out locally-prepared . . . programs . . . to rebuild and revitalize large slums and blighted areas." Nevertheless, we continue to stand by while the physical plant of most of our cities further decays or moves toward obsolescence and the postwar suburbs of the '40s enter the first stages of severe deterioration.

The Economic Opportunity Act of 1964 declared it "the policy of the United States to eliminate the paradox of poverty in the midst of plenty in this nation by opening to everyone the opportunity for education and training, the opportunity to work and the opportunity to live in decency and dignity." Six years later, some 25 million Americans are still locked in poverty.

The Omnibus Crime Control and Safe Streets Act of 1968 recognized the urgency of the nation's crime problem, calling it a matter that threatens "the peace, security and general welfare of its citizens." The Act made it "the declared policy of the Congress to assist state and local governments in strengthening and improving law enforcement at every level by national assistance." But year after year, the crime rate continues its persistent rise, while the Safe Streets Act is funded at 50 percent of its programmed level.

Time and again, presidential commissions, made up of distinguished leaders of American life, have pointed out the same set of unfulfilled obligations.

In 1967, the President's Commission on Law Enforcement and the Administration of Justice, headed by Attorney General Nicholas deB. Katzenbach, called for "a greatly increased effort" on the part of Federal, state and local governments against the rising tide of crime. "The most urgent need of the agencies of criminal justice in the states and cities is money with which to finance the multitude of improvements they must make," the report said, and added: "If this report has not conveyed the message that sweeping and costly changes in criminal administration must be made throughout the country in order to effect a significant reduction in crime, then it has not expressed what the commission strongly believes."

A year later came the report of the National Advisory Commission on Civil Disorders, headed by Illinois Governor Otto Kerner. Starting from the stark assertion that "our nation is moving toward two societies, one black, one white—separate and unequal," it argued that this fateful division "can be reversed" only by "a commitment to national action on an unprecedented scale." The commission's comprehensive plan for improving education, employment, welfare, housing and law enforcement in the riot areas was set forth in several stages, but the additional costs of the first stage alone were estimated by the Johnson Administration to be at least $30 billion a year.

Late in 1968, the National Commission on Urban Problems, headed by former Senator Paul H. Douglas of Illinois, concluded its two-year study of the cities with these words: "If there is a sense of urgency and even alarm in our report and recommendations, it is because the commission saw the cities of our country first-hand and listened to the voices of the people. The commission members were certainly not less concerned or knowledgeable than the average citizen, but after our inspections, hearings and research studies, we found problems much worse, more widespread, and more explosive than any of us had thought." The commission gave no overall cost estimate for its recommendations; however, it said one of them alone, for revenue sharing with the states and cities, would add about $6 billion a year to the Federal budget.

Finally, in late 1969, the National Commission on the Causes and Prevention of Violence, headed by Dr. Milton S. Eisenhower, president emeritus of Johns Hopkins University, "solemnly declare[d] our conviction that this nation is entering a period in which our people need to be as concerned by the internal dangers to our free society as by any probable combination of external threats" and called for doubling the spending on law enforcement and criminal justice and a $20 billion increase in Federal financing of "general welfare" programs aimed at the social needs of the metropolitan areas.

Whatever their special focus, these four high-level commissions came to essentially the same conclusion: To save the nation from the scourge of crime and violence, of riot, disorder, of social decay, racial antagonism and human waste spreading from its great cities, a vast increase in public spending for essential services—law enforcement, housing, education, income maintenance and job training—will be needed. Otherwise, the outlook, they all said, will be grim. The alternative picture was presented most starkly in the Eisenhower Commission report, in this description of the "way these cities will likely look" if, instead of effective public action, individuals try to obtain a modicum of security by their own individual efforts:

Central business districts in the heart of the city . . . will be largely deserted except for police patrols during night-time hours. High-rise apartment buildings and residential compounds protected by private guards and security devices will be fortified cells for upper-middle and high-income populations living at prime locations in the city. Suburban neighborhoods, geographically far removed from the central city, will be protected mainly by economic homogeneity and by distance from population groups with the highest propensities to commit crimes.

Lacking a sharp change in federal and state policies, ownership of guns will be almost universal in the suburbs, homes will be fortified by an array of devices from window grills to electronic surveillance equipment, armed citizen volunteers in cars will supplement inadequate police patrols in neighborhoods closer to the central city, and extreme left-wing and right-wing groups will have tremendous armories of weapons which could be brought into play with or without any provocation.

High-speed, patrolled expressways will be sanitized corridors connecting safe areas, and private automobiles, taxicabs and commercial vehicles will be routinely equipped with unbreakable glass, light armor, and other security features. Inside garages or valet parking will be available at safe buildings in or near the central city. Armed guards will "ride shotgun" on all forms of public transportation.

Streets and residential neighborhoods in the central city will be unsafe in differing degrees, and the ghetto slum neighborhoods will be places of terror with widespread crime, perhaps completely out of police control during the night-time hours. Armed guards will protect all public facilities such as schools, libraries and playgrounds in these areas.

Between the unsafe, deteriorating central city on the one hand and the network of safe, prosperous areas and sanitized corridors on the other, there will be, not unnaturally, intensifying hatred and deepening division. Violence will increase further, and the defensive response of the affluent will become still more elaborate.

That is the nightmare future that awaits us if we continue to starve our public services.

Private Affluence, Public Penury

Despite the multitude of warnings we have been given, the necessary commitment of public funds has not been forthcoming. Over a year after his commission's report was issued, Dr. Eisenhower noted that of the estimated 10 million serious crimes that had occurred in the previous year, only 12 percent resulted in the arrest of anyone; only 6 percent led to a conviction, and only 1½ percent resulted in anyone going to jail. "And of those who were incarcerated," he added, "most will return to prison another time for additional offenses."

And yet, he said, "our entire criminal justice system in this country—federal, state and local—receives less than 2 percent of all government revenues and less than three-quarters of one percent of our national income."

The truth, said Lloyd Cutler, the lawyer who served as the commission's executive director, is that "our criminal justice system as presently operated does not deter, does not detect, does not convict and does not correct." By way of illustration of his generalization, *Life* magazine reported in 1970 that for a person committing a felony in New York City, the odds of being arrested, indicted, found guilty on the original charge and then going to prison are considerably less than one in two hundred.

Inadequate police forces, jammed court dockets, overworked prosecutors are all part of the problem, but the clearest example of the costliness of our starvation of the criminal justice system lies in the area of corrections. The annual cost of crime in America has been estimated to be somewhere between $50 billion and $100 billion. Almost 80 percent of the felonies are committed by repeaters—persons who have been through the corrections system at least once. But our prisons are so inadequate for the task of rehabilitation that Norman Carlson, director of the Federal Bureau of Prisons, has said, "Anyone not a criminal will be one when he gets out of jail."

Senator Edward J. Gurney of Florida, in pleading for greater Federal help, said four jails still in use in 1971 had been built before George Washington's inaugural and 25 percent of all the local jails around the country are more than fifty years old.

A survey by the Census Bureau of city and county jails in 1970 found over half—52 percent—of their inmates had not been convicted of any crime, but were simply awaiting trial. Not surprisingly, considering the conditions of the jails and the grievances many of these men feel, riots and violence are commonplace. In September, 1971, the nation was shocked when thirty-seven men—twenty-eight prisoners and nine guards—were killed at Attica state prison in New York by state policemen ordered in to quell a demonstration against the jail conditions. But there had been ample warning. More than a year earlier, Chief Justice Warren

Burger had said, "The American people would not tolerate the conditions that exist in most prisons if they could see them and see the frustration, the waste and the absence of facilities and programs to change men who are there."

But they were tolerated, even though many of those in jail had not even been convicted of crimes. In March, 1971, the *New York Times* reported that about 80 percent of the inmates in Philadelphia's four jails, where rioting had occurred the previous year, were awaiting trial. The average wait was four months, during which time, prison superintendent Edward J. Hendrick noted, the inmates could not be forced to work or take vocational training. "I'm candid to admit," he said, "we're running a human warehouse."

Reporter Walter Rugaber then described the routine:

Each day about 150 people are awakened at 6 A.M. to get ready for the one-hour bus ride to City Hall. There they are packed into four extremely small cages on the seventh floor to await a summons to court.

The largest of these cells was estimated by a guard to measure 6 feet by 14 feet. Inside there are hard narrow benches and balky toilets. There is no drinking water. Roaches scurry over the debris.

The ventilation is so limited that on a single hot day late last summer seven men, including two of the guards, fainted. After a day of this, defendants often return to jail without even glimpsing a courtroom.

Mr. Hendrick's records show that Ophus Lampkin has been hauled to court 24 times since March, 1970. John L. Sanders has made the trip 19 times since August, 1970. Robert Briscoe has gone to City Hall 44 times since August, 1969.

If the immediate needs of the criminal justice system are not being met, neither are the underlying problems of the cities where most of the criminals are bred. The U.S. Conference of Mayors said in March of 1971 that, even if Nixon's revenue-sharing plan was passed, the states and cities would be at least $5.7 billion short of their basic needs. Later, of course, the promised $6 billion of revenue sharing was scuttled in favor of the economic stimulus of tax cuts.

Meantime, the cities were making desperate economies. The

lead stories in the *New York Times* of April 20, 1971, were head-lined: "Mayor Threatens to Cut 90,000 Jobs Unless State Aids," and "State Is Dismissing 8,250 with Wide Cuts in Services. 4,000 Vacant Jobs Also Abolished—Psychiatric, Narcotics, College and Conservation Programs Curbed."

Cities large and small felt the same squeeze. Atlanta rejected a gift of $27,000 worth of trees to beautify its central shopping area, because it could not afford the men to water them. Little Portland, Maine, cut off its $3,000 annual contribution to the city symphony and a $2,000 grant for a children's theater.

Claremont, California, eliminated its street maintenance pro-gram. Los Angeles canceled plans for a new central library. Philadelphia shuttered nine more recreational facilities, bringing the total of such centers closed for lack of staff to thirty-two. It cut the food and clothing allowance for dependent children and re-duced the daily food budget for city prisoners to eighty-nine cents. Cleveland shut its police academy and eliminated its police cadet program. Detroit eliminated its weights-and-measures-inspection force and all its industrial and social hygiene programs.

What was true of the cities was also true of the major institu-tions and services within them. In May, 1971, the President's Commission on School Finance applied the all-too-familiar word "crisis" to the condition of the public and parochial schools.

Rising teacher salaries and the same general inflation that played havoc with municipal budgets also plagued school boards. At the same time, voter resistance to higher property taxes rose significantly. The Investment Bankers Association reported that in 1970 only 48 percent of the school bond issues were approved by voters, compared to a 77 percent approval rate in 1965 and an 89 percent rate in 1960. Los Angeles, forced to cut its school spending $20 million at the start of 1971, reduced the high school day from six to five periods and laid off about fifteen hundred employees. Detroit cut its teaching staff by two hundred and stopped painting school buildings, and there were similar stories in dozens of other cities. Even Montgomery County, Maryland, one of the wealthiest suburbs in the country, was forced to adopt a policy of hiring only inexperienced teachers in order to stay within its budget. The *New York Times* quoted Dr. Orlando Furno, a Baltimore school official who makes an annual survey on school expenditures in the major cities, as saying it is inevitable that "Americans are simply going to have to accept lower quality education."

The college picture is no brighter. The Carnegie Commission on Higher Education reported in 1971 that after a decade "characterized by the most rapid growth and development in . . . American history," a "depression [is] now settling on American colleges and universities." A sample survey indicated that 61 percent of the institutions, accounting for 76 percent of the total enrollment, were either in financial difficulty or clearly headed for financial trouble. A quarter of the nation's private colleges were dipping into endowment principal to meet their current expenses. In 1971, Harvard, Yale, Princeton and the University of Chicago, among others, were operating at a deficit. Cutbacks in curriculum, delays in building plans, and salary freezes are the order of the day. Clark Kerr, chairman of the Carnegie Commission, calls it—yes, that's right—"the greatest financial crisis colleges have ever faced."

There is a similar crisis, so everyone from President Nixon on down has agreed, in the health field, stemming from a shortage of personnel, skyrocketing costs and a "delivery system" that denies all but the most affluent the kind of early, comprehensive, preventive care that represents the best investment in the future health of the individual and the nation.

Nationwide, the supply of doctors is estimated to be at least 50,000 short of needs, with comparable scarcities in other health professions. But the overall shortage is compounded by the tendency of medical personnel to concentrate in the suburbs and the affluent big-city neighborhoods, leaving both small towns and lower-income city populations in dire straits. In 1970, there were 132 counties in the United States, ranging up to 18,000 population, with no resident doctors. New York had almost three times as many doctors per 1,000 residents as did Mississippi. Jack Star reported in *Look* magazine that in the Chicago area the doctor-patient ratio was four times as high in the upper-income suburbs as in the central city. He also reported that the Sears Roebuck Foundation had given up trying to lure doctors to small towns after 52 of the 162 clinics it helped build for them were left vacant or were converted to other uses. Conditions of patient care in Chicago's Cook County Hospital, once regarded as one of the great training grounds of American medicine, have deteriorated to the point where its residents and interns have threatened several times in recent years to resign and force its closing. Star described it as a place where emergency-room patients wait two hours for a preliminary examination, another two or three for an x-ray; where patients stumble to the nurses' station to seek help, because emergency call buttons have been removed from their beds, there being far too few nurses to answer them; where fly swatters are part of the equipment in un-airconditioned operating rooms, because windows must be kept open to keep the temperature even mildly tolerable for the sweating surgeons and patients, but the screens have gaping holes.

The American transportation system is in no better condition. As John Burby described it in his 1971 book *The Great American Motion Sickness,* it is an "indifferent, inefficient, dirty, smelly, noisy and often destructive and deadly beast of national burden that goes where the spirit of speculation moves it or where it is driven by vested interest." Traffic in downtown New York, he noted, "which in 1906 crept along behind horses at an average speed of 11.5 miles an hour, was by 1966 creeping along at 8.5 miles an hour behind the most powerful engines Detroit could mass-produce." Public transportation systems in many of the large cities are in a state of disrepair and decline, and in some they are virtually nonexistent. In the Watts section of Los Angeles, site of one of the major riots of the 1960s, Burby said "public transportation was so thin that the only way to reach the County

Hospital was by taxi. The round-trip fare by cab was $10. And when a man in Watts complained that he didn't feel well, the bitter question was whether he felt 'ten-dollars bad.'"

He quotes former Secretary of Transportation Alan Boyd's observation: "It's a sad commentary that if you say you have seen a city where the skies were black with smoke, with ambulances rushing to help the wounded and planes circling overhead, where men in helmets were digging trenches in the streets, and where people were pushing and shoving in a desperate attempt to escape, I'd have to ask whether it was a city at war or at evening rush hour."

Facing Up to the Costs

In recent years America has not met the costs even of those services which anyone would regard as the basic necessities of community life: police and fire protection, a system of courts and law enforcement; schools; doctors and hospitals; a transportation system.

Gaps exist in many other areas, which can hardly be thought less consequential for a stable, civilized society: decent housing; an adequate income for families in poverty; clean air to breathe; clean water to drink; proper care for the aged and indigent; at least a modicum of support for the artists and intellectuals, the scientists and scholars.

What would it cost? No one really knows. In 1967, after months of hearings, Senator Abraham A. Ribicoff of Connecticut appalled people by suggesting that a trillion dollars of public and private investment would be needed over a decade to make the American city habitable again. The National Urban Coalition, in its 1971 "Counterbudget," a detailed five-year plan designed to meet the needs of which we have been speaking, projected total Federal outlays rising to $353 billion by 1976—a 66 percent increase in constant dollar terms in five years.

Realization of the magnitudes involved has made almost all

serious political leaders in both parties talk of the necessity for a "reordering of priorities." Most often, this has come to mean a shift away from defense and overseas spending and an increase in domestic welfare categories. The Counterbudget, for example, spelled out plans for a $20 billion reduction in the defense budget over the next five years.

The practicality and the risk of such a strategy is hotly debated. There is little agreement on what a frugal but prudent defense budget would be. One should observe, however, that the "reordering of priorities" has begun; the defense share of the fiscal 1972 budget, 32.1 percent, is the lowest in twenty-two years, and the Nixon Administration projects it to decline further in years to come.

Meantime, our development assistance to the nations of the Southern Hemisphere, which has been allowed to dwindle in the last decade, almost certainly will need to increase. The economic stability of those lands is probably as important to future world peace as the quality of our national defense; and America, like most of the other developed nations, has not been meeting its obligations to assist them.

It was popular a few years ago to suggest that these accumulated needs could be met from the "peace dividend" that would follow the Vietnam war or from the "fiscal dividend" resulting from the automatic increases in government revenues generated by a growing economy. Neither of these hopes seems likely to materialize. The "peace dividend" has been lost in higher military salaries and the rising cost of weapons and matériel. The "fiscal dividend" has also vanished like a mirage, at least for the near future. Inflation, unexpectedly high welfare and medicaid costs and the built-in increases in existing programs have pushed its arrival off to some time in the hazy beyond. The President's 1971 Economic Report, the independent budgetary analysis of the Brookings Institution and other studies see no unallocated funds available between now and 1974; even in 1975 or 1976, they are problematical.

So the choice we face is not simply one of how we divide up the government budget, but how much more we are willing to take from our private consumption, by way of taxes, to meet these national and community needs. And this is an issue few national political leaders are willing to raise, knowing the climate of public opinion to be what it is.

Instead, the leaders of the two parties have been vying in their race to cut Federal taxes. In 1969, President Nixon called for the phase-out of the 10 percent surtax President Johnson had belatedly asked Congress to impose in 1967. The Democratic Congress immediately went Nixon several billion dollars better in misguided generosity, voting an $8 billion tax cut at a time of roaring inflation. That action was taken in the same month that the Eisenhower Commission drew its stark portrait of what America faces if it seeks private solutions to the community problem of crime and violence. It represented an abdication of political responsibility. Charles L. Schultze, the tough-minded scholar and former budget director, was right in upbraiding his fellow Democrats, who, he said, "talked about priorities for pollution control and education and an end to hunger but voted for beer and cosmetics and whitewall tires."

As a result of that tax cut, personal income increased $52 billion in 1970 but Federal government receipts went up only $400 million. The 1969 tax cut was as clear a case of a deliberate decision to subsidize individual spending (and to feed inflation) at the cost of public services as our history affords.

Unfortunately, that has been the pattern. Walter Heller has calculated that the cumulative effect of the Federal income tax cuts of the 1960s was to reduce Federal revenues by $23 billion in 1970. And in 1971 Nixon's solution to the strains on the American economy was to cut corporate and individual taxes again by $8 or $9 billion a year, while deferring such important public spending as revenue sharing with the states and cities and overhaul of the welfare system. And, once again, Congress outdid the President in misguided "generosity" to the taxpayers.

Somehow this trend must be reversed, unless, as Andrew Brimmer, a member of the board of governors of the Federal Reserve System, has said, we are willing to accept a further "serious deterioration in the scope and quality of our public services." One of the crucial tasks of leadership in the 1970s, I believe, is to secure public agreement to finance those public services at an adequate level. This almost certainly means raising Federal taxes. It also means increasing use of state income taxes; as Walter Heller has noted, if all fifty states used the income tax as effectively as the ten largest do, revenues from that source alone would double.

To make increases in these taxes palatable, indeed, to make them politically possible, the political parties would have to link them to a program of tax reform that convinced the average voter that those who have been avoiding taxes would now be made to pay their proper share. Tax resistance is high today, because people know the tax system is inequitable, and has been growing more so, as the burden of financing government has shifted increasingly from the progressive Federal income tax to regressive payroll, sales and property taxes.

A variety of methods are available to make the tax system both more productive and more equitable. But, before the tactical question can be reached, political leaders and the political parties must first decide if they have the courage to put the basic question—the question of values—to the people. Taxes are, as Justice Holmes first said and as Walter Heller has kept reminding us, "the price of civilization." The question that needs to be put to the American voter is, How high a price are you willing to pay to make neighborhoods safe and livable, to end poverty, to meet our medical and educational needs, to halt the deterioration of our environment, to meet our world responsibilities? These are not goals we can obtain for ourselves, by individual effort, earnings or savings. If we are to meet these needs, we will have to do so as a nation, as a community. And it will cost us money.

7

Reforms

The source of greatest resistance to higher taxes, and the easiest justification for opposing them, is, of course, the argument that government is wasteful and inefficient. Former Senator Kenneth B. Keating of New York liked to ridicule the "Washington reflex," which, he said, is "to discover a problem and then throw money at it, hoping it will somehow go away."

In the same vein, President Nixon spoke in 1971 of the "fed up with government" syndrome, based on the feeling that "government as usual too often means government which has failed to keep pace with the times."

To those who maintain that money alone will not solve our problems, who are aware, as the President said, that "government talks more and taxes more, but too often fails to deliver," the only honest answer is to acknowledge they are right. In almost any area you care to mention, the existing structure of government is wasteful and inefficient, and ought to be reformed, overhauled or reorganized, along with, if not before, being more adequately financed.

Nowhere is the problem of governmental reform more evident than in the locus of the most severe financial crisis—the cities and metropolitan areas. The examples of waste in local government are legion. The very cities whose mayors have been asking most loudly for help are the sites of unconscionable boondoggling. The *Wall Street Journal* in the spring of 1971 ran a roundup of such practices: In Philadelphia's City Hall, fifty-five elevator operators were making $350,000 a year to run automatic, push-button elevators. Cleveland was spending $50,000 a year, mostly in wages, to collect $16,000 in launching fees at city boat ramps. In New York, an antiquated work rule, dating from the years before air conditioning, let city employees leave work an hour early each afternoon during the summer months at a cost of about $2 million a year. In city after city, phony overtime charges, payroll padding, kickbacks and fee hikes, restrictive work practices and a dozen other dodges boost the costs and deplete the quality of municipal services.

Citizen complaints, exposure by the press and watchdog groups, and an occasional shakeup in control of city hall can have some effect on this kind of waste. More serious is the kind of inefficiency and malfunctioning that results from the structure of government itself.

The Local Government Jungle

The Committee of Economic Development, a businessmen's organization studying public policy questions, noted in its 1966 report, "Modernizing Local Government," that "overemphasis on waste, inefficiency and incompetence may obscure the main point: most American communities lack any instrumentality of government with legal powers, geographic jurisdiction and independent revenue sources necessary to conduct local self-government in any valid sense."

If that seems an overstatement, it is because we have become accustomed to the crazy-quilt pattern of local government with which we all live. The 1967 Census of Governments counted 81,248 units of local government, of which 20,745 were crammed into the 228 major metropolitan areas, where two-thirds of our people live.

The average citizen paid taxes and drew services from four

separate local jurisdictions, but the number could be much greater than that. Park Forest, a Chicago suburban development less than twenty-five years old, had thirteen governmental units taxing its residents for various services. The CED report cited the horrible example of Fridley, Minnesota (population 15,173), whose citizens, it said unbelievingly, "are expected to exercise an informed control, through an electoral franchise, over 11 separate superimposed governments and are taxed for their support."

What are these fragmented governments like? They are tiny. In 1967, two-thirds of the metropolitan area municipalities had populations of less than 5,000; one-third were smaller than 1,000. Half the municipalities were less than a single square mile in size; four-fifths had land areas under four square miles. About one-third of the school districts in the metropolitan areas operated only a single school. And yet the appalling fact is that the local governments in the 228 metropolitan areas had over 134,000 *elected* officials in 1967. Few of them, of course, were professional, full-time administrators known to their constituents or responsible to the electorates they served. Indeed, the whole notion of democracy in such a fragmented scheme is mocked by the fact that fewer than 30 percent of the potential voters cast ballots in separately-scheduled local government elections.

Not only are such governments costly, inefficient and undemocratic, their jurisdictional disputes directly interfere with efficient delivery of the services they are expected to perform: When a fire breaks out, the closest firehouse is often in another town, and will not respond; a motorist whose car is stolen may have to call half-a-dozen units to find the one which will accept jurisdiction of the case. A suburb that enforces strict water-pollution standards on its residents may find its river poisoned by sewage dumped from an upstream town whose policies are beyond its control.

These tiny, overlapping governmental units serve only to confuse and frustrate everyone, including the motorist simply seeking a destination. As Representative Henry S. Reuss of Wisconsin noted in a recent book, "If you drive the eight miles from Philadelphia . . . to suburban Media, you cross into and out of and back into Yeadon, Upper Darby (three times), East Lansdowne, Lansdowne, Clifton Heights, Springfield (twice), Morton, Swarthmore and Nether Providence."

How did we come to be so far from Nether Providence in our local governmental structure? Up through the time of World War II, American cities enjoyed a population and fiscal balance comparable to that of the country as a whole. If they did not contain all the population of their metropolitan areas, they at least contained a large and representative slice of it. They approximated Aristotle's ideal of "the most perfect political community," in which "those of the middle rank," as he called them, are of sufficient number to control social and political conflict between "the very rich and the very poor." But after World War II two great tides of migration occurred that led to today's seriously unbalanced situation.

One was the movement of Negroes from the Southern farms to the Northern cities, spurred by the mechanization of agriculture and the promise of better pay in industrial jobs. It was a massive shift. Between 1950 and 1970, the proportion of the nation's Negroes living in the South fell from 68 percent to 53 percent, while the proportion living in the thirty cities with the largest black population rose from 30 percent to 41 percent.

At the same time, there was a heavy movement of whites from the central cities to the suburbs, which became the fastest-growing areas of the nation. Between 1950 and 1970, the suburbs' share of the national population rose from 27 percent to almost 40 percent—virtually all of it (95 percent) white. Blacks who sought to follow the pattern of earlier immigrant groups found their path from the big-city ghetto to suburban neighborhoods blocked by both economic and racial barriers. City governments, too, ran into barriers in expanding their borders to include the burgeoning suburbs. Rural-dominated legislatures, fearful of city power in state government, made annexation difficult, incorporation of independent municipalities easy.

When one-man-one-vote reapportionment finally came to the legislatures, it was too late to help the cities, for by the mid-1960s, the population pendulum had swung to the suburbs. Suburban communities used zoning laws to their own benefit by including tax havens and excluding high-cost residents.

The result has been a fragmentation of metropolitan areas, not on a random basis, but in a way that creates severe disparities between the neighboring jurisdictions, and particularly between the old central city and its newer suburbs. The Douglas Commission on Urban Problems reported that a range of 10 to 1 in relative fiscal capacity often appears between units of government in a single metropolitan area; the gap between the richest and poorest of Cook County's 120 elementary school districts was 30 to 1. Concern over these disparities has reached such a point that the California Supreme Court ruled in a precedent-making 1971 decision that the inequalities of school financing in that state deprived pupils in the poor jurisdictions of their rights.

Increasingly, the central cities have seen their more affluent residents, the businesses and industries that employ them and the stores they patronize moving to the suburbs, while the city has become the unhappy home of the elderly, the poor and the minorities. Declining tax bases and rising social costs are at the root of the urban fiscal crisis, but they are, in large part, a product of the structural fragmentation of the metropolitan area. As the Advisory Commission on Intergovernmental Relations (ACIR) has pointed out,

> The metropolitan areas of the United States account for 80 percent of the nation's bank accounts, three-quarters of Federal personal income tax collections, and 77 percent of the value added by manufacture. Yet it is in these same metropolitan areas that civil government faces its fiercest challenge with rising crime and delinquency; city schools that are becoming jungles of terror; neighborhoods that are blighted; poverty and disease that are rampant; and, gravest of all, with millions of citizens feeling completely alienated from government and the whole concept of liberty with order.

In brief, most of America's wealth and most of America's domestic problems reside in the metropolitan areas. Why, then, cannot this vast wealth be applied through vigorous, social measures to meet the growing problems? Because the resources exist in one set of jurisdictions within the metropolitan areas and the problems in another.

Contrary to popular myths, the tax burden is not heavier in the suburbs than in the cities. ACIR in its survey of the metropolitan areas found local taxes in central cities averaged 7.5 percent of income; the suburbanites paid only 5.6 percent of their income. Yet basic services are worse in the city, and the gap between city and suburb is growing. In 1957, per pupil expenditures in central city schools averaged $312, compared to $303 for their suburban neighbors. In 1965, those same suburbs were spending $574 per child; the central cities, only $449.

Even more ominous in its implications for the future of American society is the racial polarization that has occurred in the metropolitan areas. "This country is on its way to total apartheid," Senator Ribicoff warned in 1971. The Census data show that is, tragically, no exaggeration.

During the 1960s, the central cities of the 67 largest metropolitan areas lost 2.5 million whites and gained 3 million blacks. At the same time, their suburbs gained 12.5 million whites and only 800,000 blacks. In both the North and South, the central cities are on their way to becoming predominantly black reservations, while the suburbs maintain or even increase their status as segregated havens for whites.

What can be done to end this fragmentation of the metropolitan areas and of American society? There is no single, comprehensive answer, but most authorities agree that a first step would be the elimination of those governments that are too small to do anything but impede solutions to metropolitan problems. The businessmen who made the CED study said that "if local governments are to function effectively in metropolitan areas, they must have sufficient size and authority to plan, administer and provide significant financial support for solutions to areawide problems." They recommended surgery that would cut the number of local government units by at least 80 percent.

The Douglas Commission, while not as specific, noted that if we could replace the present hodge-podge with a set of comprehensive units, each responsible for all public services for a population of at least fifty thousand people, we could cut the number of governmental units in the typical metropolitan area from ninety-one down to six.

Most students of government oppose any solution that is mechanistic. Instead, they recommend *consolidation* of some government functions on a metropolitan area basis, *coordination* of many more, and *decentralization* of still others. The problem is that reform of any kind encounters almost insuperable resistance. The affluent, low-tax suburb is not interested in sharing the problems of its impoverished, high-tax neighboring city. The hordes of local officials are not dedicated to reforms that will put them out of work. The average citizen too often is complacent or indifferent.

True, there have been occasional, isolated gains. The ACIR in its latest report noted that the first year of the decade saw county home-rule statutes strengthened in Colorado, Maryland and Missouri, an effective Metropolitan Council created for the Twin Cities area of St. Paul and Minneapolis, Minnesota, and weaker advisory or planning bodies established in twenty-five other areas. But overall, it said, "efforts to civilize the local government jungle met with limited success" and "the chaotic local government pattern in the nation's metropolitan areas continued to be largely ignored." Surveying the record of the 1960s, the Douglas Commission came to the same doleful conclusion. Except for school districts (which were cut significantly in number) there was little thinning of the governmental overgrowth. Between 1962 and 1967, the number of special-purpose districts in the metropolitan areas increased by 899, while only 3 counties and 27 townships were merged. From 1947 through 1970, only 10 city-county consolidations occurred in the whole country.

Revenue Sharing and the Governmental Jungle

In recent years, an effort has been made to have the national government exert its influence for reform in local government. The argument is that Uncle Sam, who has become a major supplier of funds to state and local governments, should use the power of his purse to nudge them into making the changes they are disinclined to make themselves.

Federal aid to states and cities has grown enormously in the last four administrations, increasing from $3.3 billion in fiscal 1956 to an estimated $30.3 billion in fiscal 1971. Virtually all of that money is channeled through 530 so-called "categorical" grants—each a specific fund for a designated, specific purpose, ranging from intrastate meat and poultry inspection to summer youth sports programs.

Each of these grant-in-aid programs represents a decision—by Congress and the President—that this objective is a matter of national priority. Individually and collectively, they have certainly influenced the pattern of state and local government growth, because they have come to represent about 20 percent of the total receipts of those levels of government.

But their influence is not working in the direction those worried about the organization of state and local government desire. In many cases, the categorical grants, with their matching formulas for state and local contributions, mandate not only the growth of state and local *budgets,* but of state and local *bureaucracies* as well. When Federal aid to education began on a large scale in the mid-1960s, the Federal Office of Education mushroomed, and so did state and local education departments; similarly with highways, health, housing and the myriad other areas the Federal government has singled out for assistance.

The result has been the proliferation of state and local bureaucrats, many of them hired specifically to move papers back and

forth to their counterparts in Washington. All of them are carried
on the state and local payroll, but many of their activities and
programs are outside the control of the elected officials to whom
they are nominally responsible. A management survey of the Ohio
government found the six departments that use the largest
amounts of Federal money submitted 98,077 reports to Washington in a single year, providing full-time work for 259 employees at
a cost of $2.6 million. The town of Cambridge, Massachusetts,
found it filed 134 separate Federal aid applications a year. A study
of Federal aid programs in Oakland, California, showed its mayor
exerted "significant influence" on barely 15 percent of the Federal
money coming into his city.

There is a real danger that these "vertical functional autoc-
racies," as ACIR called the chains of education or highway or
urban renewal bureaucrats at Federal, state and local levels, will
undercut the authority of responsible elected officials. It is in part
in response to that fear that President Nixon has made revenue
sharing the keystone of his governmental reform scheme. The proposal, in essence, is that the national government channel significant amounts of new aid to the states and cities through broad
grants of funds to their elected officials, for use as they determine.
The President in 1971 proposed that an initial $5 billion a year in
new funds be distributed among the states and cities, with no
strings on its use. He also suggested that another $11 billion of
Federal aid, $10 billion of it previously distributed through 130
categorical aid programs and $1 billion of fresh money, be given to
those same governments for use in designated broad categories—
education, law enforcement, transportation, community development and the like.

The proposal has several principal objectives. The first and most
obvious is to provide a degree of relief from the fiscal miseries
many cities and states face. The second is to reduce bureaucracy
at all three levels of government and to cut down on the costly,
time-consuming processing of applications by specialists in Washington and their counterparts in the field, under the separate,

detailed regulations for each categorical aid program. A third objective is to increase the share of their budgets which elected officials—governors and mayors, legislators and councilmen—have authority to allocate, and thus to improve their ability to meet their responsibility to their own constituents. A fourth objective is to give the individual citizen a feeling of greater participation in decision making, by focusing that governmental responsibility on elective officials, close at hand, to whom he can direct his requests and his complaints, and whom, unlike the bureaucratic specialists in the categorical aid programs, he can turn out of office if he is dissatisfied.

The revenue-sharing proposal ran into severe opposition in 1971. Some of it came from men who are philosophically persuaded that the national government has the wisdom and courage to set spending priorities more effectively and more equitably (particularly with a view to the needs of the poor and the minorities) than do the state and local governments. More of the opposition came from those with a stake in the existing arrangement of Federal aid: the Congressmen who control the authorizations and funding for particular programs, and can direct their benefits to their favored clientele; the bureaucrats who manage those old-line programs; and the recipients, who do not wish to see their favorite programs disappear.

But there is another group of critics, more interesting for this discussion, who have faulted the Nixon proposal on the grounds that it tends to subsidize, rather than reform, the archaic pattern of local government we have described.

Max Frankel, the Washington Bureau chief of the *New York Times*, in a brilliant article in the *Times Magazine*, called "Revenue Sharing Is a Counter-Revolution," ridiculed Mr. Nixon's argument that his plan would invigorate local government.

Whoever presumes to talk of invigorating these local governments and their state counterparts is talking about many governors condemned to serve only one brief term, often alongside independently chosen, unresponsive, perhaps even disloyal, cabinet officials. He is talking about state legislatures, a number of which still meet only in alternate years, and most of which are ill-paid, ill-staffed and ill-housed. He is talking about multiple systems of state justice in which judges are often subject to partisan election without regard for their professional qualification. He is talking about mayors, managers, executives, councils, school boards, directors, commissioners, assessors and the Lord knows who else with wholly uncoordinated mandates, all scrambling for taxes and loans and subsidies, and carving out their own areas of sovereignty and authority.

Custom, confusion, regulation and debt seem to have petrified this overgrown forest. The states themselves have been passive about reorganization. The public has been apathetic, turning out no more than 25 percent of the electorate for the few occasions when local reform has come to a vote. President Nixon grandly asserts his "trust" in the people and local office holders to reorder their affairs once they are given a little more money. Revenue-sharing is being pushed on them with all the promise of a quick fix.

It is much more likely that the hasty injection of miscellaneous moneys into this structure will only reinforce its worst habits. And the very worst are the tendency to keep enlarging the tax burden of those least able to pay while sparing those who could afford to pay more and the toleration of scattered administrations that mostly wall off the people with the most money from the people with the greatest problems.

Frankel's article was answered the following month by Elliot L. Richardson, the Secretary of Health, Education and Welfare, in a speech at the National Press Club, notable for its un-Bostonian bite.

It is argued that the Administration has been remiss in not proposing to use the leverage of revenue sharing to reform state and local governments—their administration, their tax structure, their districting. Our efforts to achieve self-determination and to decentralize governmental powers are supposedly doomed to failure because public discussion and participation decline as one moves from the national to the local level. And it is reputed that the Administration has failed to take a broad view of national interests and to protect national purposes.

Would that one critic had but asked why such reforms were not embodied in the revenue-sharing proposals, and had probed a bit further to see whether in fact the national interest was being protected. . . .

We are well aware of the faults of state and local governments. We are well aware of inequities in taxing and in special districting. We are well aware of occasional corruption and of deficiencies in public services.

But we have refrained, consciously and deliberately, from imposing single-minded reforms upon the states and localities. We do not confuse equality with either uniformity across the Nation or conformity to a single standard.

We are firmly convinced that if debate and participation gather only on national issues, then that is wrong, and should be reversed.

And if all local issues elevate to the national level because that is the only place they can receive attention, then that is wrong, and should be reversed.

And if it is believed that this nation will somehow be better off if every community and every state resembles each other in more than 3,600,000 square miles of homogeneous nationalism, then that is wrong, simply wrong.

There is no amount of cavil that will persuade me that Americans at the state, county and municipal level are incapable of governing themselves, or incapable of administering substantial amounts of their money to treat social ills.

It was a good argument, by Washington standards, between two of the brightest men in town, but in fact the revenue-sharing plan did not take quite such a posture of "benign neglect" toward the jungle of local government as Frankel claimed it did and Richardson argued that it should. While reform of local government was not its principal or even secondary aim, Nixon's plan did have built into its design certain features aimed at both the fiscal and organizational mess in the metropolitan areas.

To the extent that it substituted revenues from the progressive Federal income tax for revenues from regressive property and sales taxes as the source of finance for local services, it would tend to shift the burden from lower- to higher-income taxpayers and from lower- to higher-income governmental subdivisions.

Second, because it would subsidize only general-purpose governments (cities, counties and states), it contained a rather strong incentive to have those general-purpose governments take over functions now performed by the proliferating and overlapping single-purpose agencies.

Third, because its intrastate distribution formula was based on population and local tax collections, the central city areas—which, in most cases, are making a greater tax effort than their suburbs— would receive proportionally greater benefits from revenue sharing.

But, if revenue sharing was not quite so "counterrevolutionary" as Frankel claimed, the point that can be made—and has been made—is that it could be altered so as to yield, if not a revolution in local government, at least a good deal greater reform.

Distribution formulas could be altered to increase the flow of benefits to the central city and away from the affluent suburbs, as Senator Edmund S. Muskie of Maine has suggested. Tiny units of general-purpose government could be excluded from its benefits, as the ACIR recommended, thus providing a powerful incentive for consolidation. Congressman Reuss developed and introduced, with co-sponsorship from Senator Hubert H. Humphrey of Minnesota, yet another promising approach. It would provide with the first year of revenue sharing a special fund to finance development in each state of "a master plan for modernizing and revitalizing state and local government." The plan would have to be filed before the second year's assistance was received.

The Catalyst for Reform

All of these schemes are based on the notion that Federal aid should be used in the future not simply to achieve specific *program objectives* deemed important in Washington but as a catalyst for *structural reforms* that will enable the aided organizations to perform their functions better, as they see fit. This redefinition of goals is likely, in my judgment, to be a recurring and important theme in many of our domestic policy debates in the 1970s. The main thrust of policy from Franklin Roosevelt through Lyndon Johnson was an effort to develop national programs to meet public needs. From that long experience, it can be seen that while the national government can do some things reasonably well—collect taxes, distribute cash benefits, raise and supply armies—it is a cumbersome, costly instrument to attempt to use to solve individual or community problems. Peter F. Drucker, in a book called *The Age of Discontinuity*, which appeared just as the Nixon Administration took office and which markedly influenced its officials' thinking, argued that the national government should concentrate on those essential tasks and try to create conditions and incentives that stimulate other organizations to handle the more complex, varied local needs.

While some of the spiritual and intellectual descendants of the New Deal still favor direct Federal action to solve all these problems, more and more people argue that the Federal government's leverage should be used, in Congressman Reuss's phrase, "as a catalyst and not as a crutch."

Thus, in many areas—employment and job training, health care, law enforcement, education—the search is on for ways in which the Federal government can both aid and stimulate the kind of organizational reforms in the agencies directly concerned with these services that will improve *their* usefulness to their clientele. That approach is evident in many of the major Nixon Administration proposals and in some offered by the congressional Democrats. President Nixon, for example, told Congress that despite a 600 percent increase in Federal financial assistance to education during the 1960s, much of it aimed at helping the educationally needy, "the best available evidence indicates that most of the compensatory education programs have not measurably helped poor children catch up."

"American education is in urgent need of reform," he said, and proposed that Congress charter a National Institute of Education to sponsor and finance educational research (which now receives less than half of one percent of the total education budget) and to aid state and local agencies "seeking to evaluate their own programs."

Nixon's manpower training proposal required that states and cities receiving Federal aid for this purpose develop and publish each year a statement of programs and objectives, which would be open to comment and criticism from other governmental units in their area, as well as from Washington. Bonus funds would be given groups of local governments which agreed to coordinate their programs for entire labor market areas.

A similar approach, started under the Johnson Administration, gave Federal aid to states developing law-enforcement plans for all their jurisdictions. In 1971, a bipartisan group of four senators, all former attorney generals of their states, recommended an improvement that would have the Federal government finance the establishment of model criminal justice systems—involving professional training and payment of police, guarantees of speedy criminal trials and provision of a modern correctional system—in as many states as are willing to develop comprehensive plans for such a system.

In the field of health, to take a final example, the Nixon plan and many of the alternatives offered in 1971 all called for Federal encouragement and subsidization of a new kind of medical institution—the Health Maintenance Organization (HMO), a medical system, sometimes run by the participating physicians and sometimes by quasi-public corporations representing both doctors and patients, which would provide comprehensive services for enrolled members for a fixed, prepaid fee. The Nixon plan aimed at developing 450 HMOs by the end of fiscal 1973, 100 of them in areas now lacking in medical services. A companion institution, the Area Health Education Center, would serve medically neglected areas both as training grounds for health personnel and as medical service centers.

The Problems of State Government

A feature of many of these reform plans is a major planning and coordinating role for state government. And that brings up a point that is fundamental to any realistic discussion of governmental reform. As we have seen, much of the crisis of the metropolitan areas results from the inability and unwillingness of their governments to plan and coordinate their activities effectively. Faced with that fact, people—citizens and experts alike—turn to the state government for help in "knocking heads together." When states are slow to respond, the demand comes for the Federal government to use its leverage to get action.

The uncomfortable truth is that no level of government can be any better in prodding another to undertake reform than it is in putting its own house in order. And here the picture is both bleak and forbidding at any level of government one chooses to examine.

We have already discussed the local government jungle. State government has pressing problems of its own. The Citizens Conference on State Legislatures is a private group sympathetic to the frustrations many legislators feel and convinced they have a vital role to play in American government. Yet its 1971 report said that the legislatures "stand high on the list of institutions that need reform." That is, in my judgment, an understatement of the case. In the years I have spent traveling this country on the political beat, I have no more horrifying memories than those of some of America's legislatures disposing of the public's business. I remember watching The Great and General Court of the Commonwealth of Massachusetts, as the legislature is styled, publicly strangle a referendum measure that would have allowed the citizens to vote a reduction in its size from 240 to 160 members. The referendum measure was approved, at one moment, but the presiding officer simply refused to announce the vote until his lieutenants had twisted enough arms so that the reform was defeated. I also remember standing in the back of the Texas House of Representatives while the speaker of that body, who had been named as a key figure in a stock fraud scheme, gaveled through two dozen bills in ten minutes, while the "Dirty Thirty," as the few maverick, conscientious legislators were called, frantically flashed their voting-board lights red to protest this travesty on the legislative process.

It is not always like that, of course. Like others, I have come to admire the pride, the independence and the high quality of the

California legislature—visible proof of what decent salaries, facilities and staff support can make of these much-scorned bodies. But California is the exception, not the rule. The Citizens Conference survey recorded that fewer than half the legislatures provide members with office space, or give leaders full-time professional help during sessions, or record and publish committee votes, or meet a dozen other basic criteria for responsible performance.

If the conscientious members of the legislatures are not the most frustrated men in American politics, then the governors may be. Terry Sanford, the able former Governor of North Carolina, concluded a two-year study in 1967 with the observation that "few institutions are as balkanized"—that familiar word—"as the executive branch of state government." Typically, dozens, even hundreds, of boards, departments and agencies clutter the state capital. Many of them have been given statutory independence by legislators fearful of executive power. Even those that are nominally under the Governor's direction tend to behave independently, if only because the Governor lacks an adequate budget and planning staff, or system of organization, to manage his own domain.

I remember visiting Lansing, Michigan, shortly after George Romney had moved over from the presidency of American Motors to his new job as Governor. His outer offices and the nearby corridors of the old state capitol were jammed with desks, files and workers overflowing the space the state fathers had decided, a century earlier, a Governor would need. Inside the office, Romney was shaking his head in disbelief at the managerial muddle he had inherited. "I have 241 separate boards, departments and agencies that are supposed to report to me," he said. "If I did nothing else with my time, I still couldn't see their heads more than 10 minutes a week."

There have been improvements in recent years; reorganization plans and constitutional revisions have been put into effect in a good many states, including Michigan. But as of 1970 the average state still had eight executive agencies headed by independently elected officials, the same number as a decade earlier. As of 1970, eighteen of the fifty states still limited their governors to two-year terms or a single four-year term. A 1970 article in the *National Civic Review* began with this bald declaration: "State governments are confronted with a management crisis of increasing dimensions. Administrative machinery and processes, inadequate at present program levels, will require major alteration if state executives are to cope with the expansion of services anticipated for the future."

The Mess in Washington

The Federal government—regarded by many as the last hope for spurring state and local reform—has yet to solve, or even tackle, many of its own organization problems. Each of the last four Presidents has had advisory task forces on governmental reorganization, and each has taken a nibble at the problem: Under Eisenhower, the Department of Health, Education and Welfare was created; Kennedy set up an Office of Science and Technology in the Executive Office and gave the chairman of the Civil Service Commission a coordinating role for all government personnel policies. Johnson pulled together scattered agencies into two new Cabinet departments—Transportation and Housing and Urban Development—and (briefly) made the Office of Economic Opportunity a clearing house for antipoverty programs.

Nixon, as noted earlier, has done more work on governmental reform than any of his predecessors. His first term has seen the elimination of the Post Office Department and its replacement by a public corporation, the U.S. Postal Service; the upgrading of the planning, budgeting and management capacity of the Executive Office; the simplification of Federal grant-in-aid programs; and a significant start toward the standardization of the field operations of the major domestic agencies. But, so far, Nixon's accomplishments have fallen far short of his aims, particularly in his major proposal for reorganization of the domestic Cabinet departments. In 1971, the President proposed that the functions of seven

Cabinet departments—Agriculture; Commerce; Health, Education and Welfare; Housing and Urban Development; Interior; Labor; and Transportation—and of several independent agencies be consolidated into four new departments, organized on functional lines. (Later, under political pressure, agriculture was exempted from the scheme.)

Under the Nixon plan, a Department of Natural Resources would manage and protect land and recreation resources, water, energy and mineral resources, and direct the government's efforts in earth, air and water sciences. A Department of Human Resources would look to the educational, health, manpower training, social, rehabilitation and income support needs of the people. A Department of Economic Affairs would be responsible for the growth and development of agriculture, commerce and industry; for regulating labor relations, developing national transportation systems and pursuing the foreign economic policies of the country. Finally, a Department of Community Development would take charge of federally-sponsored programs for both rural and urban areas, for housing and for highways and mass transit programs. The four new departments, along with the old standbys, State, Treasury, Justice and Defense, would comprise the new compact Cabinet.

In arguing for the new scheme, Roy Ash, head of Nixon's Advisory Council on Executive Organization, said that the old-line departments, "originally created to emphasize the distinctions between rural and urban interests, industry and agriculture, small business and large business, management and labor," no longer fit the planning needs of government. So long as that structure continues, he said, "it is inevitable that departments . . . will reflect and continue to stress their inherent differences, however anachronistic, and resist recognizing the pervasive importance of their interdependency." While emphasizing conflict, the present scheme, almost everyone agrees, fragments authority and makes responsible government almost impossible. Health programs are divided among thirteen departments and agencies; education efforts are not concentrated in the Office of Education but sprawl across the bureaucratic spectrum from the Agriculture Department to the Pentagon. The Ash council found no less than 850 interagency coordinating committees in the domestic field, but the very number made it obvious they could not succeed.

The Nixon proposals were the most ambitious effort in a generation to break out of that bind, but they were greeted with enormous skepticism and a great deal of outright hostility. The reasons vary. A few cynics agree with the late Charles F. Kettering of General Motors, who said, "We should be grateful we don't get all the government we pay for." Others take the view expressed by Robert Moses, the New York parks and road builder, who said airily, "If the President wants to get some specific thing done, he has only to put first-rate men in immediate charge, regardless of department labels."

But even those who accept Ash's view that "structure is critical to performance," remain skeptical that the effects of executive reorganization will be as glorious as he described:

With departments organized around the major purposes of government, and each equipped with the authority and means to fulfill its mission, the department heads will be able to integrate programs, consider cost-benefit alternatives, select program strategies, and resolve conflicts. And since the department heads will be charged with broad, purpose-oriented mandates, their views will be less those of special pleaders for narrow causes and more those expressing the interest of the whole public they serve.

The skeptics have to go no farther to find a talking point than a mile from the White House, to the headquarters of the Eisenhower Administration's great experiment in comprehensive, mission-oriented reorganization, the Department of Health, Education and Welfare. From their two sprawling buildings on Independence Avenue, the top HEW officials are supposed to coordinate the activities of 107,000 bureaucrats scattered across the nation. But the department has had nine secretaries in its first eighteen years of life and most of them have gone away muttering that it is "an anthill" or "anarchy in government." Everything conceivable has been tried to bring order out of the chaos, but the chaos remains.

In a 1970 study of the department, a team of Washington *Post* reporters counted 270 offices, bureaus, divisions and other major units that had been created during the past decade's reorganizations, while 109 others were abolished, 61 transferred and 109 changed in name. Since 1953, it said, the Office of Education has undergone six major reorganizations, the Public Health Service seven, and the Food and Drug Administration eight. Still, the fragmented authority the department was supposed to repair remains. Senator Ribicoff, who tried for two years to tame the HEW monster himself, said in 1970 that nine separate bureaus were still making health grants and the Assistant Secretary for Health, who was called the nation's top health officer, had direct responsibility for only $2.8 billion of HEW's $13.6 billion health budget.

The reasons HEW has stubbornly refused to be unified, in fact as well as in name, are the same reasons that underlie the opposition to Nixon's executive reorganization and revenue-sharing plans. Every existing bureau and agency, every existing program has a constituency and clientele of its own that will fiercely resist efforts to subordinate or merge it into a larger entity.

As Johnson's domestic affairs assistant, Joseph A. Califano, Jr., noted in urging public backing for the Nixon reorganization plan, "You get no support from the people you're moving. No matter how often you tell them they're not going to lose their jobs, they get worried."

Even more critical than the bureaucrats' reflexive opposition is that thrown up by the interest groups and the members of Congress who have a stake in the status quo. They resist change, just as they resist any effort to exert policy direction from above, be it from the President or the departmental secretary. John Gardner, another of the battered ex-HEW bosses, discussed his experience in a frank comment to a congressional committee:

As everyone in this room knows, but few people outside Washington understand, questions of public policy nominally lodged with the Secretary are often decided far beyond the Secretary's reach by a trinity consisting of 1) representatives of an outside lobby, 2) middle level bureaucrats and 3) selected members of Congress, particularly those concerned with appropriations. In a given field, these people may have collaborated for years. They have a durable alliance that cranks out legislation and appropriations on behalf of their special interest. Participants in such durable alliances do not want the departmental secretaries strengthened. The outside special interests are particularly resistant to such change. It took them years to dig their particular tunnel into the public vault, and they don't want the vault moved.

Gardner was talking about one of the most powerful facts of life in Washington—the concentration of power in the hands of appropriations subcommittee chairmen. Jamie L. Whitten of Mississippi, who has been elected to sixteen terms, usually by about seventy thousand people and usually without opposition, has been called "the permanent secretary of agriculture" by virtue of his position as chairman of the House Appropriations Subcommittee that controls the Department of Agriculture funds. The permanent bureaucrats in that department, who have seen secretaries of agriculture come and go for years, know that their well-being, their funds and their advancement depend far more on Whitten's good will than on the favor of the presidential appointee temporarily occupying the secretary's office. So do the lobbies that want things from the Agriculture Department. Both learn to make their arrangements with Whitten and to accommodate themselves to his tastes in programs and priorities.

One principal reason that few recent attorneys general have had any effective policy control over the Federal Bureau of Investigation, which is nominally a subordinate part of the Department of Justice, is the fact that none of them has had as close ties as FBI director J. Edgar Hoover to Representative John J. Rooney of New York, a fifteen-term veteran who heads the appropriations subcommittee that finances the Justice Department. Rooney always gives Hoover every nickel he asks for and makes it plain to whoever is attorney general that financing of other Justice Department activities depends in part on the degree of cooperation the department head extends to Hoover.

In the particular case of HEW, the inability of the successive secretaries to bring their domain under control is linked directly to the same problem. As Wilbur J. Cohen, a former Secretary who was considered more successful than most in solving the bureaucratic maze, has said,

Secretaries come and go with relatively short tenures [while] the men and women in Congress who control the legislative and appropriations committees have long tenures. Most Secretaries leave office before they find out who does what in the Department, while influential Members of Congress know more about the Department and how it really works than the Secretary. Staff members of congressional committees know how to get the information they need before the Secretary and his staff know what the problem is.

What Cohen might have added was that HEW secretaries are simply outnumbered by the legislators who supervise their domain. When HEW was formed, Congress did not designate a single committee in each chamber to deal with the new department; resistance to change in committee jurisdictions is at least as fierce as the opposition to merger among executive branch bureaucracies. Instead, all the old lines from the bureaus and agencies to their parent subcommittees were kept intact, and the Secretary, who was supposed to coordinate their activities, found himself hopping around Capitol Hill, trying to answer to the twelve separate House and Senate committees, each of which claimed a major piece of the HEW pie, and each of which was determined to protect its own particular programs and bureaus from interference by the Secretary.

These jurisdictional jealousies among the congressional committee chairmen are themselves a major obstacle to executive branch reorganization. Moreover, as the HEW case shows, any executive reorganization that is to achieve its objective ought to be accompanied by a similar consolidation of legislative authority. But

Congress itself is the victim of fragmentation of authority every bit as severe as we have seen in metropolitan government, state government and the Federal executive branch. The legislative reorganization act of 1946 had among its major goals a simplified, coordinated committee structure. The number of standing committees in the House and Senate was reduced from 81 to 34. But the gain was short-lived. New demands on government, combined with the insatiable empire building of individual lawmakers, the desire of every man to be "king of his own dunghill," sent the number of permanent subcommittees, each with its own chairman, its own staff, its own jurisdiction and its own special interest, soaring to 267 in the quarter century since the "reform" took place. The 1970 congressional reform bill, while making many other useful improvements, did not touch this fragmentation problem, except to add to it by creating a new jurisdiction for a separate Committee on Veterans Affairs in the Senate, which promptly spawned five subcommittees of its own.

Along the way, the centralized congressional budget-making operation provided by the legislative reorganization act of 1946 has been lost, and Congress now looks at its most important function—appropriating funds—not as a single, interlocking process, but as a series of separate, log-rolling operations, extending in recent years over a period of almost twelve months, and becoming increasingly uncoordinated with either executive-branch budget making or the fiscal-year calendar on which the departments and agencies must operate.

What this dismal survey of the organization problems of government adds up to is a simple, fundamental political lesson. At any level one examines, the obstacles to repair of our fragmented, inefficient, unresponsive governmental structure are terribly difficult to overcome. In addition to the simple inertia of the massive bureaucracy, there are strong jurisdictional jealousies and a powerful array of particular interests that will come to bear against any effort for reform. Those who despair of solving the problem at the local level turn to the state governments or to

Washington. But the state capitals and the national capital are caught in the same trap themselves. Even at the top, the record of recent Presidents—and particularly of Nixon, who has made reform of government a major priority—indicates the prospects for short-term gains are small. As Califano remarked, "It takes an awful lot of presidential capital—time and political capital both," to fight a reform battle. "Any president may have one or two big shots at it in his career, but that's all."

Meaningful reform will require a concerted effort over a considerable period of time, longer than the term of a single President, governor or mayor. The logical agency for focusing the required energy is the political party. Before we can reform government, we must revive our parties. And that is a formidable task in itself.

8

Leadership

One can say of the American people today what Walter Lippmann said in the Depression year of 1932:

> They are looking for new leaders, for men who are truthful and reso-
> lute and eloquent in the conviction that the American destiny is to be
> free and magnanimous. . . . They are looking for leaders who will talk
> to the people . . . about their duty, and about the sacrifices they must
> make, and about the discipline they must impose upon themselves, and
> about their responsibility to the world and to posterity, about all the
> things which make a people self-respecting, serene and confident. May
> they not look in vain.

The year after Lippmann wrote those words, help arrived, so most Americans believed, in the form of Franklin D. Roosevelt. And, as one travels America today, one hears, time and again, the expressions of hope for the leader who will somehow rescue us from our problems and provide the energy that will start the system functioning again. The notebooks of my door-to-door interviewing are filled with these expressions: "We didn't have this kind of trouble when Ike was President." Or "If only we had someone like President Kennedy who could inspire the young people." Or "By God, when Harry Truman was President, you knew right where he stood. He didn't give you all this double-talk."

The easiest explanation for our continuing political impasse is to say that our leadership has failed us. The myth dies hard that America is God's favored nation, and that somehow, in times of crisis, great leaders will come forward to rescue it. I do not mean to scoff, but when I hear this said, I cannot help remembering that mocking song at the end of *The Threepenny Opera,* in which we are reminded that in real life, unlike musicals, the "end is not so fine," the condemned man is not always "repriev-ed," and "Victoria's messenger" does not always "riding come, riding come," in time to rescue poor Macheath from being hanged for his crimes.

Analogy, either historical or literary, is not really very helpful. The fact is that when we are in the midst of a political crisis we cannot judge how much of the problem is in the atmosphere of the times, how much is in ourselves, how much in the system and how much in the men who are running it. It may well be that some of the shortcomings we impute to our scheme of government are simply the fault of the men we have put in power, or of us for putting them there. Rich as this nation is in human resources, it is not so rich as to be able to afford the profligate waste of our finest leadership we have seen in the past decade. Some of our best men have been murdered. Others have been driven from office and from public service by our impatience, or their frustration, with a system of government which obstinately thwarts the best efforts to solve our common problems. We pay a price—an incalculable price—for every such man we lose.

And yet, even acknowledging this, it is too easy to say that our problem is simply one of needing better leadership. For all those who have died too young, for all those who quit too soon, or were defeated when they had more good service to give, or who had the bad luck to be running against the wrong opponent in the wrong place in the wrong year; for all the waste of human talent that is part of our competitive political system and our accident-prone, violent country; for all that, it is still just too easy an evasion of responsibility to throw up our hands and declare that we are in trouble because we lack proper leadership.

It often seems to me that we have better political leadership in this country than we have any right to expect. The legislators, the congressmen, the mayors, the governors and senators whose campaigns and whose work I have reported are not more venal, crass, selfish, short-sighted or crooked than their predecessors of earlier generations. On the contrary, they are, as a whole, as well educated, well motivated and as earnest in their pursuit of the elusive public good as anyone could reasonably expect them to be. The Presidents we have had in this past generation have not been hacks; they have been men of extraordinary and diverse talents and backgrounds. Each of them has sought in his own way to meet Lippmann's test of statesmanship, to treat government not "as a routine to be administered," but as "a problem to be solved."

John Gardner was right in contending that "contrary to the public impression, good men do go into politics and government . . . [but] they find themselves hamstrung, caught in antiquated institutions that cannot be made to function effectively." We tend to overpersonalize our political hopes and thus to build ourselves up for the letdown that comes when mortal men fall short of the godlike myths we construct around them. Particularly is this true of our Presidents. Political scientist Thomas J. Cronin has written an intriguing essay called *The Textbook Presidency*, showing how exaggerated are the attributes we impute to the occupants of our highest political office. From our early school days right through college, he says, we are taught to think:

1. That the President is the strategic catalyst in the American political system and the central figure in the international system as well.
2. That only the President is or can be the genuine architect of United States public policy and only he, by attacking problems frontally and aggressively, and interpreting his power expansively, can be the engine of change to move this nation forward.
3. That the President must be the nation's personal and moral leader; by symbolizing the past and future greatness of America and radiating inspirational confidence, a President can pull the nation together while directing us toward the fulfillment of the American Dream.

4. That if only the right man is placed in the White House—all will be well. . . .

Cronin argues persuasively that this romantic view of the presidency carries some fairly high costs for the efficacy of our political system. It raises impossible expectations and therefore brings inevitable disillusionment. It lifts the President too high—exposing him to both the flattery of his advisers and the vituperation and not-so-occasional violence of his critics. It feeds the let-George-do-it apathy of the public and causes voters to forget their own responsibilities and to neglect the other political channels for achieving their goals.

Strength and inspiration in the presidential office will always be desirable, of course, and may even be necessary for the proper functioning of our system of government. But it is unreasonable to think we can solve our problems simply by electing the "right" President. No President can order the needed reform and reorganization of government by himself. All of the recent Presidents have tried to improve the operations of the Executive Branch, but, even in that area, none has achieved his aim. The President's writ does not extend to the organization of Congress or the state and local governments, which need reform at least as badly.

No President, under our system, can change the tax level to provide adequate resources for our dollar-starved public services. He can propose changes in Federal taxes, but Congress and the state and local taxing authorities have the final say. Similarly, no President, by himself, can cure the malaise of the public spirit, or heal the growing cynicism about politics and government that afflicts our land. He can do something—but not everything—about his personal "credibility quotient," but he cannot dictate candor and honesty to others in government whose behavior affects the level of public trust or distrust of the system. Public cynicism, underfinanced services and ill-functioning institutions are all symptoms of the single disease from which our political system is suffering: the decline of responsible party government. It is as unrealistic to expect the President to cure the disease as to eradicate the symptoms.

Two of the last four Presidents, Kennedy and Nixon, have tried to move toward responsible party government, but both were forced to defer that effort in favor of more pressing demands. A four-year term may seem a long time, but it melts away rapidly for a President pledged to "get the country moving again" or to "end the war and win the peace." Constantly, a President must weigh the advantage of working with the situation he has, seeking to achieve his goals by patching together some sort of temporary alliance, as against the long-term strategy of building support through his own party. Douglass Cater, in his 1964 book *Power in Washington,* explained well why the President often chooses the short-term expedient rather than the long-term effort:

A President, Democrat or Republican, finds himself measuring Congress in terms of the coalitions for him or against him on specific issues. His task of building a winning coalition provides a constant temptation to devise means of persuasion other than appeals to party loyalty. He often feels the urge to pick up support where he can find it—even when it means fuzzing the party issues by wooing opposition members who have shrewdly calculated their own political stakes in being wooed.

Cater then mentions other reasons why "a President is tempted to rise above his party," including the tendency to insulate foreign policy from partisanship and to recruit nonpartisan technocrats to manage foreign policy and other complex fields of government, like defense and economic policy, for him. He concludes that

these are some of the reasons why a President hesitates to sound the clarion call for party reform. Any effort to rejuvenate the system must require increased involvement by him. How does he begin the work of rejuvenation? . . . As he surveys the fragile network of state and local organizations he has good cause to doubt whether he can forge an army capable of winning supremacy over the party warlords in Congress. . . . He can perceive only dimly the far-off prospects, but he sees with stark realism the immediate consequences.

Obviously, to ignore the presidency would be to ignore a vital—perhaps *the* vital—institution for focusing the energies we need to break the long impasse in our politics. But the presidency is not the beginning and the end of our political system, and Cronin is right in reminding us that there are other kinds of institutions that can help provide the catalyst for the action we so badly need.

Two of these are particularly important: the pressure groups and the political parties. In the last sixteen years, responsible party government has all but disappeared from the United States. We have muddled through, rather unsatisfactorily, because there have been occasional prods to action on one problem or another from the interest group most concerned with it. If we are going to solve our governmental crisis in the 1970s—which is by no means certain—we are going to have to find ways to use the parties more effectively to energize the political process.

Pressure Groups and Government

The classic, academic distinction between parties and interest groups was given us by the late V. O. Key, Jr.

Pressure groups seek to attain the adoption of those policies of particular interest to them; they do not nominate candidates and campaign for control and responsibility of the government as a whole. Their work goes on regardless of which party is in power in the state, city or nation. Theirs is a politics of principle. "We must be partisan for a principle and not for a party," said Samuel Gompers, speaking for the American Federation of Labor. "Labor must learn to use parties to advance our principles and not allow political parties to manipulate us for their own advancement."

Interest groups are as American as apple pie. They represent one form of those voluntary associations which De Tocqueville said we almost instinctively turn to whenever we want to accomplish some objective. The latest Washington phone book lists almost seven full pages of associations, ranging from Action on Smoking and Health and the Ad Hoc Housing Coalition right on down through the alphabet to Zero Population Growth, Inc., and the Zionist Youth Commission. To run your eye down those listings is to remind yourself what pluralism means in this incredibly diverse country: the Aircraft Owners and Pilots Association; the Bituminous Coal Operators Association; the Council of State Governments; the Disabled Officers Association; the Emergency Committee for Full Funding of Education Programs; the Federal Statistics' Users Conference; the Friends of Rhodesian Independence; the Government Employee Association; the Horsemen's Benevolent and Protective Association; the Independent Petroleum Association of America, Inc.; the John Birch Society; the Kidney Foundation; the League of Women Voters of the United States; the Magazine Publishers Association, Inc.; the National Association for the Advancement of Colored People; the Organized Bible Class Association; the Peace Center; Planned Parenthood, Inc.; the Rachel Carson Trust for the Living Environment; the Sierra Club; the Teamsters Union; the United States Anti-Communist Congress, Inc.; the Veterans of Foreign Wars; the Western Wheat Associates, Inc.; the Wilderness Society; and the Young Americans for Responsible Action, Inc.

As the names suggest, most of these interest groups have rather narrow objectives. We think of the "gun lobby" fighting weapons registration, the "education lobby" seeking more money for schools and teachers' salaries, the "textile lobby" trying to restrict textile imports. From permanent headquarters, paid staffs lobby for their causes, and send bulletins to the members telling them how and when to apply pressure to the government. One theory of democracy is that from the competition of these myriad special interests will evolve—through the "unseen hand" of the political marketplace—a set of decisions, of priorities that somehow add up to "the national interest." Frankly, I do not think that is likely. Everything I have seen in covering Washington over the past four administrations points to a contrary conclusion. There is no "free market" in the political influence game. Some interests are far more powerful than others, so powerful that they can almost rig the game to assure a favorable outcome for themselves. When one group makes campaign contributions to every member of the legislative or appropriations subcommittee handling its program; when another provides a regular supply of jobs for retiring staff members and commissioners of the agency that is supposed to regulate its industry; when still a third group enjoys a near-monopoly on the "seed money" for liberal Democratic senatorial aspirants' campaigns; and when a fourth employs a Washington law firm whose former partners sit in key White House staff jobs, or even the Oval Office itself; when the influence game is played as it is in Washington today, I am not willing to trust the future of my country to the unregulated, unmediated clash of interest groups.

I say that not because I hold to any of the "conspiracy" theories about how this group or that is secretly manipulating the government. The power game in Washington is complex; those who attempt to explain it as if some vaguely sinister force, be it the "military-industrial complex" or the "effete Eastern liberal Establishment," is pulling the strings on those who hold public office, simply betray their own unwillingness to confront the problem of government in its true complexity.

There is competition for advantage and influence in government at every level from City Hall up to the White House—spirited, often deadly competition. And no interest wins all its battles. But there are certain kinds that are far more apt to be successful than others. A group trying to preserve the status quo has an advantage over one seeking change; inertia, the strongest force in any large organization (and government is a very large organization), is working on its side, without pay.

An interest group that is old and well established has an advantage over one that has just been formed. One that has a single narrowly-defined objective, directly related to the economic well-being of its members, is likely to be better financed and more successful than a group with a long agenda and an altruistic approach to issues. The first rule of interest group government is to "look out for yourself." This means that to the extent we rely on interest groups we resign ourselves to a significant degree of stagnation and of selfishness in our public policies.

Mass Movements and Government

But there are other kinds of pressure groups working on government, groups which seem to be much more beneficial in their effects. They do not look like the special interest groups, with their permanent headquarters and professional staffs. Some of them are no more than loose coalitions, of variable life span and floating membership, brought together by some shared concern over an issue that may be, not just the special problem of a small group, but central to the politics of the time. These are not new in American life. The abolitionists, the prohibitionists, the antimonopoly and anti-immigration movements of the nineteenth and early twentieth centuries represented such broad ad hoc coalitions. They tend to be particularly important in carrying issues at times like ours when the political parties are weak and flabby.

In our time, the course of national policy on two of the most emotional, important controversies we have faced has been decisively shaped by the civil rights movement and the Vietnam peace movement. These movements arose out of conditions of broad national concern: in one case, the persistent discrimination against our largest minority; in the other, a war which has claimed more than 350,000 casualties. They were brought into focus by tactics developed by leaders with no previously established mass constituency: the sit-ins, the bus boycotts, the Freedom Rides, the mass marches of the civil rights movement; the teach-ins and demonstrations of the antiwar movement.

The impact of these movements on national policy can hardly be overstated. At a time when the political parties and their leaders seemed reluctant to act on either of these critical problems, these mass movements used a combination of publicity and pressure tactics to shift public opinion so dramatically that the political process had to respond to their demands.

Their example has spawned a wide variety of other ad hoc coalitions, known by the causes they espouse: the consumer movement; the environmental movement; the save-the-cities movement; the movement to cut defense spending and to eliminate the draft. The techniques vary with the personalities of the leaders and the objectives these groups set for themselves. Ralph Nader, the young lawyer who sparked the consumer movement, favors lawsuits, lobbying and investigative disclosures by a few highly skilled professionals and volunteers. John Gardner, whose Common Cause organization has tackled a broad agenda of reforms, has assembled a mass membership (200,000 members after one year) to back a highly professional lobbying effort.

The emergence of these ad hoc coalitions, bringing pressure on the political system from outside, has led to the use of similar coalitions for promoting change within the system. The anti-Vietnam war movement has been as bipartisan or nonpartisan in Congress as it has been in the streets. The various amendments to restrict the use of American troops in Indochina or compel their more rapid withdrawal have all been hybrids: the Cooper-Church amendment, the McGovern-Hatfield amendment, the Nedzi-Whalen amendment have paired Republicans from Kentucky, Oregon and Ohio with Democrats from Idaho, South Dakota and Michigan.

Similar bipartisan coalitions in Congress have been responsible for the passage of civil rights bills, the reform of congressional procedures and campaign spending practices, the extension of the vote to eighteen-year-olds and the defeat of the supersonic airplane project. Operating sometimes in support of, and sometimes in opposition to, the President, and sometimes on their own initiative entirely, these coalitions are responsible for some of the notable victories for good government and wise policy in the past sixteen years. It is doubtful whether we would have managed to meet the challenges of the period without them.

But I am not convinced that we can count on these pressure groups and their allies in government to pull us out of our present difficulties. They may help energize the political parties, but I do not think they can substitute for the parties, or compensate entirely for the parties' failings.

Limitations of Pressure Group Politics

The problems that now confront the United States are fundamental and systemic. They will yield only to sustained, comprehensive efforts at reform. We are confronted with a *general* underfinancing of public services; a *general* deficiency in governmental structures; a *general* public disillusionment with government and politics.

These are not the kinds of problems which interest groups are particularly well equipped to solve. These coalitions provide too unstable a platform from which to attempt to prop up the sagging structure of American government. Characteristically, they have problems of leadership—in finding it, in keeping it, in settling rival claims for it. They have problems with recruiting, utilizing and maintaining their membership. They have problems in tactics—choosing between short-term payoffs and long-range advantages.

These problems were discussed, with remarkable candor and perception, by Sam Brown, the youthful leader of the Moratorium and other antiwar coalitions, in a *Washington Monthly* article in 1970. Reflecting on the forces which kept the peace movement from reaching its potential, Brown noted, among other critical factors:

> There was a serious lack of long-term commitment among many students. . . . Canvassing operations and education campaigns require a great deal of organization and commitment to work which is generally tedious. A demonstration, on the other hand, only requires going someplace for a few hours. . . . The Moratorium also had severe bureaucratic problems. . . . There was the normal amount of scrambling for leadership posts in all the Moratorium offices. People always debunked and frequently deposed the leadership if they felt they could do a better job. . . . Our strategy was right but . . . our base was wrong. I am

convinced it is not possible to build a successful peace movement simply on a student base.

There are two other problems with pressure groups. They tend to define their objectives in excessively narrow terms, and, if they do not disappear after the members' first burst of interest wanes, they run the risk of being captured by the more extreme advocates of their particular cause.

There is a reason for their narrowness of focus. Initially, the pressure group finds it easiest to recruit members around a specific objective or a specific grievance. Obtaining a single objective or blocking a single threat also appears easier than tackling a whole range of problems.

If it develops, however, as it inevitably does in many cases, that even with the objective so narrowed the group cannot achieve its goal, there is always the danger that its leaders, out of frustration with the lack of quick results or in hopes of whipping up again the emotions of their followers, will resort to tactics of extremism, of confrontation or even of violence. Parts of the civil rights movement went through that development, and the antiwar movement was seriously sundered by the split among its leaders over the legitimacy of violence. As Sam Brown said in his *Washington Monthly* article:

> The failures of demonstrations as a peace tactic tended to restrict the morally-based anti-war movement to the campus. And, during gestation on the campus, it continually moved toward the left. The enemies became generalized into the System and the solution into revolution. Anyone who added a new plank to the canons of the left was considered purer than his predecessor and the movement shifted in order to identify with its purest elements.

As a result of that process, Brown said, it became possible "for people on the left—whose internal ethic calls for a loving ethos, an understanding of human weaknesses, concern for the poor, and non-violence—to direct blind hatred toward Middle America, to call people pigs, to glorify militance" and to indulge in what he called "sectarian violence."

Increasingly, the politics of our time has become a politics of confrontation. I do not think this is unconnected with the increasing role of the pressure groups and the decreasing role of the political parties, as the energizing force in government. Our political parties are old, and they expect to be in business a long time. Neither of them has any great temptation to kick down the walls, or to pursue tactics when temporarily in power that will invite revenge from the opposition when it (inevitably) returns to power. Party politics is almost by definition accommodation politics.

But pressure groups, particularly of the ad hoc variety, have different standards, which make it much easier for them to push any dispute to the point of confrontation. They are more likely to be evanescent than permanent, more likely to be engaged in a single issue of overriding importance to them than in a whole range of issues. Therefore, they are constantly tempted to go "all out" in order to achieve their objective, or to prevent their "enemy" (not, as the politician would say, "opponent") from achieving his.

When the antiwar demonstrators came to Washington in the spring of 1971, their leader proclaimed, "If the government doesn't shut down the war, we're going to shut down the government." They tried (without much success) to tie up Washington by disrupting its traffic with human roadblocks. Similar obstructive tactics have been used by the ad hoc pressure groups inside the government. The filibuster once was thought of as the tactic for the diehard opponents of civil rights, but in recent years it has been used by liberal legislators of both parties in efforts to block the extension of the draft law, to defeat the SST and to cut defense appropriations. In October, 1971, three liberal legislators—Senators Alan Cranston of California, Frank Church of Idaho and Charles McC. Mathias of Maryland—announced they had changed their minds about the desirability of curbing filibusters, because they had found unlimited debate so useful in frustrating the designs of President Nixon. But, with our governmental system already suffering from paralysis, there is a limit to how much disruption and obstruction the society will tolerate—whether it takes place in Congress or in the streets—before the frustrated citizens blindly clamp down on all forms of dissent.

Societies are funny creatures. So long as there is a presumption that disagreements will be settled civilly, that each dispute will not be carried to the ultimate test of strength, the naked force that is at the root of government—the police power—need not be invoked. But when that assumption is no longer made, when every issue has the potential of becoming an "ultimate issue," the police power will become much more evident. Already we have had mass arrests, not by some foolish provincial sheriff, but by the police force of the nation's capital, acting with the approval of the Attorney General of the United States. On the other side, we have had guerrilla raids on draft headquarters and FBI offices, bombings of the Capitol and other government buildings and other acts of terrorism.

To the extent that our dependence on pressure group tactics leaves us open to increasing civil strife and the danger of reflexive repression, it represents yet another limit on how far we can rely on them to get us through our governmental crisis—and a most serious limitation, indeed.

The Prospects for the Political Parties

Do the political parties offer us a way of energizing the system without such high risks? A generation ago, when I took political science courses at the University of Chicago, few of my fellow students even at that precociously skeptical institution would have doubted that the answer was "yes." Our mentor was Charles E. Merriam—whose faith in the two-party system was such that he even ran for Mayor of Chicago as a Republican—and our text by V. O. Key, Jr., said:

For government to function, the obstructions of the constitutional mechanism must be overcome, and it is the party that casts a web, at times weak, at times strong, over the dispersed organs of government and gives them a semblance of unity.

I was greatly influenced in my thinking by a book written at that time, Heibert Agar's *The Price of Union*. Agar argued that

the special problems of the American government derive from geography, national character, and the nature both of a written constitution and a federal empire. The government is cramped and confined by a seemingly rigid bond; yet it must adapt itself to a rate of change in economics, technology, and foreign relations which would have made all previous ages dizzy. In good times the government must abide by the theory that its limited sovereignty has been divided between the Union and the several states; yet when the bombs fall or the banks close or the breadlines grow by millions it must recapture the distributed sovereignty and act like a strong centralized nation. The government must regard the separation of its own powers, especially those of the executive and the legislature, as an essential and indeed a sacred part of the system; yet when the separation threatens deadlock and danger, it must reassemble those powers informally and weld them into a working team. Finally, the government must accept the fact that in a country so huge, containing such diverse climates and economic interests and social habits and racial and religious backgrounds, most politics will be parochial, most politicians will have small horizons, seeking the good of the state or the district rather than of the Union; yet by diplomacy and compromise, never by force, the government must water down the selfish demands of regions, races, classes, business associations, into a national policy which will alienate no major group and which will contain at least a small plum for everybody. This is the price of unity in a continent-wide federation.

What made this experiment in continent-wide, constitutional government workable, he argued, what "saved the system from stagnation" was the fact that political parties emerged to bring the necessary cohesion and flexibility to the formal scheme of divided authority.

These parties are unique. They cannot be compared to the parties of other nations. They serve a new purpose in a new way. Unforeseen and unwanted by the Fathers, they form the heart of the unwritten constitution and help the written one to work.

It is through the parties that the clashing interests of a continent find grounds for compromise; it is through the parties that majority rule is softened and minorities gain a suspensive veto; it is through the parties that the separation of powers within the federal government is diminished and the President is given strength (when he dares use it) to act as a tribune of the people; it is through the parties that the dignity of the states is maintained, and the tendency for central power to grow from its own strength to some extent resisted.

Agar concluded his panegyric:

Over such an area, where there is no unity of race, no immemorial tradition, no throne to revere, no ancient roots in the land, no single religion to color all minds alike—where there is only language in common, and faith, and the pride of the rights of man—the American party system helps to build freedom and union. . . .

Even in the heady climate of twenty years ago, there were scholars who realized the political parties were not in *that* good shape. Indeed, in 1950, the same year Agar's book appeared, the committee on political parties of the American Political Science Association published a report titled "Toward a More Responsible Two-Party System," with a lengthy catalogue of reforms it said were needed for the parties to meet their responsibilities.

The committee's view, then widely shared by students and practitioners of politics, was that effective government in America "requires political parties which provide the electorate with a proper range of choice between alternatives of action."

"An effective party system," the report said, "requires, first, that the parties are able to bring forth programs to which they commit themselves, and, second, that the parties possess sufficient internal cohesion to carry out these programs." The test of an effective party system, in other words, would be its capacity to give the voters a credible pledge to pursue a certain agenda or program and its possession of sufficient cohesion or discipline to act on that agenda once in office.

What is striking today is that the concept of responsible party government is dismissed as incorrect, impractical or irrelevant by many, if not most, of those professionally involved in the study and practice of politics. Responsible party government has not just disappeared from the face of America; it is in danger of being erased as an ideal in the minds of those most concerned with American politics.

Nowhere has the backlash against the idea of responsible party government been more evident than in the profession that spawned it—political science. In 1970, on the twentieth anniversary of the issuance of the political parties report, the APSA annual convention devoted its main discussion session to a reappraisal of the document. For the occasion, Evron M. Kirkpatrick, the longtime executive secretary of APSA and a junior member of the original committee, delivered what was, in effect, the profession's highly critical look back at its own "baby." Criticizing its "lack of analysis, justification or clarification" and "its popular, missionary tone," Kirkpatrick laid down a three-point rebuttal of its main tenets.

First, he said, "It is by no means clear that political parties are competent, efficient or appropriate institutions for the formation of policy which is to be binding upon legislators and executive leaders." They lack sufficient expertise to devise solutions to our complicated problems, he said.

Second, even if they could develop policies, it is likely the parties "would not provide the voters the clear choice the committee felt essential," Kirkpatrick said, because "it is a commonplace in the literature of comparative political institutions that programmatic parties exist only in times and places characterized by significant ideological cleavages" and this "nation . . . has been famous—at least until recently—for ideological unity."

Third, he declared, "Even if two programmatic but nondivisive parties were conceivable in the United States, the likelihood that their programs could be communicated to a mass electorate which would then choose in terms of the two alternatives, as structured by the parties, is not conceivable. . . . The committee model of electoral choice requires a higher level of voter information than exists in any known mass electorate." Kirkpatrick did not cite examples but there is no shortage of evidence that seems to support his point. A Gallup Poll in 1970 showed only 62 percent of the voters knew the party affiliation of their representative in Congress; only 53 percent knew his name; and only 21 percent knew how he voted on any major bill. Donald E. Stokes and Warren E. Miller of the University of Michigan reported that a 1958 survey showed less than half (47 percent) of the voters knew the Democratic party had controlled Congress during the previous two years. They reported that 59 percent of the voters in contested congressional districts said they had neither read nor heard anything about either candidate for Congress, and less than 20 percent said they knew something about both.

Voting studies, Kirkpatrick said, show that voting decisions are shaped by habit, by group interest, by family, class, ethnic, religious, racial and party identification—all strong, stable, enduring and nonrational factors, hardly comprehended by the committee's rationalistic scheme. "The cumulative impact of voting studies on the committee model of responsible party doctrine," he said, "is, quite simply, devastating."

Many journalists, government officials and politicians share the attitude that it is ridiculous to talk about responsible political parties. George Reedy, an able Washington correspondent who became Lyndon Johnson's press secretary, has written that "the arguments for responsible party government are compelling. But their logic is totally irrelevant" to the current condition of American politics. "In the United States," he said, "true ideological discussion is something that never takes place at the political party level."

These debunking statements are cited, not for the purpose of debate, but to indicate that in today's intellectual climate the prevailing attitude is disparagement of the parties and of their capacity to help solve our governmental crisis.

Is Responsible Party Government Possible?

But I do not want to leave the impression that the case for responsible party government has been abandoned, either among the academicians or among the practitioners of politics. It has not. Professor Key, in *The Responsible Electorate*, a book cut short by his death in 1963, went over the same survey research data on which Kirkpatrick relied and made "the perverse and unorthodox argument," as he said, "that voters are not fools." The dean of the profession argued that "the portrait of the electorate that develops from the data is not one of an electorate straitjacketed by social determinants or moved by subconscious urges triggered by devilishly skillful propagandists. It is rather one of an electorate moved by concern about central and relevant questions of public policy, of governmental performance and of executive personality." Building on Key's argument, and using more recent data, political scientists Walter DeVries and Lance Tarrance, Jr., in their 1971 book *The Ticket-Splitters,* argued that those key voters base their electoral decisions on their judgment of the candidate's ability, his personality, his competence to handle the job and his stand on the issues. At the same APSA panel where Kirkpatrick presented his critique of the theory of responsible party government, Gerald M. Pomper of Rutgers University argued that "the nation is more ready for responsible parties today than in 1950," in part because the voters are more aware of the "difference between the parties and . . . the relative ideological position of the parties." I cannot judge the merits of this academic dispute, but I think it fair to say that the voting behavior studies which Kirkpatrick said were "simply devastating" to the notion of responsible party government are not so viewed by many of his fellow political scientists.

As for his contention that it is impossible for the parties to behave as the APSA committee said responsible parties should, that too is open to dispute. James L. Sundquist, the Brookings

Institution scholar, in his excellent book *Politics and Policy*, argues that "the Democratic party in the 1950s and 1960s did exactly those things" which the APSA committee said a responsible political party should do. "It *did* develop a program to which it committed itself—and which it put into effect after winning office." Sundquist traces the story of the development during Eisenhower's second term of an ambitious domestic economic and social welfare program, concocted by what he calls the "activist Democrats" in the House and Senate. He shows how it was publicized by Paul Butler's Democratic Advisory Council and ratified as party policy in the platform of 1960. He argues that it was "the mandate for a redirection of the course of government on domestic problems" that accounted for Kennedy's victory in 1960; and he notes that, although it took five years to pass parts of that program, most of it did eventually become law.

The trouble with these academic disputes is that they *are* academic. I would like to believe that responsible party government is possible, but in honesty I have to concede we have seen precious little of it in America in the past generation. Even Sundquist was forced to admit that two years after Kennedy took office, his "domestic program was in shambles." Large parts of that program were not passed until after Kennedy's assassination had created an emotional climate which enabled Johnson to get the laggard Congress to act. It is not very satisfactory to rest the case for the feasibility of responsible party government on the circumstances of a presidential assassination, but other examples are hard to find at any level of government. The pattern of divided government has spread to the states. In 1971, twenty-three of the fifty states had a governor of one party and a legislature controlled, wholly or in one chamber, by the opposition party. Government in those capitals was as frustrated as it was in Washington.

One place where the conditions for responsible party government have existed is Albany, where for fourteen years Governor Nelson A. Rockefeller has been pursuing an activist program as head of a state Republican party which has controlled the legislature for all but two of the years he has been in office.

Rockefeller's record in the fields of higher education, civil rights, consumer protection, housing and urban development, commuter and mass transit systems, air and water pollution abatement, state aid to the arts, and reorganization of government have earned him the respect of many of his colleagues in the fifty states. The retrenchment of some welfare programs, as Rockefeller has responded to conservative pressures in recent years; the plight of New York City, a creature and dependent of the state; and the Attica prison shootings in 1971 have all marred Rockefeller's record in the eyes of some observers, but his achievements in his long tenure make New York probably the best laboratory experiment in responsible party government one can find.

Rockefeller has used his personal and family connections to enlist the talent and aid of individuals and groups another governor might not have been able to reach. But he has also used the tools of political leadership available to any skillful executive whose party controls the government. The successes he has achieved are a practical demonstration of the advantages that derive from responsible party government.

At the local level, the obvious example of the use of the political party as the energizing force for government is Chicago. For sixteen years, Richard J. Daley, as Mayor of Chicago and head of its Democratic party, has marshaled his political power to advance his governmental purposes and has used his control of government to enhance the power of his political party. Daley's record as Mayor, like Rockefeller's as Governor, is open to criticism on very serious grounds. Chicago can hardly be a model for responsible politics, because an effective political opposition has not existed there for many, many years. But it is clear that the linkage of political power and governmental responsibility in that city, as in New York State, has made it possible to go ahead on major projects —ranging from mass transit to governmental reorganization—

which are quite literally beyond the capacity of political leaders whose effectiveness is crippled by the lack of a real party base.

Responsible party government is a concept which can rarely be fully achieved in real life. In America in the past generation, even an approximation has been hard to find at national, state or local levels. Nonetheless, it is responsible party government we must seek if we are serious about ending the frustration of the American people with the performance of their public institutions. It is not enough to turn away from the impasse in government, shrug our shoulders and say, "We need better leadership." Nor is it realistic to believe we can re-energize the system through some new pressure group which, while disdaining politics, will attempt to direct the government into the necessary courses of action.

We have to use the tools that are available, and of these the political parties still seem the best adapted to the work at hand. A dozen years ago, Stephen K. Bailey, the Syracuse University political scientist, wrote, with what seems now to have been prophetic wisdom, that "so long as we lack strong national parties operating as catalysts in the Congress, the executive branch, and the national government as a whole, and between the national government and state and local governments, power will continue to be dangerously diffused, or, perhaps what is worse, will whip-saw between diffusion and presidential dictatorship."

We have been through that dreadful cycle once since Bailey wrote those words—from the diffusion of power under Eisenhower to the excessive concentration under Johnson and now back to divided government under Nixon. With Nixon, we may be starting on a second run through that frustrating course. It is time to stop the game, and revive responsible party government—if we can.

9

Realignment

In the view of many experts, we cannot expect responsible party government in America again until we have another major voting realignment, comparable to that which brought the "Roosevelt coalition" into existence in 1932. Such realignments have been recurrent features of American politics. Political historians are fairly well agreed that there have been five such major realignments in the past, each initiated by what they call a "critical election."

The first was the election of Thomas Jefferson in 1800, which ended the Federalist party dominance of the young Republic. The second was the election of Andrew Jackson in 1828, a triumph for the frontier democracy, which remained in power almost continuously until the Civil War. The third, obviously, was the election of Abraham Lincoln in 1860, which brought the new Republican party to power and precipitated the Civil War. The fourth was the election of William McKinley in 1896, significant as a victory for the areas of post–Civil War industrialism over the insurgent agrarian populism which captured the Democratic party with the nomination of William Jennings Bryan. And the last was the election of Roosevelt in 1932, a turnabout caused by the Great Depression, which inaugurated the period of welfare state liberalism we now know.

These "critical elections" have certain common characteristics. They have been associated with genuine and widely perceived crises in our national life: the slavery controversy, the populist revolt, the Depression. They have been marked by an increase in the size of the vote, by the sharpness of the issues within and between the parties, and by major breaks with the past voting habits of millions. As James L. Sundquist has written in *Interplay* magazine:

A realignment occurs when the electorate is subjected to an overriding new issue or set of issues—issues powerful enough to dominate political discussion and polarize large segments of the population for a sustained period of time. The voters who are attached, or driven, to each of the new "issues poles" necessarily find or fashion a political instrument to express their views. Either they capture one of the existing major parties or they form a new one. Eventually, if the new issue or set of issues maintains its force, the two-party system realigns to reflect the new polarity.

At the moment of realignment, the voter's attachment to his party is emotional, or even passionate. It is *his* party. It expresses his will on that burning issue of the day, whatever it may be, because it was formed or reformed for just that purpose. He is loyal to it because it is loyal to him.

As time passes, these feelings fade. But not quickly. In the case of realignments that arise from the most traumatic issues . . . a generation must pass and a new one must arise before the old attachments are seriously eroded.

There has been a striking rhythm to the pattern of party realignment. The intervals between past critical elections ranged from twenty-eight to thirty-six years—a period of time, as Sundquist notes, that is just about the minimum required for those "whose political views were fixed during a period of realignment" to be "supplanted as a majority of the voters by those who were too young to have been deeply influenced at that time."

Further, there seems to be a sort of "natural history" to each of the political cycles. It was traced by A. James Reichley in a *Fortune* magazine article in 1971:

Each began with a relatively short period of intense creativity, inspired by a great national leader (Jefferson, Lincoln, Franklin Roosevelt). Then came a span of gradual development, during which an older spirit reasserted itself and for a time gained the upper hand (the administrations of John Quincy Adams, Grover Cleveland, Dwight Eisenhower). After this moderate reaction, the dominant force of the era confronted and decisively defeated some fossilized remnant of the preceding age (the triumph of Jacksonian democracy in the 1830s; McKinley's smashing victory over agrarian populism in 1896; Johnson's rout of Goldwater in 1964).

Toward the end of each cycle, politics takes on a confused and rather dispirited character. The opposition party may return briefly to power, by taking advantage of splits in the dominant coalition, as the Whigs did in the 1840s and Democrats did with Woodrow Wilson in 1912 and 1916. But essentially it is a period of political drift. The old issues fade at this stage of the political cycle, and the party rhetoric, based on them, seems less and less meaningful. Voters complain that they can see little difference between the old parties. They switch parties almost at random, from election to election, or they simply don't bother to vote, feeling there is no meaningful choice. Characteristically, a strong third-party movement arises, based on a complaint against the established parties and the interests they serve. Walter Dean Burnham mentions as the precursors of past realignments "the anti-Masons in the 1820s, the Free Soilers in the 1840s and 1850s, the Populists in the 1890s and the LaFollette Progressives in the 1920s."

The idea has struck almost everyone that our politics today indicates we are ripe for realignment. It has been forty years now since the Roosevelt coalition took form. The issues of that election—the welfare state and the responsibility of the government for the health of the economy—no longer divide the parties. The Republican opposition accepted the New Deal social programs when Dwight D. Eisenhower became President and has expanded them under the presidency of Richard M. Nixon, who has declared himself a "Keynesian," has adopted deficit spending and wage-price controls, and has carried on a foreign policy of accommodation with the Communist powers that is indistinguishable from Roosevelt's.

Meantime, a post–New Deal generation has come to form the majority of the electorate. The percentage of independents and ticket splitters has risen markedly in the past half-dozen years; almost half the prospective first-time voters for 1972 refuse to declare an affiliation with either of the old parties. The appeal of the old parties has diminished to the point that in only three of the last six presidential elections did the winning candidate receive more than 50 percent of the total vote. George Wallace's third party, avowedly anti-Establishment in its outlook, drew a very heavy vote in 1968 and has shown considerable staying power as a force in national politics. Struck by these parallels, Reichley suggested that some of the leading political figures of our day had their counterparts at the same stage of previous cycles:

Nixon seems one of those Janus-like figures, like Henry Clay and Woodrow Wilson, who look simultaneously toward both past and future, but are rootless in their own period. Hubert Humphrey belongs with the temporizing "doughface" politicians like Stephen A. Douglas and William Howard Taft, who tried to mend fissions within the dominant force. Robert Kennedy was a member of the ruling order who, like Martin Van Buren and Theodore Roosevelt, broke with orthodoxy to plunge toward the spirit of an age yet unborn. Barry Goldwater calls to mind those strangely appealing prophets of reaction, John C. Calhoun and William Jennings Bryan.

If the cyclical pattern continues, there lies in the not so distant future the onset of a new era and the emergence of a new Lincoln or Franklin Roosevelt. We can hardly expect to identify the future leader as yet. At about this point in earlier cycles, Lincoln was an obscure Congressman from Illinois, protesting the Mexican War; and Roosevelt was an official of the second rank in the Wilson Administration, soon to run unsuccessfully for Vice President. By scrutinizing the political realities, however, we may gain some hint of the kind of base upon which the leader will form his new majority.

The search for that new majority has become almost a national sport in the past three years—a game that has produced several best-sellers, hundreds of newspaper columns and innumerable Washington cocktail party conversations. Kevin Phillips has described *The Emerging Republican Majority*. Richard M. Scammon and Ben J. Wattenberg have delineated *The Real Majority*. Frederick G. Dutton has pointed out *The Changing Sources of Power*. Walter Dean Burnham has been both historian and prophet in *Critical Elections and the Mainsprings of American Politics*. And Samuel Lubell, who began the whole game a few years ago with *The Future of American Politics*, has brought his theories up to date with *The Hidden Crisis of American Politics*.

The Search for the Real Majority

Whatever their background or bias, all of these observers except Scammon and Wattenberg suggest the likelihood of a major political realignment. The co-authors of *The Real Majority* are considerably more cautious, saying "it is conceivable, although by no means definite, that we are in for a tidal political era." Their view offers a convenient starting point for this discussion of possible political realignment, because it emphasizes the stable elements in a political scene that seems precariously unstable to many others.

While most other elections analysts were struck by the volatile character of the 1968 election, by the marked decline in the Democratic vote between 1964 and 1968, by the return of the Republican party to the White House after the Goldwater débacle, and by the emergence of the strongest third-party movement in half a century, Scammon wrote (for the Washington *Post*):

Actually, 1968 saw a good deal more of Roosevelt Coalition type voting than might have been imagined. Most of the cities voted Democratic, as before; most of the suburbs and the northern country areas voted Republican, as before. The majority of the wealthy voted Republican, as before; the majority of the poor voted Democratic, as before; and the middle class voters split, as before.

In an epilogue to *The Real Majority*, he and Wattenberg made the same point about the 1970 election, which, they said, showed

the powerful theme of stability and continuity in the ongoing American political process. After all the talk about the breakup of the two-party system, about the new politics, about emerging Republican majorities, and the disintegration of the FDR coalition, a look at the election data is positively startling as the familiar patterns re-emerge.

The Democrats got 54 percent of the vote, compared to 51 percent in the last congressional election. Labor went Democratic. The Chamber of Commerce types went Republican. Blacks, Jews and Chicanos went Democratic. The majority of high-income voters, WASPs, and suburbanites went Republican.

Analytically, Scammon and Wattenberg stressed the centrist tendencies of two-party politics, arguing that a party interested in winning must "play within the 35 yard lines" of the political field.

It is the judgment of the authors that there are no two strategies for victory—they are the same strategy with different rhetoric. This single strategy involves a drive toward the center of the electorate. . . . The winning coalition in America is the one that holds the center ground on an attitudinal battlefield. In the years until the election of 1968, the battlefield had been mostly an economic battlefield, and the Democrats held the ideological allegiance of the machinist and his wife from the suburbs of Dayton, and tens of millions of other middle-income, middle-educated, middle-aged voters who wanted a high minimum wage, social security, medicare, union protection, and so on. That seems to be changing. For the seventies, the battlefield shows signs of splitting into two battlefields: the old economic one and the new social one that deals with crime, drugs, racial pressure, and disruption. To the extent that this transformation occurs, then the party and the candidate that can best occupy the center ground of the two battlefields will win the presidency.

Prescriptively, Scammon and Wattenberg warned the two parties away from any radical proposals that would take them outside the 35 yard lines. As Democrats, their main concern was, of course, that their own party take as firm a stand on law and order as the Republicans and not let the "militants," as they called them, gain such influence in Democratic party affairs that the GOP could run off with "the Social Issue." When Democratic candidates in 1970 put American flag pins in their lapels, and filmed commercials of themselves riding in squad cars with policemen, Scammon and Wattenberg applauded their astuteness.

But, being generous, they also offered a prescription for victory to the Republicans. They told the Republicans to "move on the bread-and-butter issues," and not let themselves be thought of "as go-slow on the problems of unemployment or the cities or transportation or pollution." Despite their good advice, Nixon allowed unemployment to rise sharply in 1970 and the Republicans suffered a setback in that election. But the authors in the post-1970 epilogue assured him that if he makes "every effort . . . to reinvigorate the economy . . . it will be a horse race in 1972." Quite explicitly, then, Scammon and Wattenberg's advice is that each party should ape the other, so far as possible. Implicitly, they reject the idea that the political situation calls out for a realignment of the parties; realignment involves sharp polarization on the dominant issues of the day, which is exactly what they advise both parties to avoid.

"Cynics may ask," they say, "what is the sense of parties that must always move toward the other-party position to gain political strength. They may be answered by noting that this is the procedure that guarantees the responsiveness of the American system."

To those who assert, as this book does, that the American political system has been notably unresponsive to our public needs and the health of our public institutions in the last sixteen years, and that public opinion is properly disillusioned with it, Scammon and Wattenberg reply that politics has only a limited connection with such problems. They assert there is an important and "newly intensified distinction between public policy and electoral politics." Their subject, they say, is electoral politics, which "deals with the processes of getting elected," not of deciding "issues that range from the location of the town dump to the basic ethics of our society."

"One can change society by getting elected," they say, but one can also change society "without getting elected, by convincing the public and then elected officials of the merit of specific causes. . . . In this era of almost total communications coverage, it seems easier than ever before to wage successful public policy campaigns."

In other words, what Scammon and Wattenberg argue is that we ought to rely not on our political parties but on what I have called pressure group politics to deal with the issues that confront us. By eliminating concern about the issues from their prescriptions for political party strategy, by separating politics from policy, and by treating our elections simply as contests to determine the identity of officeholders, they sidestep what seem to me to be the most serious problems in contemporary politics. The Scammon-Wattenberg book is an accurate description of the behavior of political parties in this formless, flabby stage of the realignment cycle. But its prescription is one that would maintain the political status quo. For those who find our present situation worrisome or frustrating, it is no solution at all.

The Southern Balance Wheel

Even with their emphasis on the stability of voting alignments, Scammon and Wattenberg concede that in the South there has been a "massive rejection of the older FDR coalition. In the Southern states, percentages of 75 and 70 and 85 were normal for Democratic tickets in the days of Roosevelt. In the postwar period, this had eroded to a norm of around 50 percent. . . . But in 1968 the Democratic share of the Southern vote dropped down to 31 percent and the Humphrey-Muskie ticket carried only Texas." While the change has been most marked at the presidential level, the Democratic dominance of Southern politics has been declining on a broad front. Between 1950 and 1970, the number of Republican congressmen elected from the eleven states of the Old Confederacy rose from two to twenty-seven. Six of the eleven states have elected Republican governors or senators. The old phrase about the Democratic nomination being "tantamount to election" now applies only in Louisiana and Mississippi.

The massive shift of voting patterns in the South is viewed by many observers as part of a national political realignment. It has been caused by the convergence of many forces. One-party rule was a by-product of the Civil War and the late-nineteenth-century stratagems to suppress the black vote and maintain political control in the hands of the white merchants and planters. With the massive movement of Negroes from the South during and after World War II, and the in-migration of millions of Northern Republicans who came South with the new industries. the social and economic climate for Dixie politics was profoundly altered. Between 1952 and 1960, Southern presidential voting came increasingly to resemble that in the North: the wealthier, better-educated whites voted Republican and the lower-class whites and enfranchised blacks voted Democratic. Many observers saw this as the South's belated adoption of the basic party alignment the rest of the country had known since 1932.

But there was another force at work, one which was pushing the Southern parties into a new and different alignment. Beginning in 1948, the Democratic party, which had been the white man's party in the South, adopted national policies which increasingly identified it with the cause of civil rights and integration. Black voters supplied the margin of victory for many Democratic candidates and a large proportion of the vote national Democratic candidates received in the South. Under pressure from the national party, Southern Democrats admitted blacks to party leadership, or, where they balked, as in Mississippi, were replaced by a black-led "national Democratic party" structure. Meantime, the Republicans, who had been the antislavery party, began moving in the other direction. In 1964, the year in which Lyndon Johnson obtained passage of the strongest civil rights bill in history, his Republican opponent, Barry Goldwater (who had voted against the bill and who was nominated as the candidate of the Southern Republicans), carried Deep South counties that had been solidly Democratic for a century.

In 1968, the stage seemed set for an even bigger Republican victory in Dixie, but it was short-circuited, as we know, by Wallace's third-party candidacy, which captured most of the segregationist vote in the South. However, Kevin Phillips argued in *The Emerging Republican Majority* that Wallace represented only a temporary "way station" for Southern voters abandoning the Democratic party and heading for the GOP. Phillips said "nothing more than an effective and responsibly conservative Nixon Administration is necessary to bring most of the southern Wallace electorate into the fold." Adding Nixon's 43 percent and Wallace's 14 percent, Phillips predicted a realignment that would make a conservative Republican party, based in the South, the Midwest and the West the dominant party in the new political era.

Phillips' theory provided the intellectual underpinning for the Administration's advocates of a "Southern strategy," but it rested on some dubious assumptions of its own. In describing the Wallaceites as proto-Republicans, Phillips forgot that they were mainly low-income workers, who still considered the GOP as inimical to their economic interests. There is strong evidence that most of them voted Democratic for other offices in 1968 and again in 1970. Second, he minimized the cost to a national Republican candidate of adopting policies designed to bring in the Wallaceites—the risk of a "frontlash" from traditional Republicans who object to any weakening of the party's historic position on civil rights. Even within the South, there are two quite distinct strains of Republicanism. While Goldwater carried five Deep South states in 1964, he lost all the "rim South" and Border States, whose Republican votes in previous elections had been economic, rather than racial, in motivation. Finally, on a long-term basis, it is by no means clear that overt or covert appeals to antiblack sentiments make sense as a political strategy even for the Deep South, where black voter registration is on the increase. In 1970, moderate Democrats, who avoided racist appeals, were elected as governors of Arkansas, Georgia, Florida and South Carolina, in most cases defeating avowedly segregationist opponents in either the primary or general election. The winners put together coalitions that included most of the black voters of their states and many of the lower-income whites who had been the mainstay of Wallace's support. In 1970, Wallace himself barely won the Democratic nomination for Governor of Alabama over a moderate Democrat who had all but unanimous black support. And, in 1971, Mississippi elected as its new Governor another racial moderate—a man who had first won notice as the prosecutor of the accused slayer of civil rights leader Medgar Evers.

The Free-Swinging Voters

What is true of the South is true of the nation as a whole: It is not a single bloc of voters, but many such blocs which have cut loose from their past allegiances and are on the move. While the South has been growing more Republican, New England and some suburbs have been growing more Democratic. Blacks have shown increasing political independence; like other minority groups—the Mexican-Americans, the American Indians—they have demonstrated their growing political consciousness by showing their willingness to shift partisan alignments in order to achieve their own specific goals. As the members of the congressional Black Caucus said in 1971, "We do not intend to have our vision obscured by partisan blinders where the interests of our constituents . . . are concerned."

Growing political independence, indeed, characterizes the electorate as a whole. Public opinion polls show that between one-fourth and one-third of all voters now classify themselves as political independents, up sharply over the figure one and two decades ago. Ticket splitting has increased significantly, with more than 50 percent of the ballots now showing a broken pattern of party preference. A Gallup Poll in 1968 reported that 84 percent of the voters said they chose the man, not the party. Howard Reiter has compiled figures showing that in the last six elections (from 1960 through 1970) 47 percent of the states simultaneously electing a governor and a senator have chosen men of opposite parties. In the previous six elections (from 1948 through 1958), the percentage of split outcomes was 21 percent. The new independents are not the rather indifferent, inattentive, inert citizens described in voting behavior studies of the 1950s. Many of them, perhaps half, are among the best educated, most alert, most active of the participants in politics, who have quite deliberately cast off their traditional party allegiances.

The volatility of the electorate is most dramatically exemplified by the record crop of potential new voters. Thanks to the World War II baby boom and the 26th Amendment to the Constitution, 25 million persons who were not eligible to vote in 1968 will be eligible in 1972—14 million who have turned twenty-one in the past four years and 11 million others enfranchised by the eighteen-year-old-vote amendment. Upward of 40 percent of them classify themselves as political independents. When one remembers that the potential first voters compose a population fifty times the size of Richard Nixon's 1968 plurality, their capacity for upsetting the political applecart is clear.

Historically, young people have registered and voted in far smaller proportions than their elders. But the new generation differs from its predecessors in many respects, and may prove to be more politically active. The young people have significantly more education than their parents—most have at least a high school education, and more than half, some college. Through television, they have been exposed to the world in a way no previous generation has been. Many are the products of affluence and have demonstrated great independence of taste and judgment, revolutionizing the worlds of fashion, entertainment and education since they entered their teens. And their numbers are greater, proportionately to the adult population, than this country has seen in this century. In the 1970s, the number of eligible voters over thirty-five will grow by about 6 million, while the number between eighteen and thirty-five will increase by about 22 million. Noting all this, Frederick Dutton says in *Changing Sources of Power:*

The large number of new voters and the high level of independence among them reinforce the probability that a critical passage in the politics of this country is at hand. . . . If an exciting individual or cause really stirs this generation, it could be activated in numbers that make irrelevant any past indicator of political participation among the young, and it would then become one of the few human waves of historic consequence.

The Missing Ingredients for Realignment

From almost any perspective one chooses, then, the conditions appear to be ripe for a political realignment. The normal time span between "critical elections" has elapsed. The political cycle has reached the point of aimless confusion and drift that in the past has always preceded major realignments. There are obvious internal contradictions in the existing major parties. Millions of voters have been cast adrift from their old allegiances. A wave of new voters is ready to enter the electorate and help form one of the parties in the new alignment.

But we cannot be sure that realignment will actually occur or, if it does, what form it will take. The possibilities are infinite. Kevin Phillips sees a new Republican majority composed of traditional Republican adherents and disaffected Southern and blue-collar Democrats. Former Senator Eugene J. McCarthy holds out the prospect of a victorious new party composed of the liberal Republicans who were beaten at their party's 1964 and 1968 conventions and the liberal Democrats who lost in Chicago in 1968. Walter Dean Burnham is intrigued by the possibility of a "post-industrial lineup" arraying the "professional-managerial-technical elite" and their "clients and natural political allies," the black and the poor, on one side, against "the great middle" of older white clerical and production workers, on the other. Dutton foresees "an opening to the future," when the new generation of voters and their chosen allies take command of politics, but he concedes that "if the nation takes a really sharp political turn in the seventies, the balance of power unmistakably indicates it will be further into repression, not revolution."

A. James Reichley, after weighing and discarding the chances of conservative Republicans or liberal Democrats forming a dominant new coalition, suggests that the progressive Republicans may emerge from the governorships of such states as Illinois, Massachusetts, Michigan, New York, Oregon and Washington to take charge of the political future.

Recent local and state elections have turned up scattered bits of evidence for and against almost all these possible realignment patterns. But nothing has yet occurred that could spark the emergence of a new ruling coalition on a national basis. The existing political leadership may simply be too weary to do anything more than drift along with the electorate. The Democrats have borne the burden of government, with the briefest of respites, for two generations. Even when they have been temporarily relieved of responsibility in the White House, they have had the job of writing the laws in Congress. The Republicans have had more leisure to develop fresh leadership, but they have not done so. The men the major parties nominated in 1968—Richard Nixon and Hubert Humphrey—had been at the center of power in national politics for twenty years. Neither looked like a plausible figure to spark a great realignment; nor do most of those mentioned as presidential candidates for 1972.

The obvious need of both parties for fresh blood explains the interest that developed in 1971 when two strong personalities showed signs of effecting a personal political realignment. Former Governor John B. Connally of Texas, the symbol of conservative Southern Democrats, joined the Nixon Administration as Secretary of the Treasury and quickly emerged as its most compelling figure. A few months later, New York City Mayor John V. Lindsay, the symbol of Northern liberal Republicanism, formally switched parties and affiliated himself with the Democrats. The two Johns— aside from being, perhaps, the two best-looking men in American politics—brought to their new associations exactly the kind of fresh political energy that might be required to trigger a major political realignment.

But something else is needed for that to occur—an issue strong enough to polarize the public and end the aimless drift of voters between the parties. It is hard to discern such an issue. In the autumn of 1971, Vietnam was fading from the forefront of the national debate, and no other foreign policy question seemed likely to replace it. Besides, as Sundquist has noted, "it is significant that at no time in the 140 years of continuous two-party politics has the party system been aligned or realigned on the basis of foreign policy."

Scammon and Wattenberg suggested that the Social Issue—concern over crime, drugs and public immorality—might become the lever to force a political realignment, but in 1970 most Democrats heeded their advice to "get right" on the issue so thoroughly that the positions of the two parties became indistinguishable. The Republican midterm campaign, keyed to that issue, failed notably to achieve its major objectives.

The economic issue—that old Democratic reliable—retains its potency, as Richard Nixon learned to his sorrow in 1960 and again in 1970, when his political ambitions were shattered by an inconvenient rise in unemployment just before election time. But by his dramatic reversal of economic policy in August, 1971, Nixon signaled his determination to deny that issue to the Democrats in the 1972 campaign. The other issues that have captured headlines in recent years—the environmental issue, the urban issue, the welfare issue—do not yet appear to have the emotional power to cause a major realignment, nor do they sharply divide the parties.

The one question in American life today that seems to pack the emotional punch necessary for a party realignment is the racial question—the same question that caused the realignment of 1860. The last sixteen years have seen a significant change and improvement in the legal and economic status of Negroes. But social equality is as far from reality as it has ever been. Residential segregation is increasing in the metropolitan areas of both the North and South. Efforts to integrate schools through widespread busing of pupils have brought strong resistance from white parents. Neighborhood housing integration, if attempted on any large scale, seems likely to generate even stronger white opposition.

So far, neither major party has forced the racial issue to the point at which it might bring a basic realignment of voters—for which we may be grateful. The Democrats, despite some individual qualms about the political risks of advocating integration, have not abandoned the strong civil rights position their party staked out in 1948. In 1971, every one of the Democratic presidential hopefuls in the Senate voted for an unsuccessful amendment which would have required integration of central city and suburban schools, on a metropolitan area basis, in this decade. All of them also supported the Federal open housing law. The national Republican Administration, for all the talk of a Southern strategy and all the symbolic gestures to white sentiment against busing and housing desegregation, has not drawn the hard line in the dust and told the Negroes, "Do not cross over." Nixon has kept Strom Thurmond, the 1948 states rights presidential candidate, in the Republican party, but he has not taken the steps that would drive Edward W. Brooke, the only black Senator, out of the GOP. As a matter of fact, the first three years of the Nixon Administration saw more court-ordered school desegregation take effect than any comparable period in our history.

Because the national parties have not pushed the race issue as far as they might, George Wallace has been able to keep his third-party movement alive since its strong showing in 1968. And as long as that issue remains unresolved in our national life—as long as the wounds of slavery are unhealed—there will remain the possibility that we will have a party realignment, of a very ugly kind, around the race issue.

Can There Be a Coalition for Political Reform?

If we can avoid the dreadful consequences of a realignment that would put an *apartheid* party in charge of the government, two of the many theoretical coalitions that have been suggested are particularly interesting for those seeking reform and rehabilitation of our public services.

One is the top-and-bottom coalition. In some ways, it is the most logical coalition for reform, but, as a practical matter, it is the least likely to occur. This version of the Reform party would unite the blacks, the more activist and progressive young people and the educated business and professional people who form what has been called the Republican Establishment (though many of them supported and served in the administrations of the last two Democratic Presidents).

The logical basis for such an unlikely alignment is quite simple: these three groups—Republicans, young people and blacks—fare badly in the existing distribution of *political* power. Whoever controls the White House or the Congress, their leaders and spokesmen, be they John Gardner, Sam Brown or John Conyers, seem to wind up on the outside, looking in. It is not accidental that the most vigorous denunciations of the existing distortions of the political process—gerrymandering, restrictive registration laws, filibusters, the seniority system—have come from Establishment Republicans, blacks and young people. These same groups are the most critical of our major bureaucracies, governmental, educational and military. All three favor a volunteer army. All three want experimentation in the schools. All three want increased local and community control of governmental programs.

A coalition of Republican Establishmentarians, blacks and young people would have less to lose and more to gain from shaking up, reorganizing and reforming the structure of government and public services than any other three groups one can think of. And the partners who seem most unlikely—the blacks and the big businessmen—have another interest in common, which should not be forgotten. They now share the big cities of America and have the largest stake in their being rescued; the blacks, because their homes are there; big business, because its investment is there.

Indeed, it is reasonable to suppose that if those groups ever came together in support of a *national* Republican administration, they would find they had almost automatically created a partnership that would give them control of many city halls as well. But, if there is anything that is obvious, it is that those three groups are not going to be brought together in support of the Nixon Administration. The President's record discourages support from the activist youths and blacks, and does not make it easy even for Establishment Republicans to be enthusiastic. So when we talk about a coalition that would include Republicans, blacks and young voters, we are talking about a different standard bearer from Nixon and a different strategy from that which he is following. But we also must acknowledge there is one fundamental factor that would make that coalition difficult to maintain, even if it could be established. Whereas Republicans, young people and blacks have a common interest in the redistribution of political power and the reform of government, they may have a serious conflict on the question of the cost of government and who should pay it.

In economic terms, both young people (students, soldiers, even young householders) and blacks represent claimant groups: they are likely to take out more in government services than they pay back in taxes. The affluent, educated, professional, business, managerial families who are Republicans, on the other hand, may well pay for more government services than they receive. If taxes go up and if the burden is shifted increasingly to the upper income brackets, as I believe should happen, they would be the ones who would feel the pinch most. We may say that they should recognize the equity of that scheme, and feel both a moral and civic obligation to make a contribution commensurate to their means. We might even argue that as their income, wealth and benefits from our society are greater, so is their stake in healing the infirmities of its social and governmental structure. All that may be true, but it is unlikely to make them happy about paying higher taxes.

If such a coalition occurred, it is safe to predict that it would soon develop conflict over the resistance of its more affluent members to the rising costs of government. But that reaction might—

perhaps—be turned to the advantage of our program, if it spurred a greater demand from the affluent, not for a cutback in government and public services, but for an improvement in their efficiency. The point is this: If the more comfortably fixed Americans paid their fair share of the costs of government (which, as we will see in a moment, they do not do now) they might be less complacent about the inefficiencies, the waste, the irrational structure of government. And, given their knowledge, their interest and their political influence, they could become a powerful force for governmental reform.

The second suggested coalition that seems most interesting is the "populist coalition." In many ways, it is a more plausible coalition, but I am not convinced that if it were in power it would prove to be dedicated to reforms of the kind I have argued are necessary.

The advocates of this coalition—notably Senator Fred R. Harris of Oklahoma—argue that a stress on economic and welfare issues can bring back millions of Southern white farmers and blue-collar workers who defected to Wallace or Nixon in 1972, and unite their votes with those of the blacks, Northern white working-class families and newly-enfranchised young people to form a powerful majority on class lines. Harris and those of like mind—including George McGovern and Edward M. Kennedy—talk of drastically reducing military spending, increasing welfare and social security benefits, providing insured health care for all, and forcing the polluting industries to clean up the environmental mess. All these are issues on which the have-nots of both races and the inflation-racked working class might well agree.

But the best issue, Harris says, is that fundamental question, neglected for almost two generations in American politics, of income distribution and tax burdens—the question of who gets and who pays in America. As he put it in a 1971 book, *Now Is the Time:*

> Much is being made these days about how blue-collar workers, or union laborers, and "Middle America" or "the Silent Majority" will not

support a public official or a political party that stands up for black people. Such an assessment fails to take full account of the fact that what is opposed most (sometimes unconsciously) by this group of Americans is having to pay a disproportionate share of the costs out of their own lives and income. Maldistribution of wealth and income in America, despite all our talk through the years, is still with us. Taxes, social welfare programs, and economic policy have made no real change in the rigid economic stratification which has been a durable characteristic of American life.

The documentation for Harris' conclusion is as ample as it is unpublicized. There are three sets of figures that are crucial, and they have been most clearly presented by Dr. Herman P. Miller, the chief of the population division of the Census Bureau, in his 1971 book, *Rich Man, Poor Man,* and a more recent paper updating some of its material.

The first set of figures shows the familiar story of American prosperity. It shows that, even discounting all the effects of inflation, there has been a big increase in the average family's income over the past two decades. Median income (in 1968 dollars) rose from $4,183 in 1947 to $7,434 in 1968. The share of families below the $3,000 "poverty line" was cut almost in half and the proportion in "affluence," over $10,000, rose from 9 percent in 1947 to 33 percent in 1968.

DISTRIBUTION OF FAMILIES AND UNRELATED INDIVIDUALS
BY MONEY INCOME (IN 1968 DOLLARS)

Total Money Income	1947	1957	1962	1968
Under $3,000	34%	28%	26%	19%
$3,000 to $5,999	37	28	24	21
$6,000 to $7,999	13	19	17	15
$8,000 to $9,999	7	12	12	13
$10,000 and over	9	13	21	33

Quite a different picture emerges, however, if you ask how this prosperity has been shared among American families. Has there been an improvement, not only in our level of income, but in the fairness with which it is divided among the American people? The answer is no. The share of the pie received by the rich, the middle class and the poor has not changed one bit since World War II. Despite all the social programs that liberals have congratulated themselves on passing, despite all the "handouts" that conservatives have condemned, the simple truth is that there has been no redistribution of income of any significance in the past twenty years. The poorest 20 percent of American families still scramble to divide 4 percent of the income pie, while the top 20 percent cut up almost half as their share. As the following table shows, these figures have barely budged in the past twenty years.

PERCENTAGE OF MONEY INCOME RECEIVED BY EACH FIFTH
OF FAMILIES AND INDIVIDUALS

Families and individuals ranked from lowest to highest	1947	1957	1962	1968
Lowest fifth	4%	4%	3%	4%
Second fifth	11	11	11	11
Middle fifth	17	18	17	17
Fourth fifth	24	25	25	25
Highest fifth	46	43	44	44

The picture revealed in that table will seem unbelievable to many people. We *know* we have vastly increased our welfare payments in the past twenty years to help families in poverty. We *know* we have boosted social security benefits to help the elderly, the disabled and the widowed. We *know* we have been putting billions into a war on poverty. All that is true. Why then hasn't income been redistributed so that the lowest 40 percent of our families get more than 15 percent of the pie—just as they did two decades ago? Part of the answer is that despite all the controversy and political battles over those benefits, or transfer payments, as the government economists call them, they have barely sufficed to let the poor hold their own in the scramble for the riches our economy produces. The second part of the answer is that, contrary to what we tend to think, those benefits—and the other costs of government—are being financed by taxes that hit the low-income and middle-income people as hard as they hit all but the very rich.

That statement will be rejected as absurd by anyone who thinks of taxes as the amount the Federal government withholds from his paycheck, and who has been taught that we have a "progressive income tax," that is, one where the rate increases as income rises. But Dr. Miller and a Census Bureau colleague, Roger A. Herriot, showed the reality in a carefully researched paper presented to a scholarly group in mid-1971. Instead of taxes falling lightly on the poor and with progressively more impact on each step up the income ladder, their analysis shows that combined federal-state-and-local levies are essentially the same for those from the poverty level all the way up to the $50,000 level; and go up significantly only for the super-rich.

Adjusted Money Income Levels	Percentage of Adjusted Total Income Paid in Taxes*		
	Total	Federal	State & Local
Under $2,000	25.6	11.5	14.0
$2,000–$4,000	24.7	13.4	11.2
$4,000–$6,000	27.9	17.1	10.9
$6,000–$8,000	30.1	19.4	10.7
$8,000–$10,000	29.9	19.6	10.3
$10,000–$15,000	30.9	20.6	10.3
$15,000–$25,000	31.1	21.4	9.7
$25,000–$50,000	33.6	25.6	8.0
Over $50,000	46.6	39.8	6.9

* Adjusted Total Income equals earnings, transfer payments, and various imputed incomes minus taxes to finance the transfer payments.

The inequities of our present tax system are so bad that there is reason to think that the candidate or the party that dramatizes the issue—with the vivid examples of tax evasion and tax avoidance that are available—might well trigger a strong reaction among the voters. After all, two-thirds of the families are below that $10,000 line, where the burden of taxes is heaviest. If they were convinced that the tax system could be changed in a way that would not only finance better schools and public services for them but would also give them relief from their property and payroll taxes—as it might well do—then there would obviously be a potential for putting together a sizable popular majority for that program.

If such a party came to power, some beneficial things would happen. The simple fact that the winning coalition would include a majority of both blacks and whites would be an important step toward repairing the most serious of our social splits. Second, a victory by the "populist" coalition should also tend to diminish the cynicism and alienation of the Middle Americans. An equitable, honest tax system, instead of the "soak-everyone-but-the-rich" system we have now, would, by itself, remove one of the most serious and legitimate sources of complaint of working-class families. And if the new President was someone sympathetic to and trusted by young voters (a mighty big "if," as the field looked in the autumn of 1971), there might even be a healing of that breach.

But I am not convinced a populist coalition would be much interested in reform and improvement of our governmental services. More likely, it would be what Samuel Beer, the Harvard professor of government, calls a "pork-barrel coalition." Particularly if the cost of government was shifted, through tax reform, onto the backs of the more affluent, I think it likely that a "populist" government would confine its program to "passing out the bacon."

Such a coalition might support vastly increased Federal aid for the cities, for schools and colleges, for farmers, for the needy and the sick. That is, after all, what the Great Society started out to do. But it is unlikely, I fear, to press very hard the question of how government, or the education industry, or the health delivery system, or the welfare system ought to be reformed, to be sure we get results for our investment. The reason is that too much of a populist Democratic government's support would come from individuals and groups with an enormous stake in the status quo. The bureaucracy is an important influence in a Democratic Administration. The unions, including the rapidly growing unions of public employees, have more of a voice when the Democrats are in power. In Congress, a Democratic victory means strengthening the veteran committee chairmen who are the most dogged opponents of congressional or executive reorganization. The bureaucracy, the unions, the congressional committee chairmen all lined up against the Nixon reform proposals—revenue sharing and reorganization of government. They would not hesitate to do the same thing even if a populist Democratic President endorsed these reforms, and they might well prevail again.

What to Do Until the Realignment Comes

In the preceding pages, I have argued that:

We are in the stage of the political cycle where party realignment is overdue.

But the issues and the leaders that might bring about such a realignment are not visible.

And if a realignment occurs in existing circumstances, it is unlikely that the dominant new party would be one committed to reform of government and adequate financing of public services.

The drift has gone on so long now that we must, if we are realistic, admit there is a possibility that our political system cannot generate the energy needed for a party realignment. Burnham suggests very strongly in his book that if the political parties "fall below a certain level of coherence and appeal" to the voters, they may lack the elasticity and vitality to rebound. In that case, it may not be possible to relieve the buildup of tension in our society through a party realignment. Party government is a tool that rusts when it is not used; we have gone a long time without using the political parties as they are meant to be used.

10

Mechanisms

Despite its neglect and disuse in recent years, the basic mechanism of party government has not been dismantled. It remains in place, protected by tradition, badly in need of reform and of more frequent exercise, but still intact. Whether one looks at the White House, Congress, state or local government, one can find the skeleton on which a responsible party system could be built—if the public demand for such a system should revive.

The presidency, which is the pinnacle of our government, and represents the most important single influence in our politics, is, despite the best precautions the Founding Fathers could devise, a partisan office.

The first step a man must take who seeks the White House is to win his party's nomination. He does not just declare his candidacy and set about securing a place for himself on the general election ballot of the fifty states. Although George Wallace demonstrated as recently as 1968 that it is possible to run for President in just that way, bypassing the party nomination process, the traditional and institutional forces of the two-party system have reserved the White House, so far, for men who submit themselves and their qualifications for judgment at their party convention before they face the voters in the general election. The inner dynamics of the convention system favor the nomination of candidates who are products of competitive, two-party states—men accustomed to operating as partisans in public office.

It is essential for the cause of responsible party government that the partisan character of the presidency be preserved. In later sections of this chapter, dealing with the election and convention rules, ways will be suggested to strengthen that guarantee. But it is no less important for the success of responsible party government that the functional capacity of the presidency be improved— that ways be found to help the President do his job. Several important steps have been taken in that regard in recent years.

For one thing, almost every recent President has increased the planning, budgeting and management capacity of the Executive Office, upgrading and expanding the staff available to the Chief Executive for the direction of government activities. There is still great need for reforming and rationalizing the structure of the entire Executive Branch, but the managerial improvements in the Office of the President are such that the incumbent can be—and is—fairly held responsible by the voters for the achievements and the failures of his entire Administration. Since accountability is the *sine qua non* of responsible party government, it is no small matter to have that condition increasingly well met in the presidency.

Secondly, the last two decades have seen a marked improvement in the congressional liaison capability of the White House. Regular, systematic contact between specially designated White House staff members and members of Congress began in the Eisenhower Administration. It was developed greatly in the Kennedy and Johnson administrations by Lawrence F. O'Brien, who served as head of congressional liaison for both Presidents, and it has continued, as extensively if not as skillfully, under President Nixon. Congressional liaison includes everything from the now-institutionalized weekly meetings of the President with his party's Senate and House leaders to the White House–coordinated lobbying for individual bills. It is an essential tool for moving a party program across the constitutional gap between the Capitol and the

White House. To the extent that it succeeds, the chances for responsible party government improve.

There are two further improvements in the Executive's relations to other parts of the government that I think would contribute to the health of our political system. We need to make executive-congressional liaison more of a two-way street. As more and more of Executive Branch decision making has been taken over by the White House staff from the Cabinet departments and agencies, Congress has complained that the men who shape national policy through their advice to the President are not available for questioning or consultation. For example, the Senate Foreign Relations Committee is frustrated by the unwillingness of the President's National Security Adviser to come before it, in open or executive session, to discuss foreign policy developments.

The demand presents genuine problems; a President does have a right to confidentiality in his dealings with his advisers, and that could be jeopardized if they were required to defend their views before a congressional panel. But the overriding reality is that there must be a single national policy in major areas—economics, international relations, defense—not separate congressional and presidential policies. If the leaders of Congress wanted to take a rigid, stiff-necked attitude and invoke the separation-of-powers doctrine, they might refuse to come down from Capitol Hill for consultations with the President and his advisers on the legislative program—which is, after all, their responsibility. Since they have shown some considerable flexibility in overcoming the constitutional barriers to unified policy formation, it would seem that equivalent flexibility might be shown by the President, in making his major advisers available for consultation with Congress, particularly on those matters that can only be implemented with the cooperation of Congress.

The second need is for improved and more formalized liaison between the presidential office and the heads of state and local government. The vertical integration of policy planning in the

Federal system is far less advanced than the horizontal liaison between the executive and legislative branches of the national government.

The last two Presidents have made their Vice Presidents their liaison men with governors and mayors. But that scheme has not worked very well, partly because the Vice Presidents have not had adequate staff to handle the job and partly because the Vice Presidents themselves are not really "insiders" in top-level White House policy making. The problem can be reduced somewhat through schemes for devolution of authority to states and cities, such as are embodied in Nixon's various revenue-sharing plans. But, whatever is done along that line, the national government is going to remain heavily involved in programs that overlap the responsibility of state and local government. There is a need to build the ideas, recommendations and experience of state and local officials into the basic legislative designs and management concepts that emanate from the Executive Office. One way of doing that would be to solicit governors and mayors for their proposals for the upcoming budget and legislative program, just as Cabinet departments are now asked to submit their ideas.

As a further bridge, it might be useful to institutionalize presidential appearances each year before the annual meetings of governors, of mayors and of county officials. These occasions—particularly if carried on television, as are the President's appearances before Congress—would dramatize for the country the reality of the shared responsibility of officials at the different levels of the Federal system. Any steps that strengthen the ability of the President to meet his national responsibilities, while maintaining the partisan character of the office, should be supported by advocates of responsible party government.

Congress and the Parties

Congress has certain traditions and institutions that strengthen it for a role in responsible party government. Partisanship is built into its basic structure, starting with the roll calls on the first day of each new Congress which elect the Speaker of the House and the President pro tempore of the Senate, on strict party-line votes.

The two parties have almost, but not quite, monopolized the right to nominate candidates for Congress. All 435 sitting members of the House of Representatives and all but two of the 100 senators were nominated by the Republican or Democratic party of their states. The major party caucuses do have a monopoly on committee assignments in Congress. While a Harry F. Byrd, Jr., may be elected to the Senate in Virginia as an Independent, or a James L. Buckley in New York as a Conservative, when they want to obtain their committee assignments one must join the Democratic caucus and the other gain admission to the Republican caucus.

Party lines and party loyalties play more of a role in the decision making of Congress than we sometimes imagine. Over the last decade—a time of decaying party loyalties in the public—40 percent of all the congressional roll calls produced partisan splits, with the majority of Democrats on one side and the majority of Republicans on the other. Many of the key issues of the decade were decided on such partisan tests. The 1961 housing law, the 1962 trade expansion act, the 1964 poverty act, the 1964 mass transit bill, medicare in 1965, the model cities program in 1966, the Supreme Court nominations of Abe Fortas, Clement Haynsworth and G. Harrold Carswell, and the supersonic airplane issue were all settled by party-line votes.

The main roadblocks to party responsibility in Congress are those rules and procedures that put power in the hands of a few individuals who are themselves not held accountable to the parties they represent. The seniority system has given this kind of autocratic power to some committee chairmen. The Senate filibuster rule also enables a minority to put roadblocks in the way of a party majority. In the last two decades, some progress has been made in removing these roadblocks, but there is still a considerable distance to go. Reformers interested in responsible party government have long recognized the party caucuses and the party leadership committees as important mechanisms that need strengthening in Congress. The Republicans have taken significant steps in this area. Senate Republicans now caucus weekly to discuss upcoming legislation, and House Republicans meet about once a month for that purpose. The Republican caucuses (or conferences, as they prefer to call them) and their elected policy committees—smaller groups that advise the floor leadership on policy and tactics—have been given good professional staffs. These groups have played an important part in strengthening the Republicans' generally high degree of party unity on legislative questions in the past decade.

Under Mike Mansfield, the Senate Democratic leader since 1961, the Senate Democratic Policy Committee has become a more representative and influential leadership group and some increased use has been made of the full Democratic caucus. But a functional policy committee and regular caucus meetings are still conspicuous by their absence among House Democrats. As a sort of proxy, the Northern and Western Democratic representatives, most of them programmatic liberals, have formed an informal caucus of their own called the Democratic Study Group. Its small professional staff helps brief its members on issues coming to the floor and runs a "whip" system to alert members to approaching votes.

The most encouraging development in the fight for party responsibility in Congress was the passage in 1970 of a legislative reorganization act, which was demanded by younger members of both parties, particularly in the House, who had been badly frustrated by impediments to effective policy making in Congress. The new bill did not change the seniority system or attack the problem of committee jurisdictions, but it opened congressional voting, both on the floor of the House and in committee sessions, to greater public scrutiny. It improved the staffing and research capabilities of Congress and spread the important committee and subcommittee chairmanships among more members by limiting each senator and representative, regardless of seniority, to a single chairmanship.

As small but significant steps toward party responsibility, the measure provided that the majority of a committee's members can call a meeting if its chairman does not schedule one on request, and it allowed the Speaker of the House to recognize a member of a committee, authorized by the majority of his committee colleagues, to call up a bill for debate if the chairman of the committee does not do so within seven days after a rule has been granted for its consideration.

Both these provisions were designed to deal with the problem of a committee chairman who obtains his post through seniority and who feels no responsibility to advance the program of the party he ostensibly represents. More direct action to make the committee chairmen responsible to their party was taken by the House Democratic and Republican caucuses at the beginning of 1971. With some variations in procedure, each party changed its rules to allow a separate vote, by the entire party membership, on each man recommended for the chairmanship or ranking minority position on each committee. In 1971, the new procedure did not alter the practice of putting the most senior men into those jobs, but a procedure has been established that makes that outcome a bit less automatic than it was previously. The new procedure should serve to remind the committee chairmen that they can be held accountable by their party for the way they meet their legislative responsibilities.

There is room for much more such reform in Congress. Neither party in the Senate has yet addressed itself to the problems of the seniority system. The House procedures are still heavily weighted in favor of seniority. The House has not yet given the majority-party leadership easy, guaranteed methods to bring important legislation to a floor vote, whatever the reluctance of the particular committee chairman or the Rules Committee. The Senate is still laboring under a filibuster rule that permits one-third of its members to block a vote.

Perhaps the most compelling need in both bodies is to rationalize the committee structure on functional lines, so as to pinpoint responsibility for action—or inaction—in major fields of legislation. The 1970 legislative reorganization bill required the House Appropriations Committee to spend the first thirty days of each year considering the budget as a whole. It also required legislative committees to provide cost estimates for the first five years on any new programs they recommended. But these are just the first steps toward comprehensive, rational program planning and budgeting by Congress. Much more needs to be done to give Congress the information and the procedures it needs to legislate sensibly on national problems.

The Loyal Opposition

For responsible party government to operate, there must not only be a significant degree of cooperation and cohesion between the President and his party in Congress, but effective machinery for policy making by the opposition party. The whole concept of responsible party government depends on the voters' being given discernible alternative programs by the two parties. But the task of extracting a responsible alternative from the opposition party is rendered very difficult by the lack of a single spokesman for the opposition. While the defeated presidential candidate is the "titular leader" of his party, he is most often a political exile, with many challengers for the role of opposition spokesman. What happens usually is that the power to speak for the opposition splits: much of it goes to the opposition party leaders in Congress (particularly if the losing party in the presidential race keeps control of Congress, as has happened so often in recent years). The party's governors, the national chairman, its elder statesmen (former Cabinet members, presidential candidates, Presidents, etc.), and its upcoming presidential aspirants all add their own comments. What the public often hears is a welter of voices, not a single, coherent opposition program.

To some extent, this confusion is inevitable. There is no way in our scheme of government to "impose discipline" on all those who claim to speak for the opposition; even a President, with all the power of his office, cannot impose rigid uniformity of view on his party; no one in the opposition has any authority to "lay down the line" to anyone else. Happily, however, the last sixteen years have seen the development of a very useful institution for debating and framing opposition-party policy: the party policy council. Starting with the Democratic Advisory Council under national chairman Paul Butler in 1957, continuing with the Republican Coordinating Committee under national chairman Ray C. Bliss in the 1960s, and now with O'Brien's Democratic Policy Council, the opposition party has institutionalized a device for speaking *as a party* on questions of current policy.

The policy councils have come to be increasingly representative of the opposition's scattered leadership elements. Butler's Democratic Advisory Council included the party's elder statesmen and many of its leading governors and state political leaders, but it was boycotted and fiercely resisted by Lyndon Johnson, Sam Rayburn and the rest of the Democratic congressional leadership. Eight years later, when the Republicans formed a similar group, the GOP congressional leadership joined from the beginning and participated actively in its work. Since 1969, O'Brien has been able to persuade those of his party's congressional leaders who are reluctant to join in the formal meetings of the policy council to take part in informal discussions with the Democratic governors, mayors and state political leaders. Indeed, one of the remarkable developments of the last two years has been the willingness of Representative Wilbur Mills of Arkansas, who as chairman of the House Ways and Means Committee is the living symbol of the independent congressional baron, to involve himself deeply in national Democratic party affairs, and to sit down for spirited bargaining with state and local Democratic officials on programs that affect their jurisdictions.

As the party policy councils have become more inclusive and

representative of the varied and widely-dispersed centers of power in the opposition, their pronouncements have been given increasing weight. The Democratic platform of 1960 and the Republican platform of 1968 were largely codifications of the positions adopted in the preceding years by the party policy councils; the same thing is likely to be true of the 1972 Democratic platform. The policy council statements are now treated with considerable seriousness by the news media. Editors regard them as legitimate expressions of the Democratic or Republican position on a current issue. Not infrequently, the *New York Times* has printed the full text or substantial excerpts from these statements, according them a weight equivalent to that of a news conference or major address by the President. As a consequence, both parties have found they are able to enlist considerable expert help from their "brain trusts" in developing these policy statements.

Because the policy councils have had a certain success in providing a "voice for the opposition" between national conventions, the old and recurring suggestion for a midterm convention of the opposition party has never been implemented. The midterm convention has been thought of as a useful device for physically assembling the scattered elements of opposition leadership and forcing the party to frame its alternative to the presidential party in some coherent fashion. Such a convention would certainly draw more public attention (particularly through television) than the policy councils have done, and it would be interesting to see whether it could function as a plenary policy-making body. But large assemblages of delegates, meeting for only a few days, are hardly ideal forums for policy making. To the extent the smaller policy councils fill that function, the interim convention idea may be put in abeyance.

There are other needs of the political parties—particularly in the areas of fund raising and technological expertise, which we will discuss later—which are most acutely felt by the opposition. But my impression is that, considering the terrible inherent problems an opposition party in the United States faces in framing and publicizing its alternative program, the record of our opposition parties in recent years has been encouraging. There remain such serious gaps, however, exemplified by the Republicans' failure as a party to develop a coherent position on the Vietnam war during the 1965–68 period, that no one should think there is not great room for improvement.

State and Local Party Government

The condition of the political parties at the state and local level is so varied as to defy safe generalization. For the most part, however, they are plagued by inadequate finances and the lack of a trained, stable cadre of personnel to man the headquarters and provide essential services for the party's officeholders and candidates. The turnover rate in state and local chairmen is appalling; the tenure of the typical state chairman is barely more than a year. Someone has said that the political parties may well be the worst-managed large enterprises in America.

That these infirmities are not inherent in our federalized governmental and political system is indicated by the fact that at certain times and in certain places party organizations flourish and perform their essential functions very well. At various times in recent years, for example, the Republican party in Ohio, Minnesota, Tennessee, California, New York, Washington and parts of Texas has done extraordinarily well at recruiting able candidates for all levels of the ballot, raising the funds for their campaigns, providing research and campaign assistance and working with them in office. There have been similar efforts, at different times, by Democratic parties in Maine and Michigan and Utah and Colorado and Minnesota and South Dakota. Locally, both parties have had effective organizations scattered around the country. In almost every instance, the success is traceable to a governor or mayor or county executive who is party-minded and who finds a collaborator as party chairman who shares his view that good government and strong parties go hand in hand.

Aside from the fatuous suggestion that we need more such men in public and party office, what one can say is that there is a definite relationship between the strength of the public office and the strength of the party organization. Weak governors and weak mayors are not going to spur strong party organizations. Strong governors and strong mayors may or may not see the value of strengthening the party system, but at least that option is open to them. It is almost impossible to imagine a strong, responsible party system emerging in Texas until the authority of the Governor's office is made commensurate to his nominal duties as head of the government; the same thing is true in Los Angeles, with the weak mayoral system there.

Thus, reforms that would strengthen state and local government would also be steps toward responsible party government. Even to begin to talk realistically about responsible party government in the metropolitan areas, we would have to reduce drastically the 20,745 separate governments and 134,000 elected officials counted in their most recent census. Broadening jurisdictions geographically would almost automatically increase the competitiveness of politics and reduce the "rotten borough" system of one-party control. Pinpointing responsibility in far fewer elected officials would give the voters a reason, now frequently lacking, for caring who won the election.

Similarly, at the state level, if the number of elective officials was reduced—as has been done most ruthlessly in New Jersey, where the Governor is the only elective officer in the executive branch—party responsibility for what happens in the state capital would be enhanced. Reduction in the swollen size of some legislatures, and improvement in salaries, staffing and facilities for the remaining members, would give them a visibility—and hence a responsibility—to their constituents which they do not now enjoy.

While some reforms have been accomplished in some states in recent years, the bulk of this task still is ahead of us. Its accomplishment could do more to invigorate the party system at the grass-roots level than anything else we might do.

The Election System and Party Government

The most encouraging development for the cause of responsible party government in recent years has been the spread of two-party competition to virtually all fifty states. Hawaii, which became a state in 1959, is now the only one that has supported the same party's (Democratic) presidential candidates in every election since joining the Union. Competition for state office has reached the point where Democrats have been elected as governor or senator in all the states of formerly rock-ribbed-Republican New England; and Republicans have managed to capture state office everywhere in the Solid South except Georgia, Alabama, Mississippi and Louisiana.

The election system is not only more competitive now than it has ever been, it is also more open to participation on an equal basis. The worst legal barriers to voting by minority races have been removed, and the process of enrollment of blacks, Chicanos and other minority groups is proceeding steadily. The minimum voting age has been lowered to eighteen, an overdue recognition of the improvements in education and civic awareness among young people. Residency requirements for voting in Federal elections have been reduced by Federal statute, and the welter of confusing and restrictive state and local regulations on registration and voting—which make ours one of the lowest-turnout popular democracies in the world—are under increasing attack in the legislatures and the courts.

The historic Supreme Court decision on one-man-one-vote in 1962 has ended the malapportionment of legislative and congressional districts that had been a major barrier to responsible government. Political gerrymandering—the drawing of district lines to reduce party competition or bias the outcome in favor of one party—remains a serious problem, however, and indeed may even have been facilitated by some court decisions stressing mathematical equality of population as the sole criterion for deciding the equity of an apportionment plan. We do not know whether the courts will go further into the political thicket to root out gerrymandering, but if they do not, pressure will have to be kept on the legislatures and Congress to tackle the problem themselves.

The reforms that have occurred have all been essentially designed to open up the electoral system and equalize the rules of the game. They were not aimed at facilitating responsible party government as such.

Some reformers have suggested we could strengthen party government by arranging ballots or voting machines so as to facilitate straight-ticket voting for President and Congress or governor and legislature. But recent studies on ticket splitting show the voters are fully capable of outwitting any mechanical scheme for inducing a straight-ticket vote. One favorite suggestion of reformers has been to extend the terms of members of the House of Representatives from two years to four years and to elect the whole House simultaneously with the President. The purpose, obviously, is to heighten the likelihood that the President's party will control Congress throughout his term.

Lyndon Johnson once recommended the four-year term, but the political impracticality of the suggestion doomed it to defeat. So long as one-third of the Senate is elected every two years, its members will oppose any change in House terms that would allow Representatives a "free ride" in challenging for a Senate seat. Moreover, many House members themselves favor the two-year term that keeps them close to their constituents and allows the public to register its political mood at frequent intervals.

The change in our Constitution that does recommend itself as fostering responsible party government is reform of the electoral college system. At a minimum, we ought to assure that the electoral votes go automatically to the winner of each state's popular votes. In 1968, a "faithless elector" in North Carolina cast his vote for George Wallace, even though the state had been carried by Richard Nixon. We can eliminate that kind of irresponsibility simply by eliminating the electors—men and women who are unknown to most voters, anyway—and providing that the winner of the popular vote in each state will receive its electoral votes. The minimum reform also should provide a better method of settling a presidential contest if no candidate wins a majority of the electoral votes. The present provisions for contingent election—in which each state delegation to the House of Representatives, regardless of size, would cast a single ballot for one of the top three candidates—is a total negation of the one-man-one-vote principle. If we ever had to use that system, the public outcry and protest would be deafening. It would be better to provide a runoff between the top two candidates or let Congress elect the new President—but with each senator and representative casting his own vote.

But I really believe it is time to get rid of the whole archaic electoral-vote system, to recognize that the presidency is a national office and to choose its occupant by direct, popular vote of all the people of the United States. A proposed constitutional amendment for direct election of the President passed the House in 1969, with overwhelming, bipartisan support, but was filibustered to death in the Senate in 1970.

Some scholars and politicians argue that direct election of the President would damage the prospects of responsible party government by encouraging a proliferation of small, ideological parties. I do not share that fear. On the contrary, I think direct election would strengthen the two-party system by encouraging each party to organize for bringing out every possible vote in every state—even those where it knows it cannot win a majority.

But, if the danger of a multiple-party system seems great, there are ways of reducing it. The proposed amendment passed by the House required only a 40 percent popular-vote plurality for election. It also specified that, if a runoff was necessary, only the top two candidates (presumably those nominated by the major parties) would be in it. That provision would have given minor parties less leverage than they now have under the electoral college system, where the winning candidate must receive more than 50 percent of the electoral votes, and there is no provision for a runoff. It was this system that gave George Wallace hope of controlling enough electoral votes in 1968 to force either Richard Nixon or Hubert Humphrey to make a deal with him in order to gain election. And his scheme very nearly succeeded.

But if there is still fear that under a direct election system minor parties would be formed solely for the purpose of achieving a bargaining position between the major-party candidates in the runoff, there is a simple expedient available. We can elect our President just as we elect virtually every other official in national, state and local government—on the basis that high man wins. I would be quite willing to support a constitutional amendment providing that the President of the United States shall be the person, meeting constitutional requirements for the office, who receives the greatest number of votes from his fellow citizens on the appointed day. The high-man-wins rule is the bulwark of the two-party system. It is that rule that forces accommodation and coalition building. And I have no doubt it would work to strengthen the two-party system nationally if it was used to elect the President.

The Nominating Conventions
and Responsible Party Government

Of all our political institutions, none is more vital to the possibility of responsible party government than the presidential nominating convention. The convention is the one time every four years when a national political party really comes to life as a physical assemblage of its leaders and its rank-and-file delegates. The rest of the time, our national parties are more ghostlike than visible. As Stephen K. Bailey once said, "The closer one gets to our two great national political parties, the more difficult it is to find them." The national committees keep the parties functioning between conventions; occasional fund-raising dinners may bring together the party luminaries. But if it were not for the conventions every four years, which nominate the presidential candidates and write the party platforms, the parties might really disappear.

For that reason alone, I am opposed to the recurrent suggestion that we nominate the presidential candidates through a pair of nationwide primaries. Such primaries would require terribly expensive, prolonged and intensive campaigns, in which personality factors and the battle for name recognition would necessarily be uppermost. Our current system of holding presidential primaries in individual states, which may guide or bind the votes of the convention delegates from those states, is a useful device for providing public participation in the nomination process and for testing the campaign abilities of the presidential hopefuls. The primary results, the public opinion polls and the judgments and commitments of individual delegates form a web of influences at convention time which shape the ultimate choice of the nominee. But to remove that choice from the convention and make it through the arbitrary mechanism of a national presidential primary would be a terrible mistake.

The convention system not only avoids the dangers of the national primary, it contributes positively to the prospects of responsible party government by putting the choice of the presidential candidates into the hands of people who understand what responsible party government means—people who are active in a political party, who understand the differences in policies between the parties, and who see the political party as an integral part of the process of government.

This point has been well-documented by University of California political scientist Herbert McCloskey, who assembled a mass of data on the backgrounds and attitudes of convention delegates. Commenting on the generally high quality of the nominees chosen through the convention process, McCloskey wrote:

> The delegates' ability to recognize and nominate superior candidates is not fortuitous. Through comparative research on the characteristics of

party leaders and voters, we have learned that convention delegates are much better prepared than ordinary voters to assess the attributes of candidates. They are more interested, aware and concerned about political outcomes. Ideologically, they are far more sophisticated and mature than the average voter. Despite their differences, the delegates to the two conventions constitute, to a far greater extent than their rank-and-file supporters, communities of co-believers. Not only does each of the party delegations tend to converge around identifiable belief systems, but they also tend to diverge from each other along liberal-conservative lines. Their respective followers, however, tend to look alike.

Thus, it is not the delegates of the two parties, but the mass of their supporters who can more appropriately be described as Tweedledum and Tweedledee. Whereas the delegates are prone to search out and select candidates who embody the party's values, the mass of Democratic and Republican voters, participating in a national presidential primary, would be likely to select candidates who are ideological twins. Nominations by primary, in short, might well afford the electorate less of a choice than nomination by convention.

What McCloskey is arguing, in other words, is that the convention system is one of the forces that puts some content into what would otherwise be an issueless void in our politics. The conventions put content into the nomination process, because those who attend the conventions are well above average in their education, political activism and political concern. Now, there is a danger that, as activists, their views may be so far from the center of the political spectrum that the candidate who best represents them may not be a candidate who has much chance of winning in the general election. This is what happened to the Republicans with Barry Goldwater in 1964. Goldwater commanded the support of the majority of the Republican activists who were delegates in San Francisco; but they represented only a minority viewpoint within the minority party of the country, and the nation rejected their choice. Usually, however, delegates have subordinated their ideological preferences and nominated the candidate they thought had the best chance to win.

At the 1968 Democratic Convention in Chicago, there were

protests that the delegates who made the choice of Hubert Humphrey were unrepresentative in another way. The major complaint was not that they were ideologically out of tune with the country (although that allegation was made) but that many of them had been chosen through unfair procedures. Some states chose delegates through party committees or caucuses that operated essentially as closed corporations; in many states, rules and procedures for electing delegates were nonexistent, vague or arbitrary; in many others, the process began (and in some was completed) before most Democrats were even aware of the names of the contenders.

Challenges to the credentials of the Democratic delegates chosen through these undemocratic processes, along with the incidents of violence that surrounded and disrupted the convention, threatened to discredit the Democratic Convention. Fortunately, however, it produced a major effort to reform the convention procedures, sparked first by Senator Harold E. Hughes of Iowa and later carried on by Senator George McGovern of South Dakota, Representative James G. O'Hara of Michigan and Representative Donald Fraser of Minnesota. As a result of the reform effort, the Democrats have adopted procedures for delegate selection at the 1972 convention that "open up" the process to much more public participation. The apportionment of delegate strength among the states and within each state has been made more equitable; rules have been recommended that should, if enforced, protect the rights of minority factions, and assure the inclusion of many more women, young people, minority group representatives and others who were seriously underrepresented at past conventions. Because these rules and procedures are made binding on the state and local parties—on penalty of losing their credentials at the national convention—they are an important step toward nationalizing the party structure—a goal that reformers interested in responsible party government have long sought. It remains to be seen, of course, how vigorously those procedural standards will be enforced; if they are enforced, there will almost certainly be more opportunity for public participation in the selection of convention delegates than we have ever known.

But, even if the national Democratic party succeeds in imposing standards of procedural fair play on the state and local affiliates, it cannot impose ideological conformity on them. Georgia Democrats will continue to look and talk a bit different from Hawaii Democrats; that is inevitable in a nation with our geographical, ethnic and ideological diversity.

One of the reforms the Democrats have adopted, however, could help close the breach between what James MacGregor Burns calls "the congressional party and the presidential party." One of the new rules requires that at least three-fourths of the delegates be selected at the level of the congressional district. In about twenty states, the district delegates will be chosen by primary elections, but in the others they will be elected by local caucuses and conventions of the party adherents. Given the concentration of our population, most Democrats will find the caucus of their party within easy range of their homes. There is a real chance, I believe, that 1972 will see the kind of political party mass meetings, at the local level, which all advocates of responsible party government have sought to establish as the base for the whole party system.

But something further may develop. It is the particular genius of this plan that it brings the party rank-and-file members together as constituents of a congressional district, which also sends a member to the House of Representatives. My guess, and my hope, is that if the congressional district mass-membership caucus is institutionalized for the election of national convention delegates, it will also become the device for selecting the congressional candidate of the Democratic party and for mandating his program. In most states, the choice would, of course, have to be ratified in the congressional primary. But, if you get two thousand Democrats meeting in a congressional district to pick delegates to the national convention, they will quickly discover their own power, and use their caucus for other purposes as well. A caucus endorsement for Congress could become decisive for winning the party's nomination in the primary; and the direct link, at the constituency level, between a presidential choice and a congressional choice could have enormous integrative effects on our whole national government.

The Democratic convention reforms, then, offer great potential for invigorating the party system; if they succeed for the Democrats, there is little doubt the Republicans will be forced to adopt similar reforms, if only to maintain their competitive position.

But there is a point about these reforms that is not often noted. While they "democratize" the convention procedure and "open it up" to easier public participation, they also tend to dilute the influence of the cadre party—the political activists who in the past have comprised the bulk of the delegates and who, as McCloskey has noted, provide much of the limited content and ideology that get into our somewhat diffuse and vague political system.

Is there any way of enjoying both the democracy the convention reforms seek and the content and cohesion the old-style convention gave? Is there a way to have the advantages of both mass participation and elitism? I think there is—if the two main functions of the convention are separated. Traditionally, the convention adopts a platform one night and nominates its presidential candidate the next. Logically, it seems to me, that is backward. As long as the platform precedes the nomination, it is bound to be subordinated to nomination politics. Delegates, if they pay attention to the platform at all, will vote for planks they think will help the candidate they are trying to nominate. If we want to get more content into our politics—which must be the goal of those interested in responsible party government—the delegates should nominate the presidential and vice presidential candidates first and then thrash out, with the nominees, the program on which the party will run.

My suggestion would be not simply that the agenda be reversed but that two separate conventions be held to perform the two functions. The second might follow directly on the first, or it might be held at the end of the summer of the presidential election year, while the first was held at the beginning. In any case, the first would be a nominating convention and the second a platform convention, and the makeup of the delegations would differ for the two functions.

For the first, it would be hoped that the kind of reforms the Democrats have adopted would be fully effective, and the delegations contain an accurate cross-section of the party rank-and-file.

For the second convention, the platform convention, I would deliberately "stack" the delegations, by filling them with the men and women who would share with the presidential ticket the responsibility of carrying out the party program. Credentials to the second convention could be issued, by some equitable system, to half the delegates from each state at the first convention. They would represent the grass-roots sentiment of their states. The other half of the seats would be given to the sitting senators, representatives, governors, mayors and state legislative leaders, and to the nominees for those offices in the coming election. They would be given direct responsibility for helping frame the party program, in the belief that what they helped compose they would feel an obligation to support. In this way, I believe, it might be possible to use the national convention as effectively for mandating a party program as it is already being used to nominate party candidates.

Campaign Financing and Responsible Parties

The power of the purse has been the most undisciplined, uncontrolled and essentially irresponsible force in our politics. Our method of financing campaigns has done more to demean the practitioners of politics and to discredit the political system in the eyes of the public than anything else. Unless the reform effort that began in Congress in 1971 is completed, it is hard to see how the political system can be saved from its corrupting effects.

Advocates of responsible party government have urged—so far without success—that financing of campaigns be done through the central party organization (for each level of office, be it national, state or local) either from tax funds or from private contributions, preferably from a large number of small givers, rather than a few major sources.

This has not been achieved. On the contrary, the rising cost of campaigns has fostered the most vicious competition for campaign dollars, with each candidate putting together his own war chest, either from personal sources or from men and groups using their pocketbooks to gain political influence. The upward climb in the cost of campaigning has been accelerated by the new reliance on television and technology. Herbert E. Alexander of the Citizens' Research Foundation, who does the most systematic study of this area, estimates that total campaign expenditures, which inched up slowly from $140 million in 1952 to $200 million in 1964, leaped 50 percent in 1968 to $300 million.

As costs have risen, candidates have been forced to turn increasingly to rich men and affluent interest groups for their funds. A Gallup Poll showed that only 8 percent of adult Americans made a political contribution in 1968. At the other extreme of the spectrum, Alexander reported that "at least one half, and perhaps more, of [Hubert H.] Humphrey's general election campaign expenses were paid for through contributions and loans from about 50 individuals." Outside organizations have become perhaps more important than the political parties as financial sources for the candidates. Labor unions, particularly, fill the financial gap for Democratic candidates, while business, industrial and professional organizations swell Republicans' coffers.

Congress, whose members are buffeted by the pressures from the big contributors, has attempted to grapple with the problem. A measure to provide for public subsidy of presidential campaign costs by a $1-per-person Federal income tax checkoff was passed in the 1960s, repealed before it could go into effect, then re-passed in 1971, with a proviso that it could not take effect before the 1976 election. Another measure, limiting spending on radio and television advertising, was passed in 1970 but vetoed by President

Nixon. A broader measure, limiting media expenditures for all Federal campaigns, offering tax incentives for small contributions and significantly strengthening the disclosure requirements for contributors and candidates, passed the Senate and House in 1971 and was awaiting only final action to become law when Congress returned in January 1972.

However, none of these measures except the first really approached the goal of responsible party government—channeling virtually all funds for general election campaigns, from the Treasury or from many small givers, through the party organization, rather than continuing the irresponsible practice of forcing each candidate to forage for himself among the big givers. Leashing the undisciplined power of money in politics remains a high-priority element in any program for reviving responsible party government.

The "New Politics" and Party Responsibility

A second and growing danger to the prospects for responsible party government is the technological revolution that has affected campaigning in the past decade. With the regular use of sophisticated public opinion polling, computer simulations of the electorate, automated and highly selective direct mail techniques, exploitation of the communications potential of telephone service, and, of course, the controlled use of mass media, particularly television, the makeup and organization of campaign staffs is changing. The directors of the 20th Century Fund study of American political parties, John S. Saloma III and Frederick H. Sontag, describe this as a move toward "technocratic parties."

For our purposes, what is significant is that the "technocratic" tendencies often work against the direction of responsible party government. It is true that party headquarters are being professionalized. Indeed, in 1970, the Republicans opened the first permanent headquarters building either party has ever owned in Washington, D.C. That step, long recommended by reformers interested in responsible party government, seemed to symbolize the coming of age of the political party. But Saloma and Sontag argued in a paper presented to the American Political Science Association convention in 1970 that what has occurred is a professionalization of technical experts, rather than political leaders.

Instead of treating elections as periodic tests of party programs before the public (the objective of responsible party reformers), the parties have further narrowed electoral politics to a contest of political skill and technique between teams of "non-ideological" professionals. Politics is reduced to a problem-solving strategy of winning elections. The mobilization and rational allocation of resources is the primary objective of the "political managers." Government is treated as a separate and incidental activity distinct from the politics of elections.

Often, those political managers are not even party officials or staff members but independent political consultants, doing their work for a fee. The business of campaign management has flourished in the past decade; frequently, the first step an aspiring candidate will take is to hire a pollster, an ad agency, and a campaign manager, or sign a contract with one of the many firms offering to package a whole campaign for him. While some of the managers specialize in candidates of one party or the other, essentially, as James M. Perry said in his book *The New Politics,* "they are mercenaries; they are willing to go almost anywhere for a buck." Conservative or liberal, high tax or low, the campaign managers must treat their client-candidates essentially as commodities to be merchandised to the voters. There are exceptions, of course, but the professional campaign managers tend to be as antiparty as they are nonideological. They talk with scorn (often well merited) of the bumbling incompetence of the old-fashioned "political pros," who rely on their intuitions or their experience to guide campaign decisions. They have an overdeveloped sense of their own power and prowess. I remember the man from the New York agency that handled Lyndon Johnson's 1964 television campaign saying smugly over lunch, "The only thing that worries me is that some year an outfit as good as ours might go to work for the *wrong* candidate."

The "hired guns" have scored their biggest successes over the old-line party organizations in primary elections, where the ability to "sell a candidate," to establish his name identification with a small and largely indifferent electorate, makes their commercial approach to politics pay off. In general elections, where issues and party loyalties play more of a part, and where the resources of competing candidates tend to be more equal, their success has been more limited.

But, of course, from the viewpoint of responsible party government, it is the nomination process that is particularly important. One of the major determinants of the degree of responsibility in a party system is the extent to which the party controls the nomination of the candidates who run under its name. In the last five years, all the major states—California, New York, Illinois, Pennsylvania, Ohio, Florida—have seen wealthy or well-financed men, with little background in party activity, little support among the party cadre, and little allegiance to the party or its programs, come in and beat the formally or informally designated organization favorite with expensive campaigns managed by outside political consultants.

To the extent that the technocratic "new politics" means the separation of governmental problems from the content of the campaign and the separation of campaign management from the jurisdiction of the political party, it represents a twin threat to responsible party government. Obviously, many decent, able and well-motivated candidates are using the "new politics" techniques to gain public office. But, if the goal is responsible party government, then these techniques, and the way they are being employed, must be a cause of concern.

Television and Responsible Party Government

Television has probably changed American politics more than any other single factor in the past two decades. It is a magnificent tool of communication, and with the mass audience it can deliver, it has become the focus of every candidate's strategy. The key events of recent campaigns have almost invariably been the televised events: Nixon's 1952 "Checkers speech," which saved him from being dumped from the Republican ticket; the Kennedy-Nixon debates in the 1960 campaign, which many consider instrumental in Kennedy's victory; Goldwater's disastrous 1964 acceptance speech and Nixon's triumphant performance, on the same occasion, at the 1968 convention; Humphrey's "stop-the-bombing" speech from Salt Lake City, which almost turned the last election around; Muskie's election-eve broadcast in 1970, which, more than any other single event, established him as the front-runner for the 1972 Democratic nomination.

From the perspective of responsible party government, television has not been an unmixed blessing, however. The "tube" has changed the political process in several ways that make it more difficult for the parties to fulfill their functions. Indeed, in one respect, television has seemed to make one of the party's old functions irrelevant—that of serving as a bridge between the candidate or officeholder and the public. The parties developed, in part, to fill in the gap between the citizen in his home and the official in his office, and to provide the audiences for the campaigning aspirants. Now, through television, the candidates and the officials can come directly into the home. True, there has been communication by other channels previously: through newsletters, newspapers and radio. But television adds the missing dimension: a visible presence, available to all, simultaneously.

The politicians, elected and aspiring, have been quick to exploit the medium. Presidential press conferences have been carried live on television for fifteen years; each of the last four Presidents has used the medium more extensively for speeches than his predecessor. Senators, governors, congressmen, mayors all do their TV "reports to the people." Political expenditures for purchased television time increased sevenfold between 1952 and 1968—one of the major reasons for the inflation in campaign costs.

Television not only bypasses the party as the middleman in political communication, it tends to de-emphasize the party as part of the political process. Above all, TV is a personal medium. In practice, that has meant it is the President's medium. He alone, of all the actors in the political drama, can command the cameras' attention whenever he wants it. While Federal regulations require "fairness" and balance in the presentation of contrasting views on television, the Federal Communications Commission (as of September, 1971) had refused to recognize a "right of reply" for the opposition party and its spokesmen to the President's appearances on television. Until 1971, the FCC and the courts had even refused to recognize that the political parties had a "right of access" to television, upholding stations' refusal to give or sell air time to the parties for comments on current questions or fund-raising appeals. In August, 1971, however, the U.S. Court of Appeals for the District of Columbia ruled, 2-1, that broadcasters could not refuse all such requests simply on the grounds that they might have to extend equal time to representatives of other viewpoints. Subsequent to that decision, however, the FCC again denied requests from both parties for equal-time appearances on the air, and the issue was returned to the courts.

Whatever the outcome of the legal battle, the likelihood is that the only opportunities the parties as such will have for sustained television coverage will be at the times of their quadrennial nominating conventions. The networks focus in hard on the conventions, with two of the three networks in 1968 giving gavel-to-gavel coverage. But the effect of that massive attention has not been to the parties' advantage. Robert MacNeil, the former NBC newsman, said in his book *The People Machine* that "since 1952, the television industry has engulfed the national conventions, not only covering them and interpreting them to the rest of the country but (with the active cooperation of the parties) reshaping them, molding them into happenings more appropriate to television."

Conventions are critically important institutions for responsible party government; the decisions the delegates make in the four days they are assembled can determine not only the identity of the next President but the direction of national policy for the next four years. The conventions are hardly a waste of time; but, like any large proceedings, involving thousands of confused and inconclusive private discussions and negotiations for every climactic public roll call or decision, they are not continuously interesting to the spectators.

But, from the time television moved into the convention halls in 1952, the pressure has been felt to reshape the proceedings in the interests of entertaining the television audience. Even the prime business of the convention, the nomination of the presidential candidate, has been affected. William Small, the head of CBS's Washington news bureau, in his book *To Kill a Messenger,* quotes Leonard W. Hall, the Republican National Chairman during the Eisenhower years, as saying that the presence of the cameras guarantees "you will never see the time come again when you have 30 ballots to select a candidate. You just can't bore a nationwide television audience that much." Hall was understating the case. Since 1952, no convention has gone more than *one* ballot to pick the presidential nominee.

Even with one-ballot conventions, the networks have been hard put to fill the air time and hold the audience simply by reporting the activities on the podium and in the various caucuses. So the TV reporters have roamed the convention floor, marketing the rumors of the moment and managing, often, to generate momentary smoke where there was no fire. The cameras and microphones are instantly available to amplify any dispute into a national controversy. And dissident individuals and party elements—of whom there are always plenty—find they have a vaster audience for their gripes than they ever imagined possible.

Small quotes F. Clifton White, the veteran Republican organizer who managed Goldwater's nomination, as expressing a view shared by many professional politicians: "Television is programming the convention. . . . To the television medium, it is a show, it's a production. . . . They want to get a rating. . . . I am reasonably convinced that it is not going to survive as an effective system or instrument for selecting people for the highest office in the land, if it is structured as a television production."

If White's judgment proves correct—and the damage the reputations of the conventions suffered in the eyes of television viewers in 1964 and 1968 indicates he may well be correct—then the most important single institution for the development of responsible party government will have been crippled. But it need not be, if the politicians and the television newsmen who recognize what is at stake treat the convention as an important political event, rather than a four-day circus. Reporters and cameramen do not roam the floor of Congress while it is in session. They are similarly out of place on the floor of the convention. Interviews with delegates can easily be arranged in adjacent areas, without disrupting convention business. All of the convention proceedings should be open to television coverage, but the agenda and schedule should be determined by the party's need, not the requirements of television's commercial sponsors. It is far more important to protect the convention as an institution than to protect the network ratings.

The Condition of Our Political Parties

There is much in this lengthy survey of the forces operating on our party system that could make anyone discouraged about the prospects for reviving responsible party government. I do not deem the situation hopeless, however. On the contrary, it strikes me as encouraging that so many changes favorable to responsible party government have been accomplished in a climate of public opinion that is skeptical or even cynical toward government and the parties. The strengthening of the presidential office; the increase in the scope of party organs in Congress; the development of opposition-party policy councils; the improvements in access to the electoral system; the reform of the national conventions—all these are significant steps forward. There is much left to do, in these areas, and in the areas of campaign finance, campaign technology and the use of television, to enhance and not undermine the role of the parties.

What is significant is that the gains that have been recorded, the improvements in the machinery of party government, have almost all come about not in response to public demand but through the efforts, the extraordinary efforts, of a relative handful of political insiders. The junior congressmen who pressured the House leaders for five years to pass a legislative reform bill were not acting in response to demands from their constituents; in fact, it is unlikely that more than a handful of their constituents even know what their representatives accomplished. They acted out of their own concern for the functioning of our governmental system. The same thing is true of those who sparked Democratic convention reform, who created the opposition policy councils, and who instigated the lawsuits that forced open the election system for millions previously disenfranchised and that ended the malapportionment of our legislative bodies.

The fact is that in the last two decades it is only the insiders—those already heavily involved in politics and government—who have given a damn about the health or sickness of the party system. It is thanks to their efforts that we even have a chance to revive responsible party government. But the insiders cannot revive it by themselves. What we make of our parties—or fail to make of them—depends on our decision, on our willingness to use the tools the parties provide to re-energize the governmental process, which has been so thoroughly stymied for the past sixteen years.

11

Conclusion:
Partakers in the Government

Many of the problems confronting America today, many of the shortcomings in the political system which this book has described, were foreseen by a group of scholars twenty years ago. In its 1950 report, "Toward a More Responsible Two-Party System," the committee on political parties of the American Political Science Association said there were four dangers to our democracy which "warrant special emphasis," dangers which they prophesied would become more acute unless the forces weakening our party system were combated.

"The first danger," the report said, "is that the inadequacy of the party system in sustaining well-considered programs and providing broad public support for them may lead to grave consequences in an explosive era."

The weakness of our party system has made it very difficult to build and maintain support for the long-term enterprises we need to pursue at home and abroad. The task of supporting international economic development, of constructing a stable world peace, of building a strong domestic economy and equitably distributing its products and wealth, of reforming our governmental structures and finding adequate resources for our urgent national needs cannot be accomplished by a single Congress or a single President. We have paid a high price for the instability and weakness of our governing coalitions. Ambitious programs have been launched, but funds to finance them withheld. Commitments made by a President have been undercut by Congress. Funds voted by Congress have been vetoed or impounded by a President. No party has been able to move ahead on its own agenda for very long, and the result has been sixteen years of government by fits and starts, with a mounting backlog of unkept promises and unmet needs.

"The second danger," the APSA committee said, "is that the American people may go too far for the safety of constitutional government in compensating for this inadequacy by shifting excessive responsibility to the President."

We have seen that happen, too. The weakness and frustration of responsible party government at the state and local levels—which is, if anything, even more serious than at the national level—has sent most of our major issues to Washington for resolution. And in Washington power has increasingly been stripped from Congress and the departments and been centralized in the White House. Bereft of the sustained support a responsible party system could provide for passage and implementation of a long-term program, each of the last four Presidents has been forced to improvise his governmental policies and tactics on a day-to-day basis, hoping some temporary alliance would permit him to overcome the inherent immobility of the vast governmental system. As the APSA committee predicted, this situation has produced the type of "President who exploits skillfully the arts of demagoguery, who uses the whole country as his political backyard, and who does not mind turning into the embodiment of personal government." But even the highly personalized presidency of our era has not managed to cope successfully with the problems challenging America.

"The third danger," the APSA committee said in 1950, "is that with growing public cynicism and continuing proof of the ineffectiveness of the party system, the nation may eventually witness the disintegration of the two major parties." That has not yet happened, but we are appreciably closer to that danger than we were twenty years ago. Popular dissatisfaction with the two-party system is manifested in many ways: by the decline in voting; by the rise in the number of voters who refuse to identify themselves with either party; by the increase in ticket splitting, a device for denying either party responsibility for government; and by the increased use of third parties or ad hoc political coalitions to pressure for change.

"The fourth danger," the APSA committee said, "is that the incapacity of the two parties for consistent action based on meaningful programs may rally support for extremist parties, poles apart, each fanatically bent on imposing on the country its particular panacea."

Regrettably, we have seen altogether too much of this kind of political polarization in the past twenty years. This has been an era of confrontation politics: whites vs. blacks; hard hats vs. students; demonstrators vs. police. The extremist parties are yet small, but the extremist movements are growing, and as our domestic political process becomes increasingly polarized, polemicized and violent, there is real danger the end result may be a totalitarian party of the left or right.

What must concern us is the rising level of public frustration with government-and-politics-as-usual. It is not just a few radical students who say and believe the political system is not working; millions of ordinary, hard-working Americans recognize that government is not dealing with the problems that are uppermost in their lives: crime and drugs and war and inflation and unfair tax loads and fear of unemployment and family budgets that do not stretch to meet the housing and education and medical and recreational needs of their families.

The ways in which this frustration is expressed are as various as the men and women who share it, but they were all summed up for me in the words of a retired furniture maker I met while polling in Nashville, Tennessee, in the fall of 1970. He was weeding his garden as we talked, and at the end of the conversation, he straightened up to say goodbye. "I'll tell you this," he said, "I'm glad I'm getting too old to live, because what's going to happen when this bubble bursts? The kettle is starting to boil, brother, and she ain't even heated up good yet."

For most of the last sixteen years, American liberals, of whom I am, I suppose, one, have been most concerned about the outsiders in our society—the black, the brown, the poor, the uneducated, the young—who are the all-but-inevitable losers in the influence game we have substituted for responsible party government. But some of these groups have learned to beat the odds by ignoring the rules. If the "big boys" and the "special interests" control city hall, or the legislature or the capitol, the "outsiders" have learned to control the streets. They have "voted with their feet," as the saying goes, and with their throats, and with their threats. And sometimes the government has responded, as it should have responded to the justice of their cause, if not to the threat of disruption that accompanied it.

But today it is not just these minority-group "outsiders" who are frustrated by the inequities of our society and the laggard performance of our political-governmental system. Millions of middle-aged, middle-class white working Americans are coming to understand that they have been victimized by the irresponsible politics of the recent era. No one asked them if they wanted their sons sent to fight in Vietnam; no one asked them if they wanted to gamble their family security on their ability to keep one step ahead of inflation; no one asked them if they wanted to swap token cuts in their income taxes for walloping hikes in the property taxes on their homes. Yet all these things have been done to them, by their government, and they are not going to take it lying down. Failing any means of registering their views through the political system, they will follow the blacks and the students and the other minority groups into the streets. And confrontation politics—with its constant threat of violence and repression—will increase.

Vietnam and the Political Parties

Is there not a better way to resolve our differences, to move ahead on our common problems? I believe there is. I have argued in this book that the instrument that is available to us—little used in the last sixteen years, at least—is the instrument of responsible party government. The alternative to making policy in the streets is to make it in the voting booth.

But, if that is to be more than a cliché answer, there must be real choices presented at election time—choices involving more than a selection between two sincere-sounding, photogenic graduates of some campaign consultant's academy of political and dramatic arts. The candidates must come to the voters with programs that are comprehensible and relevant to our problems; and they must have the kind of backing that makes it possible for them to act on their pledges once in office.

The instrument, the only instrument I know of, that can nominate such candidates, commit them to a program and give them the leverage and alliances in government that can enable them to keep their promises, is the political party.

But, even as I say that, I recognize that the notion will be greeted with enormous skepticism. The parties, it will be said, have been around for years; if they are the answer, then why do we have the problems we have now? My reply, of course, is that we have not seen responsible party government in this country—in Washington or in most states and cities—in the sixteen years I have been covering national politics. Instead, we have had fractured, irresponsible, nonparty government, and we have paid a fearful price for it.

I have dwelled in this book on the domestic consequences of our long period of governmental stalemate. the unmet needs of our major public services, the deteriorated condition of our governmental machinery. My emphasis was natural; it is in this area that my own reporting has concentrated and on which public attention now centers.

But I do not want to leave the impression that the most serious or costly consequences of the breakdown of responsible party government are in the domestic field. Still less do I want to leave unchallenged the argument, so often made, that politics should stop at the water's edge. For it is my firm conviction that if one wants to sum up in one word what can happen in the absence of responsible party government, that word is Vietnam.

For twenty-five years, respectable opinion in this country has held that the great questions of foreign policy should be kept sacred and inviolate, far removed from the sordid considerations of partisan advantage. The notion had a specific historic justification. In 1946, when Democrat Harry Truman was President, the Republicans captured Congress in an election that represented a strong public reaction against the wartime controls associated with the Democratic Administration.

The Republican congressional victory made responsible party government impossible. Faced with the necessity of securing support from a Republican Congress for major postwar international policies—including the Marshall Plan—Truman entrusted his foreign policy to a group of successful lawyers and businessmen, many of them liberal Republicans from the New York Establishment. The prominence given such men as Robert Lovett, Paul Hoffman, John McCloy, Allen and John Foster Dulles facilitated the course of bipartisanship that was necessary under the historical circumstances.

Unfortunately, the notion became permanently enshrined that such nonpolitical men had a natural right to manage the nation's foreign policy. Dwight D. Eisenhower, whose statements quoted in the second chapter of this book show how thoroughly he was imbued with the myth of bipartisanship, let the Dulles brothers run foreign policy for him. And, as John Kenneth Galbraith has noted, even when the Democrats returned to power in 1961, "instead of Adlai Stevenson, W. Averell Harriman or J. W. Fulbright, with their Democratic party associations," John Kennedy gave the key international security jobs to such nonpolitical Establishment men as Dean Rusk, Robert McNamara, Roswell Gilpatric and the Bundy brothers, McGeorge and William.

"Foreign policy was thus removed from the influence of party politics . . . from the influence of men who had any personal stake in the future of the Democratic party, the President apart," Galbraith noted. Elections are held and party control of the presidency shifts, but the technicians and "experts"—the Walt Rostows and Henry Kissingers—never seem to lose their grip on the foreign policy machinery.

When protest over foreign policy arises from the ranks of the President's party, as it did from some Democratic senators in the Lyndon Johnson years and from some Republican legislators since Richard Nixon has been in office, it is the nonpolitical "experts" in the key foreign policy jobs who always rush forward to defend existing policies. It is these men, with their marvelous self-confidence and their well-developed contempt for politicians and public opinion, who wrote the clever scenarios and the cynical memoranda that comprise the history of Vietnam policy under three administrations contained in the Pentagon Papers. It is they who stand ready to advise a President how he can dupe the Congress and the public and maneuver the nation into war without disclosing his intentions.

How have they been able to maintain their control over foreign policy? Because the political parties, at critical junctures, have failed to meet their responsibilities. In none of the national elections during the whole course of the escalation and de-escalation in Vietnam were the American people given a choice of defined, coherent policies toward the struggle in Indochina. Either the issue was ignored entirely or smothered in a blanket of bipartisan generalities. For six long years—between 1964 and 1970—the leadership of both parties in Congress failed to try to bring to a vote a policy declaration on Vietnam. Vietnam is a classic instance of the costliness of isolating a basic foreign policy question from examination in partisan, political debate. It is a terrible measure of the failure of responsible party government in our time.

Letting the Parties Go

I am not optimistic about the prospects of reviving responsible party government in the near future. The momentum of current trends, the drift of the public mood seem to me to point in the opposite direction: toward the further fracturing of the already enfeebled party structure in this decade. The survey that Haynes Johnson and I did at the time of the 1970 election convinced us that "not only are voters splitting their tickets and moving back and forth from election to election, but their perception of party differences is growing visibly weaker." That habit of partisanship, once lost, may be very difficult to regain.

If that proves to be the case, and if the young people entering the electorate remain as independent of the party system as they now appear to be, the major parties may no longer enjoy a monopoly on high office. Three or four or half-a-dozen serious presidential candidates may run each election year, posing a constitutional crisis whether we are operating under the existing electoral college system or a plan for direct election of the President. More minor party or independent candidates may find their way into Congress, weakening the existing party structure there.

If the distrust of politicians and parties continues to grow, it may be reflected in the deliberate crippling of responsible leadership, by dividing the branches of government between the parties and by turning officeholders out as soon as they show signs of amassing any significant power. While the masses of alienated voters use these tactics to cripple government, the activists for one cause or another may continue to press their demands through confrontation tactics—lawsuits, demonstrations, strikes, boycotts and the other weapons in their arsenal. The result would be an increase of domestic turbulence and violence.

I do not think it is inevitable that we go down this road, but I am afraid that there is as yet no widespread understanding that this is what we face unless we make a deliberate effort to reinvigorate our political party system. There is as yet no broad appreciation of the fact that the aggravations and frustrations each of us feels is part of a single crisis—the malfunctioning of our governmental-political system. We still delude ourselves by thinking we can treat the symptoms and ignore the cause. If we find ourselves stuck in a traffic jam, we start for work fifteen minutes earlier in futile hopes of beating the crowd. If the cities become unsafe, we take our businesses and our families to the suburbs, hoping the problems will not follow us. If we find ourselves as a nation fighting a lengthy, undeclared war, our reaction is to pull the troops out and hope it will not happen again.

For a long period, we have tried to buy time by this kind of retreat from reality, but we cannot play the game much longer. Unless our basic population patterns are reversed, most of us will find ourselves living in a compact mass of humanity in one of the concentrated metropolitan clusters, where we will have only the choice of trying to solve our problems on a community basis or attempting to survive by the law of the jungle. When the time comes—and it is not that far off—when most Americans live constantly with the threat of breakdowns that have plagued New York City residents in recent years, when teachers and policemen and sanitation workers and subway and bus and taxi operators strike, when taxes rise while municipal services deteriorate, and filth piles up in the streets, when jobs become more scarce and inaccessible and welfare rolls soar, while schools turn out more addicts than graduates, when personal security is no greater than one's own strength or weapons provide, then we may recognize that we face a genuine crisis of government.

If we are very fortunate at that moment, we may find leadership in one party or the other capable of mobilizing the nation through democratic means to confront what will by then be an almost overwhelming challenge. In our desperation, we may by our ballots give that party a mandate for governing commensurate to its task, and we may even be fortunate enough to find its leaders responsible and responsive in office. My guess is that if we find such leadership it will come, not from the Senate, but from that most scorned of political offices, the governorship. The best hope I can see for the short term is that one of the major states may provide a showcase example of responsible party government in action—with a governor, a legislature and a party leadership successfully working in tandem to meet the urgent needs of that state. Such a demonstration would not only validate the concept of responsible party government; it might elevate its practitioner to the presidency.

But there is a darker possibility we cannot overlook. When frustration reaches the breaking point, when inflation and economic uncertainty, work stoppages, civil disturbances, crime, drugs and the breakdown of public services can no longer be tolerated, a different sort of man with a different solution may present himself. A plausible demagogue may appear and say, "Give me power and I will make things work again. I will restore order to your lives. I will see that there is discipline again. I will make the streets safe and I will remove those who are disturbing our peace of mind. It may not be pleasant, but I promise you it will be effective. If those demonstrators try to tie up our cities, my police will know how to deal with them so they will not try again. If those unions try to raise wages, my men will see to it that there are no more strikes. We will control prices, even if it means we have to run those big businesses ourselves. Congress will pass the necessary laws, because its members will understand it will not be wise for them to go home unless they act. And the press will cooperate with us, and stop its carping and sniping, if it understands what is good for it. And we will save our country"—but, of course, destroy freedom and democracy in the process.

That possibility sounds like scare talk. Some will dismiss it as apocalyptic nonsense. But things have been happening in this country that I would not have believed when I came to Washington sixteen years and four Presidents ago. I have seen a President and his brother, a presidential candidate, murdered by assassins. I have seen the Capitol of the United States blasted by explosives, on one occasion, and ringed by arson fires on another. I have circled our national monuments in an airplane carrying the Vice President of the United States and watched the tears in his eyes as he saw the magnificent capital city set to the torch by its black residents, venting their rage and frustration at the murder of Martin Luther King, Jr. Time and again, I have heard from that same Capitol, and lately even from the White House, powerful men speak as if they did not understand that unless we obliterate the tragic heritage of slavery, it will obliterate us.

I have seen speakers shouted down and heckled into silence by student mobs at our oldest university, and I have seen police in a dozen cities use their clubs with savage delight on the heads and arms and backs of peaceful demonstrators.

Above all, I have heard the conversations of hundreds of average Americans, who see their world, their plans, their hopes crumbling, and do not know where to turn. I cannot forget the doctor's widow in Richmond, Virginia, who said, "You can't tell from day to day, but if it doesn't do better than it is now, it won't be much of a country. This is the saddest situation I've ever seen. I've seen this country go through four wars and a depression and this is the worst." I remember all too well the young husband in New Rochelle, New York, with his arm around his wife's shoulders, who told a visitor of the fears for the future that have caused them to delay starting a family. "We've even thought seriously of moving to some other country," he said, "but we don't know where to go."

Taking the Political Option

Where do we turn? To ourselves. Obviously, that must be the answer. There is no solution for America except what we Americans devise. I believe that we have the instrument at hand, in the party system, that can break the long and costly impasse in our government. But it is up to us to decide whether to use it.

What would it entail on our part if we determined to attempt responsible party government? First, it would mean giving strong public support to those reform efforts which in the recent past have been carried on entirely by a small group of concerned political insiders, aimed at strengthening the machinery of political parties and government.

We should seek to strengthen the liaison between the presidency and Congress, on a mutual basis, and between the presidency and the heads of state and local government. We should elect the President in the same way we elect all other officials, by direct vote of his constituents, with high man winning.

We should expand the role and responsibilities of the party caucuses and the party leaders in Congress. The caucus should choose the floor leaders and policy committee members, the legislative committee chairmen and committee members, not on the basis of seniority but on the basis of ability and commitment to the party program. That leadership ought to be held accountable for bringing legislation to which the party is committed to a floor vote in orderly and timely fashion, with adequate opportunity for debate and particularly for consideration of opposition party alternatives. But procedures for due consideration should not justify devices like the filibuster, which prevent the majority party from bringing its measures to a final vote.

In state government, we need to reduce the number of elected officials, to provide governors with adequate tenure and staff to meet their responsibilities, and particularly to strengthen the legislatures, by limiting their size and by improving their pay, their facilities and their staffing, and to recognize they have a full-time job to do each year.

In local government, too, we need to reduce drastically the number of elected officials and make sure the jurisdictions they serve are large enough to provide a base for two-party competition and to bring resources together with problems along a broad enough front to give some hope of effective action.

We need to take every possible measure to strengthen the presidential nominating convention as the key device for making the parties responsible. The current effort to open the Democratic delegate-selection process to wider public participation is a promising start, and its emphasis on the congressional-district nominating convention offers corollary benefits for integrating congressional and presidential constituencies. Both parties should experiment with devices for putting heavier emphasis on the platform-writing phase of the convention's work, including the possibility of a separate convention, following the nomination, where the party's officeholders and candidates debate the program on which they pledge themselves to run and to act if elected.

Most important of all the structural reforms, we need to follow through the effort to discipline the use of money in politics, not only by setting realistic limits on campaign spending and by publicizing individual and organizational gifts, but also by channeling much more of the money (including, in my view, all general election spending) through the respective party committees, rather than through individual candidates' treasuries.

We need to strengthen the party organizations and their staffs, and recapture for them the campaign management functions that have been parceled out to independent firms which tend to operate with a fine disdain for the role of party and policy in government. We need to devise ways to make television—the prime medium of political communication—somewhat more sensitive to the claims of the parties to be a regular part of the political dialogue, and to protect the vital institution of the nominating convention from being distorted by the demands of the television cameras.

All these reforms would help, I believe, but they would not accomplish the invigoration of responsible party government unless they were accompanied by a genuine increase in the participation by the public in party affairs. The cure for the ills of democracy truly is more democracy; our parties are weak principally because we do not use them. To be strong and responsible, our parties must be representative; and they can be no more representative than our participation allows. Millions more of us need to get into partisan political activity.

We need also to become somewhat more reflective about what we do with our votes. We need to ask ourselves what it is that we want government to accomplish, and which candidate, which party comes closest to espousing that set of goals. That may sound so rationalistic as to be unrealistic. But this nation has more education, more communication, more leisure available to it than ever before. In the nineteenth century, James Bryce wrote of us, "The ordinary citizens are interested in politics, and watch them with intelligence, the same kind of intelligence (though a smaller quantity of it) as they apply to their own business. . . . They think their own competence equal to that of their representatives and office-bearers; and they are not far wrong." Are we to think less of ourselves today?

Finally, we need to examine some of our habits. It seems to me we should ask, before splitting a ticket, what it is we hope to accomplish by dividing between the parties the responsibility for government of our country, our state or our community. Do we think there is no difference between the parties? Do we distrust them both so thoroughly that we wish to set them against each other? Do we think one man so superior in virtue and wisdom that he must be put in office, no matter who accompanies him there? Why are we splitting our tickets? My guess is that, if we asked those questions, we would more often be inclined to give a temporary grant of power to one party at a time, rather than dividing responsibility so skillfully between the parties that neither can govern. If we were willing to risk this strategy, knowing that we would be able to throw the rascals out if they failed, we might even discover to our amazement that they are not always rascals.

The Questions Beyond Politics

These are the things we could do if we wanted to attempt responsible party government. But they would not, of course, be a panacea for our problems as a nation. There are limits to what parties can do, limits to what politics and government can do. We need to remember the point Pat Moynihan made in an essay for *The American Scholar* called "Politics as the Art of the Impossible." Government, he said,

cannot provide values to persons who have none, or who have lost those they had. It cannot provide a meaning to life. It cannot provide inner peace. It can provide outlets for moral energies, but it cannot create those energies. In particular, government cannot cope with the crisis in values that is sweeping the western world. It cannot respond to the fact that so many of our young people do not believe what those before them have believed, do not accept the authority of institutions and customs whose authority has heretofore been accepted, do not embrace or even very much like the culture that they inherit.

The twentieth century is strewn with the wreckage of societies that did not understand or accept this fact of the human condition. Ours is not the first culture to encounter such a crisis in values. Others have done so, have given in to the seemingly sensible solution of politicizing the crisis, have created the total state, and have destroyed themselves in the process.

The party system is essentially a device for making choices between candidates and programs, and for enabling those who prevail at the polls to seek to put their policies into action. It is a way of expressing choice; and choice implies division, which will be ever present in a large and diverse nation like ours. But, for the two-party system to work, there must be not only division but large areas of agreement. There must be agreement on the rules of the game, so that losers accept defeat and winners do not attempt to abuse the advantage of victory. There must also be a high degree of agreement on the values and goals the society cherishes, so that political defeat does not seem to carry intolerable penalties for the losers. A party system must reflect the political community it serves, and when that community loses its sense of identity, the party system cannot fabricate one for it.

Whether we Americans still retain a vision of ourselves as one people, one continent-sized community, is the ultimate question. And that is a question beyond politics. I can speak of it only in very personal terms. During the summer of 1971, when I was completing this book, I became aware of a paradox. For a period of about ten days, when I was at my typewriter, attempting to describe the shattering of the party system, the frustration of government, the crisis of unmet needs and unreformed institutions that I think confront us, something quite extraordinary was happening. Three Americans were making a voyage of exploration to the moon. Even as I was writing that the history of the last four presidencies was essentially a record of unkept promises, of goals set but not achieved, of government by fits and starts, the evidence on the television set and in the daily newspapers seemed to mock those generalizations. The expedition of Apollo 15 was the triumphant achievement of a governmental enterprise that spanned four presidencies—the same four Presidents of whom I have written in this book. The space program began in the Eisenhower Administration; the commitment to go to the moon was made under President Kennedy; it was given impetus by President Johnson; and it was President Nixon who was in office when the goal was finally accomplished.

"We found what we came for," said astronaut David R. Scott, when he spied the "genesis rock," the piece of matter dating from the birth of the solar system some 4½ billion years ago. How rare it is that we can say of any of our shared enterprises: We have done what we set out to do.

To find comparable experiences, one must go to the tiny, isolated communities that are vestiges of an earlier America. My family spends its summers on Beaver Island, an island in the center of Lake Michigan, west of the Straits of Mackinac, where the remnants of a once-flourishing fishing community cluster in weatherbeaten frame houses around the church, two stores and a tavern that comprise the town of St. James. During our 1970 visit, I wrote a column for the Washington *Post* which I think is pertinent here.

It is back-to-school time here on Beaver Island, just as it is in the rest of the country, and at the tiny school across from Holy Cross Church, a crew of volunteers has been working with the sisters to scrub and paint the classrooms for the new year.

It took no great effort to line up the help, for on this island . . . where children and old people comprise most of the 230 souls remaining from a once-thriving fishing center, cooperation and improvisation are requisites for survival.

The school itself is a unique hybrid. It is a public school, financed by public funds. But since few lay teachers could be persuaded in recent years to spend the long winters on this isolated island, the teaching is done by the nuns—which is fine with the largely Irish Catholic community, anyway.

The new school building, the historical museum, the new medical center and the new dock all represent the same mixture of public funds and private effort—signs of vitality in a community which, although cut off from its original economic base, remains too proud to die. . . .

The problems of Beaver Island are certainly not those of America, but the qualities that have made its survival possible are those we need as a nation—particularly that sense of community that makes individuals respond instinctively to shared responsibilities. It is striking to me that the sense of community has survived only at the smallest and largest extremes of our national life. In the small society of Beaver Island, shared family ties, a shared religious faith, and the fierce shared determination to survive impel men and women almost spontaneously to clean and paint the schoolhouse, build a medical center and put up a new dock.

At the other extreme of the scale, when we Americans, gazing up at our companion in space, the moon, as men have done for millennia, grasped the idea that this nation in this generation had the capacity for the first time in man's history to walk upon its surface, to see and touch its primitive material, to learn from it the secret of our own planet's birth, the decision to make the journey was almost instinctive. Once the possibility was understood, there was no question but that we would go. And we have gone, in a real sense, all of us, on that fabulous voyage, and seen our own green earth as a small, round ball in space; and shared the accomplishment that, above all others, is likely to make this time, this people remembered. The pride we feel in that accomplishment is the same pride the Beaver Islanders feel in their shining schoolhouse, their new medical center and their dock: the pride that comes from community accomplishment.

But in the vast range of needs and concerns and goals that lie between the microcosm society of Beaver Island and the deep space of the moon voyage, our sense of community cannot be found. Every thoughtful man, every politician whose perspective goes beyond the next election has recognized this as our fundamental problem. They differ only in the language and metaphor they use to describe it to us.

Nelson A. Rockefeller said in 1968, "We have become an incongruous society—at deep odds with itself. We somehow have contrived to be, at one and the same time, the Affluent Society and the Afflicted Society. . . . We have tried to find the core of—and give a name to—the ordeal and the turmoil of our society. We have—many of us—come to call it the crisis of the American city. This is true enough, but we must also understand its full meaning—a crisis of the American conscience."

John Gardner said in 1970 that he was "not interested in indicting the President" for any shortcomings, "because I believe that virtually all of us have failed in our duty as Americans. . . . While each of us pursues his selfish interest and comforts himself by blaming others, the nation disintegrates. I use the phrase soberly: the nation disintegrates."

And in that same year, Edmund S. Muskie remarked, "Every American I have met wants this to be a whole country and one with a place for him and his family. The difficulty is that we have grown so far apart, in every way, that what one man does to secure a place for himself strikes another as a threat to his own place—and so fear and distrust undermine the sense of wholeness that keeps us secure."

At about the time that I was reflecting on the meaning of Beaver Island and the loss of the sense of community in the larger society of America, on which all these leaders were commenting, I came across a passage in De Tocqueville that seemed so apt as to be prophetic.

Epochs sometimes occur in the life of a nation when the old customs of a people are changed, public morality is destroyed, religious belief shaken, and the spell of tradition broken, while the diffusion of knowledge is yet imperfect and the civil rights of the community are ill-secured or confined within narrow limits. The country then assumes a dim and dubious shape in the eyes of the citizens; they no longer behold it in the soil which they inhabit, for that soil is to them an inanimate clod; nor in the usages of their forefathers, which they have learned to regard as a debasing yoke; nor in religion, for of that they doubt; nor in the laws, which do not originate in their own authority; nor in the legislator, whom they fear and despise. The country is lost to their senses; they can discover it neither in its own nor under borrowed features, and they retire into a narrow and unenlightened selfishness.

I thought of what the Katzenbach and Kerner and Douglas and Eisenhower commissions had told us about the decay of our system of justice and of our cities; how they had warned us of the danger of becoming two societies, separate and unequal; and of the folly of seeking personal safety by arming ourselves against every stranger. I thought of how these warnings had been given and been heard but not heeded. And I thought of the fear so many of my fellow citizens feel and express for the future of our country. In such a situation as ours, De Tocqueville said, it is not enough to call forth the "instinctive patriotism" of the people, "that instinctive, disinterested and undefinable feeling which connects the affections of man with his birthplace.

"While the manners of a people are simple and its faith unshaken, while society is steadily based upon traditional institutions whose legitimacy has never been contested, this instinctive patriotism is wont to endure."

But we are not so fortunate; ours is a time of turbulent change, what Walter Lippmann in his eightieth-birthday interview called "the most revolutionary age that man has ever lived in." "So swift is the pace of modern change," said *Time* magazine in an essay written for Richard Nixon's inaugural, "that in terms of common experience, America has a new generation every five years."

In such times of turbulence as our own, De Tocqueville advised relying on the "patriotism of reflection," which, he said, "springs from knowledge . . . is nurtured by the laws . . . grows by the exercise of civil rights, and, in the end . . . is confounded with the personal interests of the citizen."

And then he wrote the sentence that I think might well serve as the keynote of our search for a solution to the terrible impasse in which we find ourselves. "I maintain," he said, "that the most powerful and perhaps the only means that we still possess of interesting men in the welfare of their country is to make them partakers in the government."

To make them partakers in the government. That is the challenge that now faces our political parties. That is·ultimately the test of responsible party government—to make all citizens feel they are partakers and participants in the government.

It will not be easy to revitalize our political parties. Even if that is done, our problems remain awesome. We must somehow rediscover our sense of community, of nationhood. We must heal the scars of slavery and generations of discrimination. We must find a way to meet our inescapably heavy responsibilities in the world, while nourishing the debilitated services on which our own welfare, well-being and peace of mind depend. And, to do all this, we must make our government functional again in the great metropolitan areas, in the states and in Washington. These are tasks that will test our democratic system and each of us as individuals.

But to settle for less is to admit defeat for our ideals and our aspirations. I said in the Introduction that when I called this book

The Party's Over, the pun was intended, but not the prophecy. I do not believe our political parties are doomed, unless by our neglect of the services they can provide and the vital role they can play in re-energizing our political system.

But, in another sense, the party is over, whether or not the political parties are revived. I do not expect to see again in America the kind of smugness, of euphoria, that gripped Washington when I came to the capital city sixteen years ago. Since then, we have gone through the New Frontier and the Great Society and the New American Revolution, each briefer in duration and more patently false in its promise than the slogan that preceded it. If there is one thing the long travail of the last four presidencies has taught us, it is to be skeptical of the easy answer.

In the dark June of 1940, when the Nazi Army had captured Paris and was poised for an assault on England, while the United States stood by, seemingly impotent to act, Walter Lippmann told the reunion of his Harvard class that "upon the standard to which the wise and honest will now repair it is written . . . You took the good things for granted. Now you must earn them again. It is written: For every right that you cherish, you have a duty which you must fulfill. For every hope that you entertain, you have a task you must perform. For every good that you wish to preserve, you will have to sacrifice your comfort and your ease. There is nothing for nothing any longer."

We face a similar challenge. The cost of being an American citizen is going up. If this nation is to survive and meet its responsibilities, many of us will have to sacrifice some of our personal luxuries to help pay for the society's neglected needs. What is more, we will have to give up the idea that we can escape from the consequences of our civic irresponsibility by purchasing private passage for our families to the segregated suburbs, to the private schools and to the protected professions. It is going to cost us time and energy and thought, diverted from our private concerns, to make government workable and politics responsible again in America. Our parties, our government will be no more representative than we make them, by our own commitment and partici-pation.

If we do nothing, we guarantee our nation will be nothing. There *is* nothing for nothing any more. Our choice is simple: Either we become partakers in the government, or we forsake the American future.

Index

Adams, John Quincy, 191
Advisory Commission on Intergovernmental Relations, 146–47, 148, 150, 154
Advisory Council on Executive Organization, 160, 161
affluent and upper class: income, 208, 209; and politics, 205–07; Republican party, 193, 194, 197, 205, 206; taxation, 116, 206, 207, 210; working-class resentment at treatment of blacks, 117–18
AFL-CIO, 37, 61; see also labor
Agar, Herbert, 181–82
Agnew, Spiro, 94, 103, 216; attacks on news media and demonstrators, 93, 100, 104; election (1970), 96
Aiken, George, 68
Alabama, 199; Democratic party, 225; election (1964), 82; election (1968), 82; Republican party, 82
Alaska: proposal for statehood, 14
Alexander, Herbert E., 235
Allen, Ivan, 127
American Political Science Association, 56; convention (1970), papers, 183–84, 185, 236–37; Democratic party influenced by, 186; report (1950) on two-party system, 182, 244, 245–46

Americans for Democratic Action, 14
Arkansas: Democratic party, 198; election (1968), 82
arms limitation see disarmament and arms limitation
Ash, Roy, 160, 161
Atlanta, 59, 125, 135

Bailey, John M. 25, 34
Bailey, Stephen K., 188, 228
Baker, Bobby, 58
Baltimore, 125
Beer, Samuel, 211
Bell, Jack, 42–43, 69
Berlin, 34, 90
blacks: in cities, 122, 145, 147, 203; Democratic party, 36, 66, 197; demonstrations and riots, 50, 52, 75, 246, 247; under Eisenhower, xiv–xv, xix–xx, 3, 4, 15; housing, integration and segregation, 83, 95–96, 104–05, 118, 203, 204; under Johnson, 42, 70, 72; under Kennedy, 32, 36; legal and economic status improved, 203; migration North, 145, 197; under Nixon, 85, 104–05, 206; racism as political issue, 203–04; racism protested by students, 111, 113; school desegregation and busing,